Gas to Europe

Gas to Europe
The Strategies of Four Major Suppliers

Edited by
ROBERT MABRO and IAN WYBREW-BOND

Contributors
ALI AÏSSAOUI
ULRICH BARTSCH
MALCOLM PEEBLES
JONATHAN STERN
IAN WYBREW-BOND

Published by the Oxford University Press
for the Oxford Institute for Energy Studies
1999

Oxford University Press, Great Clarendon Street, Oxford OX2 6DP

Oxford New York
Athens Auckland Bangkok Bogotá Buenos Aires
Calcutta Cape Town Chennai Dar es Salaam
Delhi Florence Hong Kong Istanbul Karachi
Kuala Lumpur Madrid Melbourne Mexico City
Mumbai Nairobi Paris São Paulo Singapore
Taipei Tokyo Toronto Warsaw
with associated companies in Berlin Ibadan

Oxford is a registered trade mark of Oxford University Press

British Library Cataloguing in Publication Data
A catalogue record for this book is available from the British Library

ISBN 0-19-730022-7

Cover design by Holbrook Design Ltd, Oxford
Typeset by Philip Armstrong, Sheffield
Printed by Bookcraft, Somerset

CONTENTS

Acknowledgements   viii

Conversion factors   ix

Key milestones in the development of the European
gas industry   x

Introduction
Robert Mabro and Ian Wybrew-Bond   1

1   **Setting the Scene**
Ian Wybrew-Bond   5

2   **Algerian Gas: Sonatrach's Policies and the
Options Ahead**
Ali Aïssaoui   33

3   **Dutch Gas: Its Role in the Western European
Gas Market**
Malcolm Peebles   93

4   **Soviet and Russian Gas: The Origins and
Evolution of Gazprom's Export Strategy**
Jonathan P. Stern   135

5   **Norwegian Gas: The Struggle between
Government Control and Market Developments**
Ulrich Bartsch   201

6   **What does the Future hold for the European
Gas Business?**
Ian Wybrew-Bond   255

Index   275

TABLES AND FIGURES

Chapter 1

Tables
1   European Annual Gas Consumption   26
2   Main International European Gas Pipelines – Existing
     and under Construction   27
3   Main International Gas Pipeline Projects in Europe   29

Figures
1   Total Primary Energy Supply, 1973 and 1997. Per Cent   25
2   Evolution of Natural Gas Imports in Europe.
     Breakdown by Exporting Countries   25

Maps
1   European Natural Gas Pipelines 1970   8
2   European Natural Gas Transmission Systems 1998   9

Chapter 2

Tables
1   Long-Term Gas Supply Contracts Between Sonatrach and its Partners   40
2   Algerian Institutional Energy Framework:
     Evolution of the National Energy Council   50
3   Algeria: 1997 Gas Balance   52
4   Algerian Gas Consumption in 1997   52
5   Algeria: Re-allocation of Proven Gas Reserves   54
6   Sonatrach's Total Commitments in 2000   54
7   Location and Development of Proven (Remaining)
     Algerian Gas Reserves   58
8   Algeria: Capital Investment Needed to Double Exports, 1990–2000   59
9   Sonatrach's Portfolio of Operational Gas Supply Contracts   73
10   Basic Petrochemical Projects Using Natural Gas/NGLs as Feedstock   75

Figures
1   Comparative Paths of Gas Exports to Western Europe   44
2   Disposition of Algerian Gas Production   53
3   The New Institutional and Energy Policy Framework   78

Map
1   Algeria: Main Non-associated Gas Production Regions,
     Pipelines and Export Facilities   33

Chapter 3

Tables
1   State Revenues, 1975–90   101
2   Total Gas Resources   107

3	Estimated Cumulative Demand Over Next 25 Years	114
4	Actual Demand by Main Market Sector	114
5	Primary Energy Consumption in 1997	115
6	Dutch Gas Exports	117
7	Gas and Oil Prices in 1998	120
8	Published Dutch Gas Export Prices 1998	121

Figure
| 1 | Corporate Arrangements for Groningen Gas | 98 |

Map
| 1 | The Dutch Gas Transmission System | 103 |

Chapter 4

Tables
1	Gazprom's Proven and Probable Gas and Oil Reserves	145
2	Russian Gas Production and Transmission Assets 1992–98	146
3	Soviet Natural Gas Trade 1970–91	148
4	Russian Exports to Former Soviet Republics 1990–98	155
5	Debts for Gas Supplies owed to Gazprom by Former Soviet Republics	156
6	Russian Natural Gas Exports to Europe 1990–98	163
7	Gazprom's Principal Gas-related Investments in Europe	167
8	Russian Hard Currency Earnings from Energy as a Percentage of Total Merchandise Exports	171
9	Soviet Hard Currency Earnings from Energy as a Percentage of Total Merchandise Exports	182

Maps
1	West Siberian Gas Fields and Pipeline Corridors	144
2	New German Gas Pipelines	165
3	Russia's Gas Export Routes	173
4	Gas Pipeline Routes to Turkey	174

Chapter 5

Tables
1	Remaining Discovered Resources and Reserves	205
2	Major Oil Fields	206
3	Major Gas Fields	206
4	The Troll Contracts in 1986	218
5	Norwegian Gas Export Contracts	219

Figure
| 1 | Institutional Framework for Norwegian Gas Sales | 222 |

Map
| 1 | Norwegian Gas Export Pipelines | 223 |

Chapter 6

Table
| 1 | Currently Contracted Gas Supplies to Europe in 2010 | 262 |

ACKNOWLEDGEMENTS

The Oxford Institute for Energy Studies would like to acknowledge with much gratitude financial support received from BP Amoco Gas, Iberdrola, In Salah Gas, Nera, Statoil and Total for the conduct of the research presented in this book. Thanks are due to other benefactors of the Institute who support all our research projects through annual grants. Those who expressed a particular interest in this project include Elf Aquitaine, ENI, Mitsubishi Corporation, Osaka Gas, Philips Petroleum, the Royal Norwegian Ministry of Petroleum and Energy, Shell and Tokyo Electric Power Company (TEPCO). Representatives of these benefactors participated in a workshop held in Oxford on 5 February 1999 to discuss the findings of the study. The comments made by participants and the debate that followed enabled the authors to improve their analysis and address further issues in their research.

The authors have also benefited from a number of interviews which they have conducted individually and from comments received on their drafts from colleagues in the industry. It is impossible to mention them all and some wish to remain anonymous. A warm thank you to everyone who has been generous with time and ideas, and to *Gas Matters* for kindly supplying maps.

In addition, Ulrich Bartsch wishes to acknowledge the valuable support received during his research from Ambassador Jon A. Gaarder, Gunnar Hognestad, Hans Henrik Ramm and officials in the Norwegian oil and gas companies. Ali Aïssaoui is particularly grateful to Nordine Aït Laoussine, former Executive Vice President of Sonatrach and former Minister of Energy, who made valuable contributions to the first draft and challenged some of his interpretations; to Abderrahmane Hadj Nacer, former Governor of the Bank of Algeria, for insights into the economic reforms of the Hamrouche government; Walid Khadduri of *Middle East Economic Survey* for helpful observations on the political and energy scene in Algeria; and, last but not least, to Nicole Foss and Peter Greenhalgh, colleagues at the Institute, who edited a first draft without complaining at the tedium of this painstaking task.

APPROXIMATE CONVERSION FACTORS.
NATURAL GAS AND LNG

	TO					
	Billion cubic metres NG	*Billion cubic feet NG*	*Million tonnes crude oil*	*Million tonnes LNG*	*Trillion British thermal units*	*Million barrels of oil equiv.*
FROM	*MULTIPLY BY*					
1 billion cubic metres NG	1	35.3	0.90	0.73	36	6.29
1 billion cubic feet NG	0.028	1	0.026	0.021	1.03	0.18
1 million tonnes crude oil	1.111	39.2	1	0.805	40.4	7.33
1 million tonnes LNG	1.38	48.7	1.23	1	52.0	8.68
1 trillion British thermal units	0.028	0.98	0.025	0.02	1	0.17
1 million barrels oil equivalent	0.16	5.61	0.14	0.12	5.8	1

Source: *BP Statistical Review of World Energy*

KEY MILESTONES IN THE DEVELOPMENT OF THE EUROPEAN GAS INDUSTRY

1946	Laying of first long distance pipeline to Moscow (845 km)
1955–7	Discovery of Algerian oil and gas
1959	Discovery of Groningen field
1963	First Dutch gas deliveries, and Gasunie established
1964	First Algerian LNG supplies to UK (Camel project)
1965	Establishment of Gazprom
1968	First Russian gas supplies to Western Europe – Austria.
1969	Discovery of Ekofisk field in Norway
1973	First Russian gas delivered to Germany ('74 Finland/ Italy, '76 France)
1977	First Norwegian deliveries to Emden
1979	Discovery of Troll field
1983	Transmed line laid
1986	First Troll contracts signed
1990	Gazprom/Wintershall form Wingas
	First non BG sales to UK industrial customers
1992	EU market completed
1995	In Salah gas marketing company formed between Sonatrach and BP
1996	Maghreb line complete
	Statoil's offices raided at the instigation of EU's DG IV competition authorities
1997	EU Electricity Directive comes into force
1998	EU Gas Directive comes into force
	UK-Continent Interconnector came into operation
	Ruhrgas, Gasunie, BEB, Gaz de France, Thyssengas offices raided by EU's DG IV competition authorities
	Ruhrgas buys 4% Gazprom stock

INTRODUCTION

Robert Mabro and Ian Wybrew-Bond

Once upon a time ...

The development of the European gas industry is in some senses very much a fairy tale. It has all the ingredients of a great story with nation states battling for territory, the gas companies behaving like 'barons' who mark out their fiefdoms and, some would say, control the lives of their 'serfs' in the form of customers. The latter have been told what is good for them provided they remain faithful and do not try to leave the fold. At the same time the environment in which the industry operated has changed as the form of the European Union took shape, its bureaucracy grew in influence and the Union itself enlarged geographically. The story of the European gas industry is one which has many tales of courage and vision particularly in its early days.

Some of the readers of this book may be well versed actors on the European gas scene, or new players yet to have their part and with contributions to make to the next act of the tale which has still to unfold. The majority, however, will be part of the audience which we hope will enjoy an important story relevant to our modern lives. To readers from different sides the story told here will inevitably carry different meanings.

These words of introduction are not meant to be in any way frivolous. When the authors of this book embarked on this study and stood back from all that has happened over the past forty years, it became apparent that in retrospect a great story is being played out. Its end has not yet been reached; in fact it lies very far ahead in time. We stand today at the beginning of a new and important chapter. Our purpose is to help the understanding of what may unfold on the basis of a study of the complex developments which shaped the gas industry of today.

The European gas industry will undergo fundamental changes as it is opened to competition. It is now subject to an EU directive issued in 1998 one year after the electricity directive which maps the path for liberalization and competition in an utility sector that is closely related to gas.

These important developments follow from the introduction of these new EU policies. First, the gas industry is no longer able to consider its future in isolation but must take into account what is happening in electricity and telecommunications. The electricity industry is responding to the legal pressures as regards competition arising from its EU directive. Trading instruments are being introduced and there are already active electricity trading pools operating in the UK, the Nordic countries, Switzerland, the Netherlands and elsewhere.

Secondly, consumers who buy gas, electricity and telecom services are becoming more price conscious and naturally come to expect the same range of options in gas as they are getting, or expect to get in other utilities. Further, the introduction of the Euro will make cross border price comparisons easier than they are today, and the effects of competition in the gas industry in one European country would become readily visible to consumers in other countries.

Thirdly, a number of relevant developments have happened in a relatively short time. Some electricity companies, for example, are deciding to move into the gas business and use their base to access gas customers.

Fourthly, long-term supply contracts which have been the bedrock of the gas industry will not continue to be accepted without qualifications by the big industrial users of gas. Thanks to these arrangements the producing companies enjoyed the security of a guaranteed offtake. This enabled them to invest in gas projects with a minimum of risk. The European gas utilities were able to balance the requirements of captive markets with the supplies obtained under the long-term contracts. Now, the gas-producing companies and the major European gas utilities are having to face the prospect of coping with a higher degree of market risk than they have so far been comfortable with. Added to this there are new entrants to the European gas market who have no established positions to defend. They can easily upset the old rules of the game by bringing to Europe incremental gas supplies priced at the margin and offering customers a wider choice of suppliers.

In the past thirty or forty years the structure of the European gas industry was stable because the gas chain from the producing field to the end-consumer was orderly and well understood with every agent along the chain in a clearly defined position. Now, the forces that will slowly transform the structure have been set into motion.

The authors of this book have delved into the history of the

European gas market in order to explain in their proper context the significance of recent changes and assess how the major suppliers – the Netherlands, Algeria, the USSR/Russia and Norway – may respond to the challenges which increased competition involves.

These four countries have provided the secure supply base from which the natural gas market has developed. The authors' purpose was to depict the characteristics of the gas industry in the four producing countries, getting as it were 'under its skin', and present to the reader a view of how each country developed its resource base, established the internal organization of the industry, and how the energy system related nationally to wider political forces and institutions. The design and implementation of gas development and supply strategies depend in part on political, institutional, even cultural factors.

The authors have endeavoured to evaluate the importance that natural gas holds within each of the four major countries. They discuss these nations' attitudes towards foreign companies. More fundamentally, they review how each country has approached the marketing of gas in changing political and economic circumstances, and how they are likely to position themselves – given the constraints imposed by their history and the capabilities developed through this same history – for an uncertain future.

Although each author has written a separate chapter they have worked very much as a team throughout the research for and the writing of this book. They have discussed together successive drafts and each of them has been influenced by the inputs of all the others.

Finally, two other aspects of this book may require a word of explanation. First, the approach is qualitative rather than quantitative although data are presented wherever necessary. No attempt is made, however, to forecast gas supply and demand as such analyses are available elsewhere.

Secondly, the UK is not included in a chapter of its own. To be sure, the UK North Sea is a major gas province now linked to the Continent via the Interconnector, but it is not likely to become a major exporter. Its importance is recognized however for the European liberalization process and is discussed in this context.

The authors hope that this book will provide a different insight to other works and serve all those who seek to understand a changing world by placing the likely transformation in context. Furthermore, the gas industry is expanding rapidly in Europe. New companies are entering the fray and both old and recent organizations are recruiting new staff with diverse skills and different business background and experience. Although the book is addressed to wide audiences, one of the authors' cherished ambitions will be fulfilled if new generations of curious men and women find in this work useful answers to questions they would like to ask: How did the European gas market develop to become what it is today? Are the old but major players able to respond efficiently to changes which they neither welcomed nor initiated? The views that readers may form about the future of this market depend very much on the answers to these questions.

CHAPTER 1

SETTING THE SCENE

Ian Wybrew-Bond

In setting the scene for the analysis that follows in later chapters, we should remember how the European gas industry has grown in little over forty years to become a major utility. Most of us have come to depend on it either as consumers or through the work we do. We take for granted the pipeline structures that have grown to provide this fuel to industries, commercial premises, and our homes. The vast majority of consumers are not conscious or concerned that this fuel has been brought to them from difficult offshore locations or thousands of kilometres from distant countries.

Oil is always in the public eye and its pricing is fairly common knowledge. The price of gasoline affects everyone and so consumers shop around. Oil is easy to transport by ship from many sources, which gives consuming countries confidence and therefore a sense of security of supply. It is now widely traded. Sadly its polluting properties are only too well known.

Gas is so different. It is not a product that we can see or are normally aware of. Unlike electricity the pipelines are all underground and out of sight. It is regarded as a safe and reliable fuel for heating and cooking. Most domestic gas consumers do not know the unit price of the gas they use. Only in the UK are they becoming price conscious as the residential market is opened to competition.

The recent legislation introducing liberalizing changes in the continental European gas market has yet to come into real effect. The intention is that competition will be introduced into all markets and consumers should have a choice of supplier. Although this sounds simple, it is complex to achieve and not welcomed by all. In particular the existing players have resisted change, for they have invested collectively and extensively in production capabilities and pipelines, and now see their revenue streams at risk. Before we discuss the likely impact of these changes in more detail, let us first look at how the industry grew to what it is today.

1.   In the Beginning ... till 1979

It is sometimes forgotten that from the nineteenth century gas was well established as a fuel for street and home lighting in many North West European countries – before electricity was widely available. It was manufactured using coal as feedstock until well into this century when oil became the economic choice. The manufacturing of gas was at that time concentrated in urban areas because the low pressure at which it was delivered limited its range of distribution. Whilst town gas was hardly the methane that now predominates, its production and utilization encouraged the development of urban distribution networks in France, Germany and the UK.

Natural, as opposed to manufactured, gas was also known in Western Europe. West Germany, France, Italy and Austria all had established reserves but their size was thought to be insufficient to justify national transport networks. Distribution was therefore restricted to the locality of the reserves or at best within the region. The former Soviet Union however was piping natural gas relatively long distances internally before the Second World War, an expertise which later had a major influence on the development of the European gas market.

The real impetus for conversion from town to natural gas was the discovery of major gas reserves in and around Europe after the Second World War, in particular in 1959 the huge Groningen field in the Netherlands. When its size began to be realized, Europe was faced for the first time with the possibility of trading natural gas on an international scale. Long distance lines coupled with compression facilities became technically feasible and export markets were at hand in West Germany, Belgium and France.

Exploration and appraisal of the North Sea established that the UK and subsequently Norway had extensive reserves. Additional, less extensive, but nevertheless economically attractive, reserves were found in West Germany, France and Italy. When the North Sea Southern Basin gas discoveries were made in the 1960s, they provided the basis for the widespread introduction of natural gas in the UK and a national grid was created which increased the use of gas in the domestic market. Algerian LNG deliveries to the UK began in 1964 and were primarily used to meet peak demand. Apart from the UK, major programmes were initiated to convert distribution systems from town to natural gas in Germany, France and Italy. Algeria developed facilities to export greater volumes of LNG to Europe and the Soviet Union was investigating the possibility of transmitting large volumes of gas from Siberia westwards.

The development of Groningen gave Europe three types of gas: (i) manufactured, (ii) Groningen natural gas which was methane with a high nitrogen content that lowered its unit heating value and (iii) gas which was essentially pure methane. Each had a different calorific value and therefore needed separate transportation and distribution systems. With their domestic market not yet fully developed, the Dutch sought exports to secure income and they set an aggressive pricing policy. There was also a concern at the time that this major resource must be sold and markets established or captured before nuclear generated electricity became a serious competitor. In the mid-60s when oil prices were $2.00/barrel, Groningen gas exports were priced at a thermal equivalent to oil, as this was seen to be its main existing competitor. A precedent in gas export contracts was thus established which had significant consequences later for exporters and importers when oil prices became volatile.

Dutch exports grew from 10 to 45 bcm/year in the period 1970–75, the foundation period for the European gas grid. Maps 1 and 2 show the development of the international transmission system between 1970 and 1998. This was a time of vision and courage. Dutch reserves were so large that supplies were considered to be completely secure when the growth of the international market began. Groningen gas was, however, incompatible with first Soviet and later Norwegian gas. When these two producers began to enter the Continental market, long distance pipelines and grids separate from Dutch gas had to be developed giving importers competing and compatible supply sources. The Dutch set about securing the Groningen gas market by extending their international pipeline network and offering attractive pricing. At the time of the first oil price rises in 1973–4, Dutch gas accounted for over 75 per cent of internationally traded gas in Western Europe. The nine-month contractual time lag in Dutch export contracts meant that they could not increase their prices in line with and at the same time as the four-fold increase in oil prices.

Because internationally traded gas price rises did not match those of oil, demand for this new fuel suddenly increased. Furthermore, following the 1973 oil price hike, gas as an indigenous European resource was regarded as a more secure energy source than Middle East oil. The necessary gas pipeline network was beginning to be put in place and there was a mutual need on the part of producers and importers for long-term contracts – secure supplies and secure offtakes.

The development of the markets, infrastructure and increased prices encouraged new supplies from the USSR, Algeria, and Norway in the late 1970s. The USSR had already planned to expand its exports, so

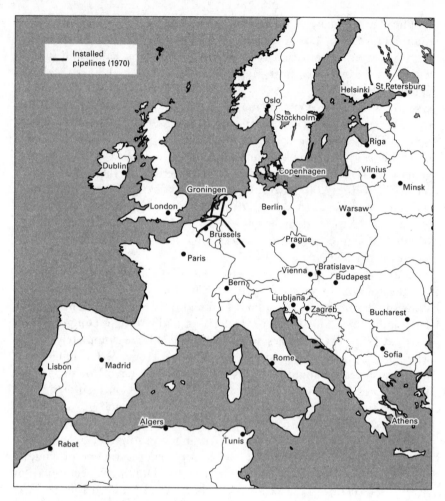

Map 1: European Natural Gas Pipelines 1970

the impact on gas prices of the 1979 oil price increase was fortunate.
Algeria had already sold a small amount of LNG to France and to a
consortium from Austria, Belgium, France, and Germany. The latter
deal subsequently collapsed because of the Algerian insistence on fob
oil price parity for its LNG. Although France and Belgium still took
cargoes, the volume of their purchases was smaller than originally
planned.

Norway saw itself primarily as an oil rather than a gas producer.
With no potential domestic market to absorb the associated gas
resulting from oil production, this could either be reinjected or disposed
of through exports. The Norwegians have a small population and their

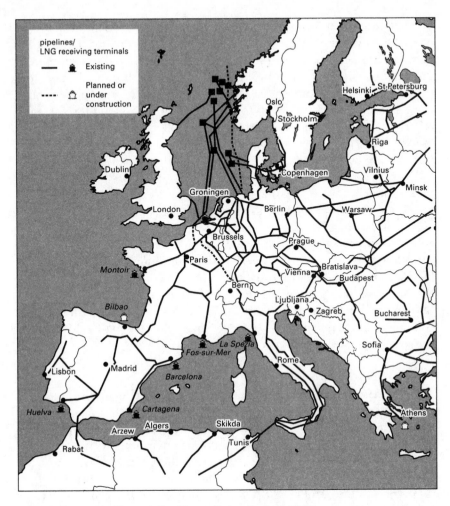

Map 2: European Natural Gas Transmission Systems 1998

relatively low overall national income needs could well be met by oil exports alone. Once the extent of their potentially huge gas reserves became apparent, they decided that if their demands were not met for higher gas prices than other supply sources – to compensate for high Norwegian offshore production and subsea transmission lines costs – then they should concentrate on the development of their oil reserves.

They also felt that they offered the key North West European markets more politically secure supplies than either the USSR or Algeria and this should be recognized in price terms. They were initially successful and a line was laid from the Ekofisk field to Emden in northern Germany in the late 1970s.

The Dutch then pressed for higher prices to bring them in line with others. They were in a strong negotiating position given that they provided some 50 per cent of the internationally traded gas supplies to the region. At the same time, having achieved almost 100 per cent penetration of the domestic market for gas heating and cooking, they were conscious of the need to ensure their own long-term supply security and to restrain any further export plans. Indeed, they went so far as to join the buyers of Ekofisk gas, both in order to conserve their own reserve base and to gain experience of international gas purchasing.

Even before the second oil price shock of 1979–80, then, all the four producers were seeking to increase prices. They traded on the importance to importers of the security of gas supplies compared to oil, each producer trying to match any gain that any of the others achieved in negotiations. The view was propagated that gas should be considered as a scarce resource and a 'premium fuel' reserved for high-value uses rather than a boiler fuel. It is a moot point whether this sense of scarcity existed because Dutch (and UK) reserves were thought to be lower than they turned out to be, or because it was commercially beneficial to sellers to maintain the high-value, scarce resource mentality in buyers' minds.

2.   Political and Business Environment in the 1980s

The decade starting in 1980 witnessed great changes, both within the gas business and its political and economic environment. It was a time of difficult US–Soviet relations, reflected in the US attempts to obstruct Soviet plans to build a new pipeline linking the massive Urengoy field to Western Europe. The USA feared that dependence on Soviet gas supplies could give the USSR leverage on importing countries' policies in other matters including defence. The fact that the USSR would then become dependent on the hard currency flows from such sales was apparently not taken into account, or it was not considered a strong argument for accepting increased Soviet gas exports. President Reagan also pressed Europe to utilize its indigenous coal and gas resources and reduce its Middle East oil liftings.

In 1982 the IEA had resolved that nuclear (and coal) should form the basis of Europe's new generating capacity. However, the 1986 Chernobyl reactor accident following that at the Three Mile Island plant in the USA in 1979, produced a change in public acceptance of further nuclear plant construction. By the end of the 1980s the Soviet Union was breaking up and the 'walls' between East and West Europe were coming down. Both these events had profound effects on the European gas industry. Countries newly emerging from the former Soviet Union now had their own agendas, either as gas producers in their own right or seeking reward as transit countries for Russian gas. This changed the relationship between the former Soviet Union and its captive East European gas purchasers. Furthermore, West European gas companies began to invest in many of the formerly state-owned utilities in Eastern European countries, introducing more commercial approaches to their business. Combined-cycle gas turbine (CCGT) power generation was encouraged as a way of reducing the well publicized pollution levels.

In 1984 the European Community set itself the daunting task of completing its formal structure by 1992, i.e. within two Commission lifetimes, based on the 'Four Freedoms' – the free movement of goods, services, people and money between all member states. This would lead to the development of a bureaucracy in Brussels to oversee the process, with growing power and influence. In turn, this was seen by individual nations and their key institutions as a threat to their freedom of action on many issues, including the governance of their gas and electricity industries.

There was a second oil price hike in 1979–80 followed by a fall in 1986, both of which had a major impact on the gas industry. This was not only in terms of pricing but also because investment in new production and transmission projects was initially encouraged and subsequently discouraged. In the latter part of the decade, new cost-cutting technologies emerged and gas projects could be developed against lower than hitherto predicted oil and thus gas price expectations.

Politically, the Thatcher administration was elected in the UK in 1979 and embarked on an ideologically driven programme of privatization of state-owned companies, including British Gas (BGC) and the Central Electricity Generating Board (CEGB), which was also broken up. The UK government had a fundamentally different view to that of many national authorities on the Continent as to the economic viability of state-run monopolies. There was total opposition to monopolies in any form by the UK government, and this was to become a source of political division within the European Union as the UK tried to impose its fervently held belief in open competitive markets on the rest of Europe. Many countries had developed their utility structures on the grounds that they were there to provide a service to the public, and as such were best managed as state or local authority owned entities.

These fundamentally different views led to a prolonged process to reach agreement on the European electricity and gas directives which the European Commission wanted in place to provide more transparent and open gas and electricity markets. The first attempt to secure a gas directive failed in 1992 and it was not until 1998 that agreement was reached – encouraged to some degree by the finalization of the electricity directive the previous year. During this time the influence of new entrants to the Community began to be felt. The southern states of Spain and Portugal, with gas industries in an early stage of development, had different concerns to the established northern markets and were open to the liberalizing ethos. There was also a growing sense that adequate supplies of gas were available and security of supply, whilst still important, was not the issue it had been in the past. The degree of compromise required to reach agreement on these two directives, particularly that for gas, is reflected in what many regard as the weak final outcomes and timetables for the liberalization of these markets.

Towards the end of the 1980s, the European Commission was also beginning to provide a forum for the development of environmental policies. Concerns as to levels of air pollution and early signs of global warming gradually climbed the political agenda as public awareness increased. This could only benefit gas, the cleanest fossil fuel, and in particular its use in the new technology of CCGT power generation. In addition to environmental gains, these plants offered more than 50 per cent efficiencies compared to some 35 per cent for coal stations. CCGT power generation stations could be sited wherever a gas supply could be made available and, compared to new coal-fired stations, they were quicker and cheaper to build. In the 1990s these developments brought the gas and electricity markets closer together, not as competitors but increasingly as complementary and interdependent activities.

3.   What the 1980s Meant for the Producers

When the second oil price hike occurred in 1979–80, a new incentive was given to importers to secure gas supplies underpinned by long-term contracts. The sellers were quick to recognize and take advantage of this. There was a feeling that oil prices would continue to increase, not entirely without foundation when one puts oneself in the position of gas industry executives in 1980 who were coming to terms with a second dramatic price rise following that of 1973.

On the Continent natural gas was beginning to be seen as a more reliable energy source than oil, and suppliers investing in transmission lines enhanced the confidence of importers that supplies would not be interrupted. Algeria established the sub-sea Transmed pipeline to Italy and therefore was no longer solely an LNG supplier; the Norwegians contracted to sell Statfjord gas and a new line was laid; and the Soviets were planning significantly increased deliveries. The Dutch had been aware from the mid 1970s that importers were willing to pay higher prices for supplies from other sources, which when aggregated with other lower cost supplies still achieved prices acceptable to customers. This left the Dutch with no alternative but to threaten to refuse extensions beyond the existing contract expiry dates. Importers agreed to pay increased prices for Dutch gas but only in return for increased flexibility in offtakes. So although the Dutch had managed to bring their prices into line with those of other suppliers, it was at the cost of Groningen becoming in effect the swing producer for the North West European gas industry – but without the Dutch securing the reward that was due for this service.

Low calorific Groningen gas had been principally supplied to industrial and electric utilities in Belgium, France, West Germany and Italy – the high base load users that make long distance pipeline investments attractive. As Dutch gas prices rose and the West German government increased subsidies to maintain its coal industry, sales of Dutch gas to the electricity utilities significantly decreased. At the same time, in the light of its commitment to Algerian LNG and their own cheap nuclear generated electricity, France reduced its offtake of Dutch gas. Germany used compatible Norwegian and Soviet gas to penetrate the domestic and commercial sectors which were willing to pay for these higher priced supplies.

This change in marketing was to have fundamental repercussions. Domestic and commercial markets have a much more pronounced seasonality in their demand than the industrial and utility sectors. More flexibility was therefore required in contracts and eventually the development of storage to meet winter demand peaks. Pipeline systems also had to be sized to handle peak demand and so were under-utilized in the summer. This, coupled with the higher cost of distributing gas to the smaller customers in the domestic and commercial sector than had been the case with industry and utilities, meant higher unit costs and lower returns to the gas companies.

Not surprisingly, producers were initially unreceptive to these signals, having become used to the sellers' market environment of 1980–81. Even before the oil price collapse of 1986, expectations of demand had fallen from those of the 1970s which resulted from extrapolations of earlier rapid growth periods. Producers, however, did not immediately accept these changes of views on demand. Some important landmarks emphasized the new realities.

The Norwegians were negotiating to sell the Sleipner field to BGC, but their pricing demands became much higher than BGC had to pay to secure UK North Sea supplies. In 1985, therefore, the UK government stepped in and refused to sanction the deal. This was a major shock to the Norwegians who until then had taken the stance that its higher costs and European base justified a price premium.

In the 1970s, the Algerians had concentrated on oil rather than gas exports. They focused on broad issues of sovereignty over natural resources and control of the hydrocarbon sector. In the 1980s they battled for a higher share of the gas rent. They stated that their LNG supplies would be priced not just against current oil prices, but against a future price which they believed oil would move to. They let it be known that they would be prepared to cut off supplies if their demands were not met – although they never in fact took this action. Nevertheless, the effect was a reduction in offtake by their customers in France, Italy and Belgium. Algeria also lost its LNG market in the USA and the overall loss of gas export volumes had an adverse impact on the maintenance of their LNG plants. As a result they were unable to take advantage of the growth in demand that began in the second half of the 1980s.

However, the economic difficulties facing Algeria after the 1986 oil price collapse contributed to reforms aimed at transforming the economy from a state controlled, oil dependent economy to one that was both market oriented and private sector led. Sonatrach attempted to re-enter the US market, but its initial deal with Shell collapsed when the latter was unable to agree with its US partner to reopen the US Cove Point LNG terminal. It then negotiated with Trunkline and Distrigas of Boston, but had to accept selling into a deregulated market with volume flexibility and market related pricing. Using this experience, Sonatrach then pushed to increase its share of the expected growth in its natural markets in Southern Europe, initially expanding the Trans-Med system to Italy and later with the Maghreb line laid via Morocco to Spain and Portugal.

The USSR was the great beneficiary of rigid pricing attitudes in the early 1980s by other producers. Whether or not they were more commercially astute, forward thinking or politically motivated can of course be debated. The fact was that they took a decision to link their massive Urengoy field to Western Europe with a 40 bcm/year pipeline with only some 65 per cent of its capacity covered by supply contracts.

It is interesting to reflect upon whether this decision would have been made in a post-perestroika Russian world with market related financing costs and commercial returns on investments being required. Undoubtedly, the fact that until now Gazprom remains a single entity and arm of the state, and has not been broken up as the Russian oil industry has been, means that its ever increasing share of the European gas market has given the state a sense of control over Western Europe. However there have been 'gas for pipes' barter arrangements in place for many years, which lock both sides into a mutual interdependency. In the 1990s, Russia's need for financial support, particularly from Germany, has further increased this dependency and the recent acquisition by Ruhrgas of some 4 per cent of Gazprom's stock could perhaps be seen partly as a reflection of this mutuality of interests.

So the second half of the 1980s saw a changing Continental market place and the move from a sellers' to a buyers' market, not only because of a reduced demand forecast, but also because the four producers were able to supply significant volumes. How would they maintain or develop their market position? What alliances, if any would they consider? Would they take control of their own downstream destiny or rely on the gas company 'barons' in each market? Before discussing these questions further we will first look at other players in the gas chain, developments in the political arena, and the major changes that would unfold in the UK.

4.　Growth of the Gas Companies

Ruhrgas, Gasunie, and Gaz de France immediately spring to mind as the great market makers and key influences in the early shaping of the Continental European gas market. However, gas companies were established in other countries with a monopoly or dominant position in the purchasing, transmission and distribution of gas in their own markets. Important amongst these were Distrigaz in Belgium and SNAM in Italy. We will now look at the way these companies in the more mature gas markets have acted and the influence they have had on producers.

Throughout the late 1980s and the 1990s most of the major companies have taken a similar line towards the opening up to competition of European gas markets, as the European Commission has increasingly sought to pursue the cause of liberalization. The companies have consistently argued that establishing the extensive transmission and distribution system was only achieved by major investments up-front, principally by themselves. In addition, they had to make long-term take-or-pay commitments to the producers to ensure customers' security of supply. They believe that in return for this they should have the security of knowing that the gas they have imported and purchased will be taken by customers. Competition in the downstream markets would put this at risk. Tacit or open support for this line was given by all governments (with the exception latterly of the UK) to ensure that security of supply concerns should not affect customer confidence in natural gas as part of their national energy balances.

The common attitude amongst the key continental gas companies towards market liberalization did not result from a similarity in the structure of their national industries but rather from a common purpose in protecting their rent chain. In Germany there is no national gas company but sixteen gas importers who are either transmission companies or electricity generators. They generally buy as a consortium led by Ruhrgas, the largest transmission company. Ruhrgas has developed solely as a downstream company without, until recently, any upstream interests. It has taken equity positions in a wide variety of downstream gas companies and pipelines, both in Germany and outside, not only to influence their commercial direction but to acquire information and market intelligence. Their knowledge of what is going on in the continental gas industry, therefore, has been without parallel and a vital component of their negotiating strength. A further strength has been the unusual voting structure between their shareholders, including German coal and industrial interests, Texaco, and BP operating as one block with some 60 per cent of the shareholding, and Shell, Esso, and Mobil holding the balance. This has the effect of giving the Ruhrgas management an unusual degree of freedom to operate. The then West Germany was also divided into a number of areas between the various transmission and distribution companies which were the subject of demarcation agreements. These were in effect 'gentlemen's agreements' not to encroach on other companies' distribution areas – thus avoiding what has been termed 'inefficient competition'. Some might say these were monopolies in all but name.

The development of Wingas (the Wintershall/Gazprom joint venture transmission and marketing company), has changed the German gas scene in the 1990s. Its stated objective was to establish a transmission system through the heartland of the gas industry but without being party to (and therefore limited by) the demarcation agreements between the existing gas companies. It was clear, too, that in addition to supplying Russian gas as feedstock to BASF, Wintershall's parent company, Wingas would actively seek other customers close to its pipelines. It has been successful in this, much to the disbelief of the existing German gas companies who found it hard to accept that such a project would ever be economic and come to fruition. It is now generally accepted that Wingas is here to stay as a major player – which is a considerable achievement on the part of Wintershall and Gazprom.

In France the situation is quite different; Gaz de France is the sole gas transmission company and it is state owned. It is closely linked to, and some see as somewhat dominated by, the state-owned Electricité de France; inasmuch as the French government deliberately decided to rely on nuclear generated electricity rather than gas as the cornerstone of its energy needs. Its financial position has in the past been weak because of the high prices it paid for Algerian gas – a political rather than a commercial decision. It takes its gas supplies from the indigenous Lacq field as well as from the Russians and Dutch. Recently it has been active outside France seeking participation in overseas distribution companies. Its attitude to market liberalization has been that of France in general – confidence in the way state-owned monopolies run their businesses and that allowing open competition could undermine their financial viability and ability to provide national security of supply.

Gasunie purchases and transmits gas for export and domestically within the Netherlands to industrial customers and municipalities who distribute locally. Owned 50 per cent by the government and 25 per cent each by Royal Dutch/Shell and Esso, it buys all the gas produced in the Netherlands and imports some from Norway. The level of Dutch production is set by the government to conserve this national resource for the long term and Gasunie's sales objectives have been governed by these limits. Any new fields that come into production are taken into Gasunie's sales portfolio under the 'small fields' policy, whereby Groningen production is correspondingly reduced to maintain the overall government production targets but new discoveries are encouraged. Throughout the 1980s and early 1990s the Dutch were implacably opposed to market liberalization but lately the government has softened this line to some extent, recognizing the inevitability of market change over time. Gasunie hopes to make up for the erosion of its virtual monopoly of the Dutch market through increased exports, within the current overall 80 bcm/year permitted production target.

SNAM is the state-owned gas transmission company in Italy, selling gas direct to ENEL, the state electricity utility, and to the distribution companies which in turn supply local municipalities. It buys its gas from Algeria, the Netherlands and Russia, as well as taking the domestic production from fields operated by AGIP, its sister company in the state holding company ENI. SNAM has sought to retain its monopoly of the Italian transmission system and gas imports, although this has been broken recently by ENEL in its purchase of Nigerian LNG, and more recently the BP-Sonatrach venture via a new pipeline from Algeria. The privatization and break-up of SNAM is now on the Italian political agenda.

Distrigaz has steadily built a very broad based gas business in Belgium. Having established an LNG terminal in Zeebrugge in 1987 it could take its Algerian LNG directly rather than relying on France for receipt and regasification. Zeepipe, which brings Sleipner and Troll gas from Norway also lands there as does the UK Interconnector, more of which later. The Belgians scored something of a coup over the Dutch in securing the Interconnector landing point. It would have made good commercial sense had it landed in the Netherlands as this would have provided the UK with access to the Dutch seasonal modulating capacity. The UK government was in favour of Zeebrugge as it felt Gasunie was more interested in preventing the construction of the Interconnector, or preferred to lay the line themselves if one was to be built. By controlling it, Gasunie hoped to hold back the UK 'infection' of market liberalization. Distrigaz meanwhile actively welcomed the new line. In addition to Algerian LNG, Distrigaz has received cargoes from Australia's North West Shelf project but takes the majority of its supplies by pipeline from the Netherlands, Russia, and Norway, having both high and low calorific transmission systems. Its shareholders include Tractobel and Shell. With a relatively small domestic market, Distrigaz has established a major European gas transit point. This will have value in the years to come when the US concept of a 'hub' and short-term/spot trading becomes more prevalent on the continent as a result of the direct linkage with the UK.

Not only have some of these gas companies sought to restrain the pace of market liberalization, but some of their shareholders (notably Shell and Esso) have been active in pressing the case in various European forums wishing, understandably, to retain the profitable status quo. Being essentially at one remove from the direct market place, their interests take the form of shareholdings in a number of key gas companies, and they perceive market changes more as a threat than an opportunity. Although outsiders see them as having con-siderable power and influence, the reality may not be as clearly defined as third parties think.

Before dealing further with formal market changes and the implications for producers, there are other issues to be discussed.

5. The Changing Nature of the UK Gas Market

The way the UK market has changed is worthy of particular attention, for the politically driven liberalizing zeal has so reformed all aspects of the industry that it   bears no similarity to that of the mid 1980s. With the UK being a member of the European Union and physically linked in gas terms by the new Bacton–Zeebrugge Interconnector, what happens in the UK cannot but have an impact on the continental gas market. Although the changes appear to have occurred in the early to mid 1990s, in fact the seeds were sown in the previous decade in both the gas and electricity sectors. It is not however clear that the UK government foresaw the interrelationship that subsequently developed between the two industries as a result of adopting gas-fired CCGT technology in order to enter quickly the electricity supply business.

It is sometimes forgotten that the extensive gas penetration of the UK energy market was a considerable achievement on the part of BGC. Before 1982, BGC had pre-emptive buying rights on all gas offered for sale and a monopoly use of its transmission and distribution grid. Producers were paid the minimum that BGC thought they needed to pay. The 1982 Oil and Gas Act gave third parties the right of access to BGC's grid but offered no way of assessing tariffs. BGC hardly encouraged the development and direct marketing by new competitors was stillborn. However between 1986 and 1989 BGC was privatized, the Office of Gas Supply (Ofgas), the regulator, was established and a Mergers and Monopolies Report recommended that 10 per cent of new gas supplies should be sold to buyers other than BGC. Although BGC resisted all changes, it was to no avail. They came to pass, embraced by many who deeply resented the way they considered BGC had previously exploited its monopolistic buying and selling positions.

In 1989 the state-owned CEGB was broken up and privatized, the distribution activities being split into regional electricity companies (RECs) and non-nuclear power generation divided between two new companies, National Power and PowerGen. A pool was established to provide a structure for bidding in supplies on a daily basis and the transmission company, National Grid, was responsible for ensuring power demands were met through its management of the pool. It is interesting to observe how the privatization process changed between the earlier one of BGC and that of the CEGB. BGC was privatized as a whole, largely due to the opposition to any break-up by its powerful chairman, Sir Dennis Rooke; but the next years have been spent effectively in breaking it apart. When it came to the electricity industry's privatization, it was split from the start into generation, transmission, distribution and marketing, with a market mechanism in the form of the pool.

After their formation in 1990 the RECs immediately set about vertically integrating and acquiring generation capability through the building of CCGTs. Since BGC had lost its buying monopoly, producers were happy to sell to the new power sector and for a time beach gas prices actually rose as a new sellers' market was created. National Power and PowerGen tried to buy a REC in order to secure the benefits of vertical integration but this was blocked by the government as they did not want the effective creation of two new CEGBs. In due course, CCGT generators found that with a contracted gas supply they could on occasion sell the gas more profitably than by using it to generate electricity and so began to trade gas. The flexibility of CCGT technology allowed them this freedom.

At the same time, in early 1990 UK producers began to market gas direct to industrial customers and, as recommended by the MMC, BGC was not allowed to sell below the prices it was obliged to publish as schedules. It was not difficult for producers to sell gas direct very profitably by undercutting a helpless BGC – the only challenge being to find the best customers and to secure from BGC a tariff established after they ceased to be a total monopoly. In addition, they were short of gas as all existing gas supplies were contracted to BGC. The government therefore stepped in and forced BGC to offer a quantity of 'release gas' which was allocated between the new marketers. In due course the RECs joined in and new gas companies were set up with no ties to a producer. The RECs could draw on the customer base in their own area, while the new companies had to establish their own computer systems and marketing organization. With slim overheads they were quick on their feet and able to find a profitable niche. Successful alliances between RECs and producers also emerged while downstream margins were large, but they came under strain when competition really developed and these margins shrank or became negative – the producer partner still having an upstream margin to cushion difficult times.

In the mid 1990s, bilateral short-term trading commenced and a spot market using newly published indices began to influence longer-term prices. When the International Petroleum Exchange published a forward contract at the end of 1996, the gas futures business began. With the domestic sector fully open for competition from the end of 1998 and BGC split up with its transmission and distribution arm (Transco) fully regulated, all the elements of a free gas market are now in place.

The establishment of a group of companies in 1993 to develop an Interconnector linking the UK to the Continent was actively supported by the UK government as a way of allowing exports of gas as well as, one suspects, the open market philosophy that it was evangelizing to its continental colleagues. This pipeline will no doubt encourage the growth of short-term and spot gas trading at Zeebrugge; although initially and somewhat unexpectedly it is being used to import gas into the UK, the strength of sterling giving rise to higher UK end-user prices than on the Continent.

Has it all been worthwhile? It depends where the reader is positioned of course. In the UK gas prices to consumers are certainly lower than they were and security of supply concerns have not yet surfaced – although a prolonged period of low oil and therefore gas prices could curtail offshore UK projects. However, there is no way back in the UK even though the Labour government elected in 1997 has decided to protect the relatively small remaining UK coal industry by placing a moratorium for the time being on further gas-fired power stations. The gas regulator has been embattled with BGC for most of the past eight years, yet without the persistence of Ofgas the market would not have changed as it has. Certainly, continental gas executives have watched with increasing concern the impact of all the changes on BGC. This has stiffened their resolve to prevent if at all possible the establishment of a potentially zealous independent regulator, particularly one based in Brussels. Without the changes in the UK's gas and electricity industries, it is questionable whether the liberalizing movement on the Continent would have moved very far forward.

6. Power Generation – a Major New Market

Although the 'dash for gas' in the UK dominates the recent power generation scene, gas had been used for this purpose in Europe before the 1973 oil price shock. As a result of the re-evaluation of its role, it was then resolved that gas was too valuable a fuel to be used in this way, a view which was reinforced by a 1975 European Commission directive to this effect. This was not reversed till the late 1980s when it was apparent that there was a plentiful supply of gas and, in the meantime, environmental pressures had grown which encouraged the use of gas to the disadvantage of coal and nuclear stations. The recent technology employed in a CCGT station results in a facility that is relatively quick and easy to build, with a low environmental impact on its immediate surroundings, and which can be developed as a combined heat and power (CHP) provider for an industry or community. There will be considerable growth in gas-fired power generation in the former Eastern Europe as these countries adopt EU environmental directives. In some countries their nuclear industries are in poor condition and environmentally unfriendly local lignite-based generation will have to be replaced.

Even in those countries where the nuclear industry is considered safe, there is public concern at the mention of building new nuclear capacity and planning approvals are hard to secure. New coal plants are expensive to build and equip with SO_2 removal facilities and with lower efficiencies than gas-fired stations they will always emit more CO_2 per unit of electricity generated than a gas-fired unit. The same is true of heavy fuel oil-fired stations. There really is no alternative to the use of gas for new power generation until renewable energy becomes both more economic and larger scale. This is evident from the plans in all countries in Europe.

It is also evident that gas can be delivered at prices that match existing fuels when environmental clean-up equipment costs for coal in particular are included. It is becoming an accepted norm that gas purchasing pricing will have to include indexation with electricity market indices so as to share market risk between the power generator and gas supplier.

As with gas, the European electricity market is now gradually opening up to competition, a process which has been formalized by the recent electricity directive providing a timetable for market liberalization and third-party access to existing transmission line capacity. It hardly represents a blueprint for rapid change, but it does formalize and recognize the need for liberalization which is now apparently unstoppable.

7.   Gas Market Liberalization – the European Union's Long-awaited Directive

The directive has indeed been a long time coming. Its foundation lies in the European Commission's four freedoms mentioned earlier, in particular the free movement of goods and services between member states. Such a simple vision but, as in most such situations, difficult to enshrine in legislation acceptable to the states themselves.

Why has it been so difficult to agree on a common set of guidelines? After all, more than 50 per cent of the gas consumed in Europe crosses national boundaries before reaching its ultimate market. So any way that the existing pipelines can be opened to access by others must help the movement of gas. Europe as a trading entity must face the emerging economies of the Far East and low energy prices would help member states becoming more competitive. There are abundant supplies of gas available and growing demand, particularly in the power generation sector, which will help Europe to meet the increasingly demanding environmental standards it has set.

Although there is no overall formal European view governing gas supplies, the common interest amongst continental buyers in ensuring security of supply has resulted in an industry that has developed at a predictable pace, so matching supply and demand. Gas suppliers and importers have had a mutual interest to enter into long-term contracts, with importers accepting a high level of 'take-or-pay' commitment to assist the producer justify high production and transmission costs to the buyers' borders. Within each market there have been effectively monopolistic organizations, often state owned, which buy and import gas and provide transmission to industry or local distribution companies. In some countries these local distributors are municipalities who make a profit on their sales of gas (and other utilities) which is then used to provide other services required by the local population. Furthermore, the UK apart, there is an acceptance in many European countries that in certain situations a monopoly is the most efficient way of operating a utility industry and it is in the national interest to retain it.

Opening up the gas market to free competition is seen as putting this complex structure at risk and the real gain has been questioned by many established players. There are however industries that wish to deal direct with producers and cut out the margin of the gas company or middle man. But without access to the transmission systems, which are often owned and operated by the same gas company that the industry wishes to cut out, there is no way to receive supplies. The costs of laying a parallel line are normally prohibitive.

Customers and some independent producers looked to the directive to lay out a blueprint for a phased opening up of the various markets, with third-party access to existing pipelines at a non-discriminatory and publicized tariff as an essential component of the process. This would be coupled with the establishment of a regulatory body to whom they could refer complaints or issues that could not be resolved between themselves and transmission companies in particular. The UK government pushed for a completely liberalized market as they did not want the directive in any way to inhibit what they wished to achieve in their own market.

The result was a fudge which was seen by many as a victory for the 'established gas club' with the phased opening of the market pushed out well into the next decade. It is left to each member state to decide whether they want regulated or negotiated third-party access. In the former there will be a published tariff for the use of pipelines and in the latter it is left to bilateral negotiations between the transporter and the customer, although the main commercial conditions have to be published. Take-or-pay contracts will normally be respected, but the final ruling as to whether or not this is being used by a gas company to prevent access by others to pipelines and markets will be taken in Brussels. So although member states have a significant degree of control over the way changes occur, they cannot sit on their hands and do nothing.

The process of change has begun and although it may move at a varying pace in different countries, the liberalizing effect of the combination of gas and electricity directives will be unstoppable. The timetables incorporated in the two directives are summarized in Appendices A and B.

8.   So Where Are We Now?

The European gas industry has grown far beyond what might originally have been envisaged. This resulted from the considerable increase over time in overall reserve assessments plus, singling out one specific action, the Soviet/Russian investment in major long distance pipelines. Compared to other major world gas markets, the European market is unusual for it is supplied principally by four producer states. This adds a political dimension which is not as marked elsewhere and which will be discussed in subsequent chapters. This political balance may change in the coming decade(s) with the potential advent of Central European and Middle Eastern supplies and the growth of LNG availability from Trinidad and Nigeria in particular. Figure 1 shows the growing importance of gas in the European energy balance, although the full impact of power generation demand is yet to come. Table 1 shows the growth in individual gas markets summarized regionally as north western, central and southern Europe. Figure 2 shows the evolution of

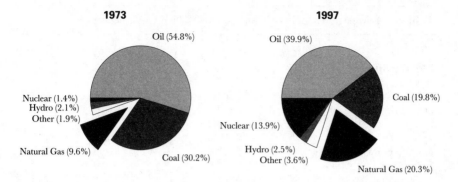

Note: Other includes geothermal, solar, wind, heat, combustible renewables and waste.
Source: *Natural Gas Information, 1997 (1998 edition)*, IEA Statistics

Figure 1: Fuel Shares in Total Primary Energy Supply, 1973 and 1997

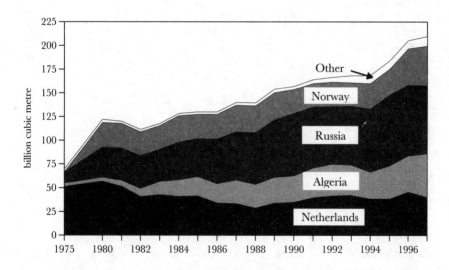

Source: *CEDIGAS*

Figure 2: Evolution of Natural Gas Imports in Europe – Breakdown by Exporting Countries

Table 1:　European Annual Gas Consumption. Billion Cubic Metres

	1980	1985	1990	1995	1997
NW Europe					
Austria	4.7	5.1	6.7	8.3	9.7
Belgium	11.6	9.4	10.6	11.8	12.5
Denmark	-	0.7	2.0	3.2	3.9
Finland	0.9	0.9	2.5	3.2	3.2
France	26.5	26.2	29.3	32.9	34.7
Germany (E&W)	58.0	55.2	59.9	74.4	79.0
Ireland	0.6	2.0	2.1	2.6	3.3
Netherlands	34.0	36.5	34.4	37.8	39.1
Norway	-	-	-	-	0.4
Sweden	-	0.1	0.7	0.8	0.8
Switzerland	0.9	1.1	1.5	2.4	2.8
UK	45.6	54.4	52.7	72.7	85.8
Total NW Europe	137.2	191.6	202.4	250.1	275.2
Southern Europe					
Italy	25.7	30.6	43.4	49.9	53.9
Spain	2.0	2.4	5.6	8.3	12.3
Portugal	-	-	-	-	0.2
Turkey	-	-	3.4	6.8	11.0
Greece	-	0.1	0.2	0.1	-
Total Southern Europe	27.7	33.1	52.6	65.1	77.4
Central Europe					
Bulgaria	n/a	-	5.9	5.0	4.2
Czech Republic	n/a	4.1	5.4	6.6	7.6
Hungary	n/a	9.6	9.6	10.2	10.8
Romania	n/a	35.5	30.8	24.0	21.8
Slovakia	n/a	4.1	5.3	4.8	5.2
Total Central Europe	n/a	53.3	57.0	50.6	49.6
Grand Total	**n/a**	**278.1**	**312.0**	**365.8**	**402.8**

Source: *BP Statistical Review of World Energy*

gas imports into Europe broken down by exporting country. Table 2 details the main pipelines that have either been built or are under construction and Table 3 shows probable and possible pipeline projects.

Market expansion may be limited by the impact of prolonged low energy prices on the provision of additional supplies. Low prices will reduce the financial returns on the exploration, production and

Table 2: Main International European Gas Pipelines – Existing and Under Construction

Projects	Start-up Date	Length (km)	Diameter (inches)	Capacity (10⁹m³/year)	Comments
Existing					
Transgas	28.12.1972	3736	48, 36, 32	79	Transport of Russian gas to Europe
TAG I and II	February 1974	1411	38, 36, 34, 42	17	Transport of Russian gas to Austria and Italy
MEGAL	1.1.1980	1070	36–48	22	Transport of Russian gas to Germany and France
STEGAL	October 1992	316	32–36	8	Transport of Russian gas in Germany
TENP-Transitgas	1974	830	38, 36, 34	7	Dutch gas delivered to Germany, Switzerland, Italy
Norpipe/Statpipe	1977/May 1986	440/880	36, 30, 28	18	Norwegian gas delivered to Emden in Germany
Trans-Med	1984	1955	48, 40, 20	16	Deliveries to Tunisia, Italy and Slovenia
Zeepipe	October 1993	850	40	12	From Sleipner to Zeebrugge
MIDAL	October 1993	600	32, 36, 40	8	Transport of Markham gas (Wintershall's network)
TransMed (extension)	June 1994	2100	48, 26	25	Deliveries to Tunisia, Italy and Slovenia
Europipe I	1.10.1995	620	40	13 (initial)	From the Draupner-E platform to Emden
Bulgaria-Macedonia	1995	165	–	0.8	From the Bulgarian network to Skopje via Kriva Palanka
Nordeutsche Erdgas-Transversale (NETRA)	1996	292	48	16–18	From Etzel/Wilhelmshaven to Salzwedel, via Wardenburg/Oldenburg
Zeepipe Phase IIA	1.10.1996	303	40	12–13	From Sleipner to Kollsnes
Maghreb-Europe (Phase I)	1.11.1996	1861	48, 22, 28	9.7	Transport of Algerian gas from Hassi R'Mel to Spain, Portugal, via Morocco
Hungary-Austria (HAG)	Autumn 1996	120	28	4.5	From Baumgarten to Győr

Source: CEDIGAZ

Table 2: continued

Projects	Start-up Date	Length (km)	Diameter (inches)	Capacity ($10^9 m^3$/year)	Comments
Existing					
Scotland/Northern Ireland Pipeline System	1996	135	24	2	From Castle Douglas to Northern Ireland
Bulgaria to Greece (Burgas to Alexandropolis)	1996	870	36, 30, 24	7	Russian gas to Greece, via Bulgaria
Zeepipe Phase IIB	1.10.1997	249	40	18	From the Draupner-E platform to Kollsnes
NorFra	October 1998	850	42	14	From the Draupner-E platform to Dunkirk
UK-Continent Gas Interconnector	October 1998	238	40	20	From Bacton (United Kingdom) to Zeebrugge (Belgium)
RTr (Belgium)	October 1998	280			Link, via the Interconnector, with the British, German, French and Dutch networks
Under Construction					
WEDAL (Westdeutschland-AnbindungsLeitung)	Autumn 1998	300	40, 48	11	From Bielefeld (MIDAL), via the Ruhr region, to Aachen. The construction of WEDAL I was completed early 1997
Artère des Hauts de France	End 1998	185	44	15	Will link Dunkirk to Cuvilly in the north of Paris
JAGAL (Yamal link)	Mid-1999	330		28	Will link Mallnow to Rückersdorf in Germany
Europipe II	1999	660	40	18	Will link Kollsnes to Emden
Yamal-Europe (Polish section)	1999	670	56	10–14	From Gorzow to Wloclawek, Ostrolenka and Bialystok
Les Marches du Nord-Est (France)	2001–2002	550	36–40	6+	Will transport Norwegian gas to Italy

Source: CEDIGAZ

Table 3: Main International Gas Pipeline Projects in Europe

Projects	Start-up Date	Length (km)	Diameter (inches)	Capacity ($10^9 m^3/year$)	Comments
Probable Projects					
Libya-Italy pipeline	2000	520	–	8	Would link the Libyan coast with Sicily
Midpipe	2000+	About 750	40	12–15	From the Haltenbanken to the North Sea network
Maghreb-Europe pipeline (Phase II)	after 2000			+9	Extension of the MEG Phase I beyond the Pyrenees
Possible Projects					
Interconnector Netherlands/UK	2002–2003	155	42	20	From Callantsoog (Den Helder) to the Corvette field in the British North Sea or direct to Bacton
Nordic Gas Grid	?	–	–	–	Transport of Russian gas via Finland and Sweden to the European Continent
Baltic Gas Transmission	?	–	–	–	Transportation network linking Denmark, Norway, Sweden, Finland, the Baltic States and Russia
Algeria-Spain pipeline	2000+				Would link Mostaganem in Algeria with Carthagena or Almeria in Spain
South-west pipeline (Germany)	after 2000	980	44, 48	–	From Frankfurt/Oder to Bavaria and Switzerland, with a branch to the west to connect with the MIDAL at Bielefeld
Polpipe		1200	–	5–10	From the British North Sea to Poland
Macedonia-Albania		200	30	–	

Source: CEDIGAZ

transmission investments that will be required. In conjunction with the inevitable uncertainties that market liberalization will bring, this will be a major challenge for individual producer states to face. This is also a challenge for the well established market players, the gas companies. However to suggest today that natural gas is a scarce resource and that security of supply is a fundamental issue in the liberalization debate, is a less credible argument than in the past.

Factors that will not change however are the increasingly demanding European environmental standards, their principal impact being a growth in gas-fired CCGT power generation, and the forces for market liberalization. Whether or not what has occurred in the UK is regarded as positive progress, the genie is out of the bottle and will not go back. The short-term trading environment is well established there and will now be exported to the Continent as a result of the Interconnector. As a stone thrown in water causes ripples to spread out, so will this – although how far it will spread has yet to be seen. The UK experience is that the publication of short-term or spot gas prices has an impact on the price expectations of all customers disproportionate to the volumes so traded – which may in fact be very small. Furthermore, such trading draws new players into the gas business who enter to make money and who have no loyalty to either a producer or the existing gas fraternity. Such players often bring highly sophisticated US experience in other commodity trading skills to bear and offer customers attractive packages of price and service levels that will change their expectations of what should be made available by all suppliers in the gas chain. For the new players, gas is not the 'premium' or 'noble' fuel it has traditionally been regarded as, but merely a commodity like any other from which money can be made.

The Interconnector allows UK producers, many of whom do not have a significant presence on the Continent, to offer for the first time long-term supplies to customers in North West Europe. The current uncertainty created by the new Labour government about the continued growth of the UK gas-fired power generation sector only adds to the potential volume of gas that may be sold to continental customers.

This need not mean all gloom and doom for existing players, whether producer or gas company. They have tremendous strengths and established positions. They can, and in some cases already do, provide the increasingly sophisticated services required by the market and see these as profitable opportunities. The producers' reactions will be discussed in detail in the next four chapters. To summarize briefly, Algeria has laid lines to Italy, Spain and Portugal to establish its supply position to these growth markets. The Dutch have made major investments in underground storage to provide profitable load balancing services. They have also signed a co-operation arrangement with Gazprom to underpin its supply undertakings in Eastern Europe and in return have secured some 4 bcm/year of Russian gas. This can be used to secure new markets, which can then be supplied by Dutch gas as Gasunie loses some of its own internal market share. This works around the Dutch government's imposed production level of 80 bcm/year. The Russians have established downstream joint ventures everywhere but the UK (although it has a 10 per cent interest in the Interconnector) of which Wingas is the most significant. The Norwegians have so far not been very active downstream, preferring to rely on sales to well established gas company customers.

In summary, the four nation states are still embattled, although there have been signs of open co-operation between two of them. The barons claim to have won their own battle to retain their power base and thereby somewhat uneasily retain the status quo. One senses however that the serfs' time to be heard is about to come, aided and abetted by some new players to the game.

Appendix A: Timetable for the Electricity Directive

February 1997: 'Implementation date' i.e. date of entry into force.

February 1999: Directive must be transposed into national laws (with the exception of Greece, Belgium and Ireland). First market opening based on a 40 GWh threshold becomes legally enforceable.

February 2000: Market opening based on a 20 GWh threshold becomes legally enforceable.

February 2003: Market opening based on a 9 GWh threshold becomes legally enforceable.

February 2006: Commission reviews Directive and considers further opening.

Appendix B: Timetable for the Gas Directive

August 1998:   Directive came into force.

August 2000:   Directive must be transposed into national laws (with the exception of those countries and regions granted derogations). First market opening for consumers with an annual consumption in excess of 25 MMcm – equating to a minimum of 20 per cent of a country's national consumption – becomes legally enforceable.

Mid 2003:   Market opening for consumers with an annual consumption in excess of 15 MMcm – equating to a minimum of 28 per cent of a country's national consumption – becomes legally enforceable.

Mid 2008:   Market opening for customers with an annual consumption in excess of 5 MMcm – equating to a minimum of 33 per cent of a country's national consumption – becomes legally enforceable.

CHAPTER 2

ALGERIAN GAS: SONATRACH'S POLICIES AND THE OPTIONS AHEAD

Ali Aïssaoui

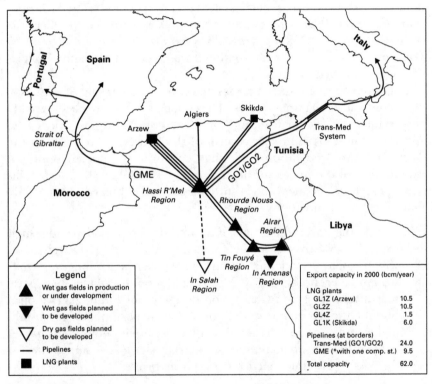

Map 1: Algeria: Main Non-associated Gas Production Regions, Pipelines and Export Facilities

1.   Introduction

This chapter aims to analyse the outlook for Sonatrach, the Algerian national oil company, in particular its gas business and ways in which it could adapt to the fundamental changes taking place in the market place. The views taken derive from a review of past and present policies. The focus is on both political and institutional changes, and on government policies.

So far, the supply of hydrocarbon has been the exclusive concern of the Algerian government, which has used its ownership and administrative control of the national company to determine successive depletion policies and to direct its marketing strategies. However, while domestic use of gas has been systematically promoted, and the gas share of total primary energy requirements has increased to reflect the structure of hydrocarbon reserves, gas exports have been affected by both uncertainties of the international markets and changing policies of successive governments.

Major changes in such policies have been the result of domestic economic and social imperatives. These policies also have been greatly constrained by ideological and political considerations. Since the Algerian state took complete control of the hydrocarbon sector in the early 1970s, a redefinition of what constitutes a socially optimal exploitation of the hydrocarbon resources has resulted in different gas strategies. Key debates and controversies have hinged around the following policy directions:

(i)   Should the government opt for a rapid depletion policy and a high export policy to secure the financing of a large industrial base, which would provide the country with a vehicle for long-term self-sustaining economic growth? Or should it opt for moderate exports that would preserve hydrocarbon resources for future generations?

(ii)   Should the government opt for a low export policy to sustain higher prices on international markets or should it opt for a market strategy aimed at increasing its market share to compensate for the loss of revenues incurred by lower prices?

The debate culminated at the end of the 1970s and early 1980s, when the rapid depletion policy of the 1970s (Abdesselam 1989) was challenged and substituted by a prorationing policy,[1] and its corresponding low export policy (Nabi 1991). While there is no convincing evidence of the soundness of the former policy, the 1986 oil price collapse and the subsequent social and economic disruptions underlined the limits of the latter. These disruptions provoked radical political and economic changes, which involved a double transition: from a one-party system to a multi-party system and from a centrally-planned economy to a market-oriented economy. As a result, ideological constraints were relaxed, allowing for major shifts in energy policies and gas strategies in the 1990s (Boussena 1989 and 1991; Aït-Laoussine 1992).

As the 1990s progressed, the debate on the share of gas in total hydrocarbon exports re-emerged (INESG 1996). The new argument put forward suggested that government fiscal objectives would be better met by expanding liquid than gas exports. Indeed, compared to oil, the gas industry generates much lower economic rent (simply defined as income above factor costs), since on a calorific basis, gas has higher costs of production and transportation, and it also fetches a lower market price. In keeping with this argument, Sonatrach's move to develop additional gas reserves further afield and from costly reservoirs, is being questioned at a moment when downward pressures on gas prices are increasing in its main European markets. Whether Sonatrach and its foreign partners, newly involved in the gas industry, will be able to lower the costs of production is a key factor in the expansion of its resource base and its gas business. Indeed, with the oil sector recovering and oil production expected to double by 2005, the 'rent' argument will finally come to bear on future gas export policies.

This new debate shifts the focus to Sonatrach's performance and new strategy. The challenges facing the company are not only upstream. The changes taking place in the market place may be a threat to its overall market share position. Also the redistribution of the rents associated with restructuring of the gas chain highlights the opportunities offered downstream. The extent to which Sonatrach can meet such challenges and exploit these opportunities will shape its course.

This chapter is organized as follows:

Following this introduction, Section 2 will provide a brief historical background starting with the creation of Sonatrach and its progressive control of the gas business. It will examine the company's first gas strategy as embedded in the Valorisation des Hydrocarbures (VALHYD) plan, before focusing on the so-called 'gas battle' of the early 1980s and its implications.

Section 3 will analyse the basic concepts underlying the 1989 gas strategy, the resulting potential long-term export profile and how major financing constraints have led to radical changes in the gas regime, which widened the scope for foreign participation. Consideration of Sonatrach-BP and Sonatrach-Amoco partnerships will illustrate the resulting different ways of developing the gas business.

Section 4 will explore the period ahead. How the company could reassess its upstream expansion is a key determinant of future export profiles. This section will also examine how the company is perceiving the changes in the market place and how it intends to move to capture some of the downstream gas value. Finally, restoration of a normal corporate structure and the extent to which Sonatrach can gain autonomy and retain more flexibility from the new institutional setting will be analysed.

2.   A Brief Historical Background

As Algeria organized its way out of war into independence, the take-over of the hydrocarbon industry from the French colonial power was put at the top of the political agenda of an Algerian leadership committed to independence and sovereign government. Hydrocarbon resources were regarded as a major asset that could be used to generate economic development and achieve social welfare.

However, in spite of the relative importance of gas, it was oil which shaped early developments of the energy sector and directed Algerian international relations. The potential for gas development would only be given full consideration in the second half of the 1970s, within the first comprehensive Sonatrach hydrocarbon development plan, VALHYD. Based on a rapid depletion policy, the underlying strategy was aimed at sustaining economic development biased towards a heavy industrialization programme. However, the plan did not materialize.

By the end of the 1970s, fundamental changes in the political leadership and governmental administration resulted in a major shift in energy policy. In a context of higher oil prices, the new administration embarked on a so-called 'gas battle' that focused on the adjustment of gas prices and price formulas. This move was underlined by a new depletion policy, which had wide-ranging geo-political ramifications since, in spite of stagnation of gas demand, it contributed to a major expansion of Soviet gas in Western Europe. The significant loss of Sonatrach's market share resulted in LNG exports falling to less than half the nominal capacity by the mid1980s. Algeria, which had, by the end of the 1970s, secured contracts to export some 70 bcm per year by 1986, was actually only exporting 21 bcm by that time. This trend combined with a downward pressure on oil prices, which culmin-ated in their collapse, led to a downfall of export revenues and rapid expansion of foreign debt. These developments, which resulted in dramatic social unrest, brought about major political and economic transformations and led to drastic measures to revive the hydrocarbon sector.

2.1   The 1960s: Towards Gas Emancipation

The early orientation of Algeria's hydrocarbon policy was constrained by French vision and interests. Following the discovery of huge oil and gas reserves in 1955–7, the French colonial authorities conferred upon SN Repal and CFP (Compagnie française des pétroles, now Total), the concession holders of the super giant fields of Hassi Messaoud and Hassi R'Mel, the development of the hydrocarbon industry. The 1962 Evian Accord between France and Algeria, which organized the transition from war to independence, instituted a quasi 'co-sovereignty' over hydrocarbon resources, thus maintaining French advantages intact. As a result, although the Algerian government had inherited a substantial equity participation in SN Repal,[2] it was prevented from genuine participation in the industry. The first attempt to obtain a controlling interest in an oil pipeline project linking Hassi Messaoud to the port of Arzew was frustrated by the French companies, which regarded it as an infringement of their privileged positions. This prompted the government to create its own company – Sonatrach – on 31 December 1963, and entrust it with the construction of the contentious pipeline.[3]

The acronym Sonatrach (for Société Nationale de Transport et de Commercialisation des Hydrocarbures) was intended to reflect its initial mission, which was limited to the transportation and commercialization of hydrocarbons. Until the revision of the conditions of exploitation of oil and gas in 1965 and the subsequent extension of Sonatrach's mission to all phases of the industry, the newly formed national company was in no position to take enterprising initiatives. Therefore, the Algerian government had to rely on foreign companies for projects on long-term marketing of natural gas. Since the major portion of the gas reserves would have to be exported, bold schemes for LNG and sub-marine pipelines across the Mediterranean were explored with a view to delivering gas to European markets. CAMEL (Compagnie Algérienne du Méthane Liquide), the world's first commercial gas liquefaction plant, originally designed to fulfil a British Gas contract, was inaugurated in September 1964. A later deal with Gaz de France led to an expansion of the project to supply additional output to France.[4]

2.1.1 Uncertain European Market
The prospects for further expansion of LNG exports were uncertain.

In September 1965, the announcement of the first commercial gas discovery by BP in the British sector of the North Sea closed a window of opportunity previously offered by the UK market. Algerian gas also faced competition from Dutch gas and, to a lesser extent, from Libyan. As it became clear that Algeria would seek to increase its control over oil and gas, prospective buyers turned their interest to NAM (Nederlandse Aardolie Maatschappij) (Shell, Esso) in the Netherlands, and to Esso in Libya.

Also uncertain were the projects for trans-Mediterranean gas pipelines to Europe. The offer made in 1963 to the Algerian government by SN-Repal and CFP(A), with French government support, put particular emphasis on an export scheme through Morocco and the Strait of Gibraltar (Pawera 1964; Abdesselam 1989). However, such a scheme was faced at the outset by a highly unfavourable political situation arising notably from the boundary dispute with neighbouring Morocco.

2.1.2   *Opportunity in the American Market*

Early competition from Dutch and Libyan gas, and the difficulties experienced with the French government and French companies, were certainly at the origin of several years of fruitless discussions with European gas companies. This led the Algerian government and Sonatrach to turn their attention to the American market.

By the end of the 1960s, the American economy was experiencing a remarkable expansion and concurrent increase in the demand for energy. However, the capacity of domestic gas reserves to cover demand was uncertain. Data for that period point to a rapid increase of natural gas reserves in the Lower 48 States, to a peak in 1967. After that a sharp decline began, which even the addition of the Alaskan North Slope reserves in 1970 could not reverse. As the ratio of reserves to production was less than twelve years, there was a general belief that there would be a severe gas shortage. Consequently, in addition to the well-established Canadian, and to a lesser extent Mexican, pipeline gas imports, long-haul LNG imports became a serious option.

In this context, the first major contract for the export of LNG from Algeria to the USA was signed in 1969 between Sonatrach and El Paso Natural Gas Company. During the 1960s, the base price of the first generation of LNG contracts was in parity or above fob oil prices (Jarjour 1990; Nabi 1991).[5] However, the context was that of declining oil product prices. Over the period 1961 to 1969, posted prices for middle distillates declined by 18 per cent and those for fuel oil by 6 per cent.[6] Therefore, gas-exporting companies favoured an indexation, or escalation of the base price with non-oil indices. In the case of the El Paso contract, such a price arrangement and the absence of minimum price and price re-opener (Table 1) proved ineffective in protecting the purchasing power of the expected revenues. In spite of these shortcomings, the El Paso contract was considered to be a remarkable milestone by the Algerian energy policy makers. Not only were the authorities persuaded of its economic spin-offs, but also they acclaimed its symbolic value, which resided in the fact that it 'consecrated Algeria's emancipation and its international credibility for marketing its gas resources' (Abdesselam 1989:161 [original French]).

2.2   *The 1970s: An Ambitious Hydrocarbon Development Strategy*

By the end of the 1960s and early 1970s, the international gas trade was still limited. Total cross-border volumes amounted to only 46 bcm in 1970, accounting for 4.5 per cent of world marketed production. Consequently, it was oil and not gas which was the main determinant of energy policy and international relations. The focus was on the mounting conflict of interests between producing countries on the one hand and international oil companies and governments of consuming countries on the other. The Algerian government, having cemented its control of the hydrocarbon industry and laid the foundation of the country's economic development (Mazri 1975), focused its international ambitions through OPEC, which it joined in 1969. Algeria played an active role in the process of fiscal and price adjustments and took the lead in promoting the idea of a new international economic order, linking the question of oil prices to much broader issues of resources allocation (Ghozali 1975).

Algeria's international ambitions were a reflection of its domestic social objectives. These were expressed in the 1976 National Charter,[7] an ideological, political and economic platform, which mirrored the dominant forms of 'statism' and 'socialism' established in radical Arab countries at that time. The Charter stressed the vital importance of the hydrocarbon industry to Algeria's economic and social development. As the country had no other revenues, the sale and export of hydrocarbon reserves were viewed by the Algerian government as the means for financing the creation of a large and integrated industrial base for the national economy. The government's view was that, once in place, 'this industrial base will provide the country with a vehicle for self-sustaining economic growth in the future' (Sonatrach 1977:1-1 of VALHYD).

Table 1: Long-Term Gas Supply Contracts Between Sonatrach and its Partners — Evolution of the Main Contractual Terms

	1960s	Mid-1970s	First half 1980s	Second half 1980s		First half 1990s
Market	Lng-UK/USA	Lng-USA/Europe	Lng-Europe	Lng-Europe	Lng-USA	Pipeline gas-Europe
Take-or-Pay	100%	100%	100%	100%	None	85%
Base price fob	$0.305/Mbtu[1]	$1.30/MBtu	$4.80/Mbtu	$2.30/Mbtu	Market-related sale price	$1.90/Mbtu
Indexation of the base price	Relative — Partial indexation (15% to 20%) to steel product prices, and wages	Relative — Full indexation to gas oil and fuel oil prices	Absolute — Full indexation to Basket of crude oil prices (official prices)	Absolute — Full indexation to Basket of crude oil prices (netback values)	None — Netback Fob price equal to 63 percent of sale price	Absolute — Full indexation to Gas oil and fuel oil prices
Minimum price	None	$1.30/MBtu indexed to a basket of currencies	None	$1.30/Mbtu not indexed	None[2]	$1.00/Mbtu not indexed
Price re-opening	None	Every 4 years	Every 4 years	Every 3 years	None	Every 3 years

1 Base price agreed between Sonatrach and El Paso in 1969. Other base prices are indicative and may vary from contract to contract.
2 Contract with Boston's Distrigas may include a time-indexed minimum FOB price.

Source: Aït-Laoussine (1979), Jarjour (1990), Barrows and MEES (several issues)

2.2.1 VALHYD

Within such a global framework an ambitious hydrocarbon strategy was devised. Sonatrach's resulting long-term development plan, VALHYD, was commissioned to International Bechtel Inc. The Plan's objectives were 'to maximize the production rates of gas, crude oil, LPG, and condensate, consistent with obtaining the highest total recovery of hydrocarbons on an economic basis' (Ibid.). A comprehensive re-assessment of the hydrocarbon reserves (DeGolyer and MacNaughton 1977), provided the necessary base to work out the long-term sustainable production, domestic requirements, and export profiles, as well as the resulting investment costs and return. Foreign exchange earnings provided the financial structure to promote the plan (Khelil and Harouaka 1979), which was presented to the government by the end of 1977.

The basic concept underlying VALHYD was that essentially all of the known oil and most of the known gas reserves, including reserves around In Amenas and In Salah, as well as NGLs in the form of condensate and LPG would be produced between 1976 and 2005. Gas export commitments, together with domestic consumption and internal requirements of the hydrocarbon industry (including the liquefaction facilities), would involve a total commercial production at field level of about 110 bcm per year, on account of proven reserves of some 3000 bcm at that time. In setting a target of 70 bcm per year of gas exports from 1985 to 2005, the government endorsed the underlying assumptions that two-thirds of current proven reserves would be allocated to exports. As with any large-scale, long-term development project, major uncertainties in the underlying assumptions were pointed out, notably those linked to the evolution of gas markets.

2.2.2 Mitigating Market Risks

To prepare for the financing programme and implementation of the Plan, by the end of 1978 Sonatrach had built a portfolio of sale contracts, amounting to 65 bcm per year of firm sales and 6.5 bcm per year of contracts signed but awaiting approval (Aït-Laoussine 1979). In addition to diversifying its markets, Sonatrach had sought to balance the risks involved across the gas chain, as well as to ensure gas competitiveness in the energy market.

The uncertainty of the American market and failure of the US administration to achieve a clear and coherent LNG import policy, led Sonatrach to depart from its initial desire to sell gas in both the USA and Europe in roughly equal volumes (Belguedj 1978). A more pragmatic approach was subsequently adopted. As a consequence, 78 per cent of total commitments went to the European market (Gaz de France, Enagas, Distrigaz, ENI, as well as Gasunie and Ruhrgas together with other German companies), and 22 per cent to the American market (El Paso, Trunkline and Distrigas). Alternatives to LNG were also considered via trans-Mediterranean pipelines; the Trans-Med pipeline to Italy was agreed by the end of 1977 and intensive maritime surveys were carried out in preparation of a direct link between Algeria and Spain.[8]

Two major characteristics of the industry had been recognized as essential features of gas contracting; firstly, the considerable up-front investment involved and the high financial risks associated with the inflexibility of the gas chain, and secondly, the need for gas to gain a competitive position in various buyer's markets with different structures, characteristics, and premiums. Therefore risk-balancing measures, as well as modifier mechanisms to enable gas to remain competitive, were agreed upon. Taking into account the Algerian pattern of ownership, where major financial risks were borne by the government, minimum prices and take-or-pay clauses offered a reasonable risk-sharing arrangement. An indexed minimum price was designed to generate sufficient revenues to cover Sonatrach's investments, and a strict 'take-or-pay' obligation was deemed necessary to protect the country's revenues against default by the buyer.

Contrary to the 1969 El Paso agreement, the modifier of the base price (the indexation formula) was proportional to the evolution of the prices of competing fuels in the buyers' market. At the same time a price reopener mechanism was introduced in the 1970s to give the opportunity to both parties to correct any deviation (see Table 1).

2.3   The 1980s: The 'Gas Battle'

President Boumedienne's death in December 1978 brought funda-mental changes in the political leadership and government administra-tion. Serious problems faced by the Algerian economy led to an economic re-evaluation of the massive industrialization programme of the previous administration, as well as its hydrocarbon strategy. As a result, the VALHYD Planning Group was dismantled, and major components of its programme abandoned, including, in the gas sector, a third LNG plant together with the supply contracts supporting it.

Under contracts signed in 1977, Sonatrach was committed to supply 11.25 bcm per year, over a period of twenty years, to Ruhrgas/ Salzgitter of West Germany and Gasunie of Holland. Deliveries were planned to begin in 1983 from GNL3 Arzew plant. As this project was not included in the five-year plan 1980–85 (and the construction contract with Foster Wheeler and Technip was cancelled), Sonatrach was instructed to renegotiate the corresponding deliveries as well as deliveries to other German companies, through the Trans-Med pipeline to Italy (Nabi 1991).

Such a move was presented by the incumbent administration as a fundamental shift away from costly LNG plants to pipeline routes (Pauwels 1983; Nabi 1991). Indeed, past experience with LNG – both during the lengthy construction period of LNG1 and since Sonatrach took over CAMEL – revealed not only the high investment but also the costly operating involved. In particular, the huge quantities of gas fuelled in the liquefaction plants were presented as being of great concern to the Algerian authorities. Also, ill-conceived and consequently inefficient foreign technical assistance did not tackle properly the intensive maintenance requirements of such plants (Djaroud 1991). However, the LNG vs. pipeline argument was rather fallacious. Both the Trans-Med and, in the face of increasing political uncertainties with neighbouring Morocco, a direct link between Algeria and Spain were integral components of the VALHYD plan (Aït-Laoussine 1979). In fact, what was at stake was more the rapid depletion policy underlying VALHYD. The choice of the appropriate level of gas exports was at the core of the national energy policy debate launched by the FLN (Fergani 1983).

The ruling party, which emerged stronger during the transition, stepped in to adopt new guidelines for the country's energy policy (FLN 1980). Particular emphasis was put on guaranteeing long-term domestic requirements and conserving energy resources. The resulting depletion policy paralleled the one adopted by the Dutch government, which prompted Gasunie to curtail its gas exports by some 15 to 20 bcm in the early 1980s.[9] The impact on Gasunie of the loss of the Algerian gas contract is not clear. What is certain, and clearly illustrated in Figure 1, is that in spite of the Reagan administration's hostility towards Soviet export pipelines,[10] Algerian and Dutch policies favoured Soyuzgazexport's aggressive penetration in West Germany and the rest of Europe.

Obviously, retraction of Algerian and Dutch gas on the one hand, and the corresponding expansion of Soviet exports on the other, were supplemented by different pricing policies. In the case of Algeria, in the euphoric context of the Iranian revolution and the belief that OPEC would be able to continue to administer oil prices at the prevailing levels, the FLN guidelines conveyed the idea that greater revenues could be generated from higher prices than from larger

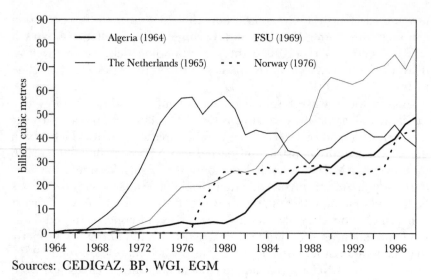

Sources: CEDIGAZ, BP, WGI, EGM

Figure 1: Comparative Paths of Gas Exports to Western Europe

volumes. However, neither the Algerian demands for a higher base price and a new indexation formula linking gas prices to oil prices, nor the final result of the subsequent negotiations in the first half of the 1980s (see Table 1) should have come as a surprise.[11] Indeed, with the exception of the 1969 El Paso contract,[12] all Algerian supply contracts provided for price re-opening, that is the opportunity to periodically review the base price and price formula or to revise them in the case of fundamental changes in the energy scene, which was certainly the case at the end of the 1970s. Secondly, as in the 1970s, attitudes to indexation had continued to evolve with increasing emphasis on international reference pricing ranging from oil to alternative fuels. What is remarkable is, first, the ambiguity regarding an oil-gas price parity, secondly the attempt to involve OPEC, and thirdly and more importantly, the direct involvement of the Algerian government.

Failing to formulate clearly the new principles underlying its claim and to find the necessary support within OPEC,[13] Algeria entered bilateral negotiations at government level. Not surprisingly, discussions with the USA failed rapidly. The new Reagan administration, ideologically committed to economic liberalism, showed no sympathy for a country which, though increasingly pragmatic, was still identified with radical socialism and Third World activism. In addition, in an increasingly liberalized gas market, independent regulatory commissions, under intense lobbying from distributors and consumers, greatly limited the room for manoeuvre of the gas-importing companies. In contrast, European governments each found a specific reason to favour a solution at government level. This was particularly the case for France, Algeria's main LNG client. Indeed, the new socialist Mitterand administration, keen to promote more balanced North–South relations, had a rather positive attitude towards Algeria's ideological orientation. In addition, France was well aware of the gain it would derive from placing gas discussions in a broader and more complex context of foreign policy, trade, and financial relations with its main Arab and African partner.[14]

Pauwels, an academic and occasional advisor to the Algerian government and Sonatrach, unconvincingly reflected the prevailing thinking in 1983:

> The enhancement of value Algeria has obtained for its gas supplies transcends simple gas economics as well as the 'rounds' of price revisions that producers have embarked upon. Such an enhancement is the result of a political will to improve relations between Algeria and the European Countries and comes within a new type of North-South relations. (Pauwels 1983:51) [translated from French]

As far as prices are concerned, Algeria's philosophy concerning the international gas trade and contractual relationship was epitomized in the following statement:

> Amongst the decisive factors for balance in relationship between the sellers and buyers of natural gas, prices are undoubtedly the kingpin. Importing countries have consistently tried to control prices directly or indirectly. In the first generation of contracts, particularly for LNG, only a fraction of the price (15 to 20 per cent) was indexed, and even then on price changes of some industrial products. The exporting country therefore saw the purchasing power of its raw material drop steadily. The second generation of contracts did provide machinery for indexing natural gas prices on those of refined products, but the base price was kept below that of energy, especially crude oil, thus creating a widening gap since the indexing was of a proportional nature. Moreover, the prices of refined products considered were those internal in the importing countries and therefore in most cases controlled by them. Corrections to the third generation of contracts (raising the base price, rejection of the proportional indexing machinery, price adjustments along with those of crude oil and oil products on the international market place) restored some measure of balance (Algerian Energy Committee 1985:30 of the English translation).

This argument was originally proposed by Yousfi (1984:4).

While the new pricing mechanism and the confirmation of clauses such as take-or-pay were instrumental in shaping a better balance in contractual relationships, it is difficult to determine whether the price agreements Algeria finally reached with its European partners, most significantly with France, were an achievement in political or economic terms.

On the economic terms, the 'absolute' indexation to oil prices did achieve higher prices than the previous 'relative' indexation to oil product prices. However, it proved to be 'a high-risk formula' (Aït-Laoussine 1990), since it benefited only from the context of increasing oil prices in the period 1979–81. Furthermore, the loss of the American market and the significant contraction of quantities with its Belgian, and more dramatically with its Spanish partner, diminished beyond immediate 'take-or-pay' compensations any longer-term economic gain.

Indeed, Algeria's move on prices took place at a time of major shifts in the pattern of energy demand and supply of the main consuming countries. In a context of deep economic recession, expansion of nuclear power and the application of a strong coal utilization strategy, as well as concentration of the use of natural gas on premium users' requirements, all affected gas demand in Western Europe, particularly in Belgium, Spain, and to a lesser extent France. In the USA, lower gas demand combined with a revival in domestic production, produced a long-lasting 'gas bubble'. As a result, Sonatrach was in no position to find other buyers for the gas it had anticipated selling to the USA and the Algerian government had to bear the brunt of the economic and social cost resulting from the non realization of revenues on which it had based its development plan (Pelletreau 1987).

2.3.1 Adjusting to New Circumstances

The oil price collapse in 1986 offered a new environment for Sonatrach to alter significantly its gas marketing policy and to adapt to the new realities of the market place. As governments from both sides adopted a lower profile, innovative new deals with Panhandle and Distrigas allowed the company to re-establish links with a deregulated US market. In Europe, after several rather difficult rounds of renegotiations with its established clients, GdF, Distrigaz, Enagaz and SNAM, new contractual arrangements translated into significant changes in the pricing mechanisms (see Table 1):

(a) a new base price of $2.30/MBtu to reflect the post 1986 low oil price environment;

(b) the abandonment of official oil prices as an index and their replacement by netback values;

(c) the reintroduction of a minimum price of $1.30/MBtu, to avoid the previous absurd situation, where as a result of oil prices collapsing, gas prices derived from the previous formula became negative (Aït-Laoussine 1990).

For new European LNG clients, such as Turkey, Sonatrach was willing to agree for the first time since the mid-1970s to an element of explicit indexation to oil product prices alongside that to oil prices.

2.3.2 The Effects of the Policies of the 1970s and 1980s

Algeria, which had focused on the 'oil battle' in the early 1970s, shifted to a 'gas battle' in the early 1980s. The difference was that in the 1970s the battle involved broader issues of sovereignty over natural resources, participation in, and ultimately control over the hydrocarbon sector, while in the 1980s, the battle was for a better sharing of the gas rent. However, the 'gas battle' single-mindedly translated into a 'fight over formulas' (Zartman and Bassani 1987) therefore failing to achieve its proclaimed objectives.

As a result, Sonatrach's rather slow development of its LNG exports in the 1970s resulted in the loss of its market in the USA, as well as a substantial market share in Europe in the 1980s. Although in the 1970s Algeria had committed to exports of up to 70 bcm per year by 1986, it was actually only exporting 21 bcm by that time – below the five-year plan (1980–84) target of 34 bcm. Sonatrach's poor performance in terms of gas export volumes had an effect on the maintenance of the LNG plants. The loss of one-third of LNG capacity was coupled with a similar loss in oil production, which, as a result of a combined FLN-inspired 'conservation' policy and OPEC-inspired shared price defence policy, fell from 1.15 million barrels per day in 1979 to 0.69 million in 1988. When world energy consumption began to recover, Sonatrach was in no position to take its share of the incremental demand. The opening of the hydrocarbon upstream sector in 1986 was too little, too late. The fall in export volume, coupled with that of the price of oil and gas, resulted in the decline of export revenues from a peak of $14.2 billion in 1981, collapsing to $7.3 billion in 1986, and even further to $7.0 billion in 1988.

For a country where oil and gas revenues represented some 95 per cent of external revenue and 60 per cent of fiscal receipts, the consequences were devastating. According to Walid Khadduri (1989:1–2):

The past decade [1979–88] has been a difficult one for the Algerian petroleum industry in many ways. The conflict over gas contracts in the early eighties meant that the multi-billion dollar LNG plants at Arzew and Skikda were working at less than half capacity throughout most of the decade. Gas contracts were either reduced, delayed or cancelled. Stringent law and inflexible policies deterred foreign firms from coming forward in earnest with the investment funds and modern technology required for exploration in a vast country that has been sparely explored so far. The global decline in energy demand and the collapse of oil prices did not help matters either.

3.   Gas Policy in the 1990s

By the end of the 1980s, Algeria's economic, financial and social situation was rapidly deteriorating, and was weakened further as a result of the expansion of external debt to a crippling level. As it became clear that oil prices would remain uncertain and that oil production recovery would involve a long time lag, Algeria shifted its focus towards expanding gas exports and developing the more readily available gas resources.

The new gas strategy, aimed at doubling exports by the end of the 1990s, introduced basic elements of flexibility in order to recover lost market share and to penetrate new markets. The focus was put on the fast-growing southern European market. In spite of the convergence of the new strategy with the EU objectives and the subsequent financial support of EU institutions, the scale of the necessary capital investment underlying the programme put tremendous pressure on the country's external financial resources. This prompted a notable move towards attracting foreign private investments in the gas sector. Unfortunately, the attempt to secure access to foreign capital conflicted with the limits imposed by the prevailing hydrocarbon law, thus necessitating a problematic policy revision.

The impetus for change came once again with a new administration, which, while continuing to disregard any orthodox solutions to the problem of foreign debt (debt rescheduling), put pressure on the oil sector to attract and generate more cash to fill the country's deepening financial gap. The shift in policy had to take into account broader long-term objectives to develop and expand the hydrocarbon sector, eventually resulting in radical changes aimed at attracting foreign investments and new technologies. In particular, international oil companies were granted the right to share in natural gas production and to invest in the transportation sector, hitherto the sole preserve of Sonatrach. The door was opened for foreign investments across the gas chain, leading to innovative partnerships and alliances and potentially new ways of commercializing gas.

3.1   The 1989 Novel Gas Strategy

1989 was a pivotal year in Algeria's gas industry. Early in that year, a novel gas strategy was approved by the newly-established National Consultative Committee on Energy (NCCE), as the centrepiece of a broader energy policy aimed at securing macro-economic balances and achieving economic growth. As a matter of fact, the NCCE substituted for the 1981 National Energy Council (NEC). However, unlike the NEC, the NCCE was ideologically and politically less constrained. Indeed its framework referred to the 1986 Charter, a new platform initiated by President Chadli, at the start of his second mandate, in an attempt to move radically away from the 1976 National Charter and President Boumedienne's 'socialist' legacy (Table 2). As there was no representative of the FLN party in the Committee, it was easier to challenge the hitherto strong influence of the FLN on energy policy issues. On the other hand, the affirmation of the Prime Minister's prerogatives was also instrumental in embarking on the reforms necessary for the success of the new gas strategy.

This strategy, whose underlying concepts are examined in later developments, was devised in a context characterized by major ideological, political and economic changes and uncertainties (Løchstøer 1990). Economic difficulties caused by the weakening of oil prices in the run-up to the 1986 price collapse and the considerable burden of foreign debt had been dictating an unpopular period of economic austerity. Combined with social and demographic pressures this resulted in social unrest in October 1988, which brought about major political and economic reforms. The February 1989 constitution deleted reference to socialism, separated the FLN from the state institutions, and allowed for the creation and participation of political associations. As such, it marked the most significant change in the ideological and political landscape of the country since its independence in 1962. On the economic front, the new reforms were aimed at transforming Algeria's economy from a state-controlled, oil-dependent economy to a market-oriented and private sector-led one.

Unfortunately, the ability of the political transition to exert a positive influence was undermined by the rapidly deteriorating economic environment. Export earnings from hydrocarbons had fallen to $7 billion in 1988, their lowest level since the end of the 1970s. Algeria, which shared in the OPEC output reduction to ease pressure on oil prices between 1982 and 1985, was in no position to claim its share of the incremental market when demand for oil began to increase again after 1986. Despite a renewal in exploration in the aftermath of

Table 2: Algerian Institutional Energy Framework: Evolution of the National Energy Council

Denomination	National Energy Council (NEC)	National Consultative Committee on Energy (NCCE)	National Committee for Energy (NCE)	National Energy Council (NEC)
Date	May-81	Jan-89	Oct-90	Apr-95
Ideological & political framework	1976 National Charter	1986 National Charter	None	Platform for National Consensus
Main missions	Definition of energy policy Co-ordination of implementation Control of execution	Definition of energy policy Co-ordination of its implementation Periodic evaluation	Evaluation of government energy policy and programmes	Follow up and evaluation of the energy policy Supervision of strategic alliances with foreign partners
Composition	President of the Republic (chairman) President of the Parliament Prime Minister Chairman of the FLN Economic Commission Minister of energy Minister of finance Minister of planning Minister of scientific research	Prime Minister (Chairman) Minister of foreign affairs Minister of energy Minister of higher education Minister of trade Head of the Prime Minister's office Delegate for planning Chairman of the Economic commission of the Parliament	Prime minister (Chairman) Minster of energy Minister of finance Minister of trade Governor of the central bank Delegate for planning Director general of Sonatrach Director general of Sonelgaz	President of the Republic (Chairman) Minister of foreign affairs Minister of defence Minister of energy Minister of finance Minister of trade Governor of the central bank
Remarks	Pronounced ideological and political character Though acted to counterbalance the heavy tutelage of the FLN party on energy policy	Affirmation of the Prime Minister's prerogatives Less ideological interference (absence of the FLN)	Absence of any ideological or political reference Involvement of financial institutions Emergence of Sonatrach and Sonelgaz as policy makers	Reference to transitory consensual arrangements Enlargement of preoccupations to foreign alliances and long-term commercial agreements with strategic implications

Source: *Journal Officiel de la République Algérienne*, various issues, and author's comments the 1986 hydrocarbon law, a sense of pessimism linked to the perception of limited oil potential and the long time lags involved, led to the clear shift of emphasis in favour of natural gas development.

3.1.1 Re-allocation of Gas Reserves

The new gas export strategy was formulated within a global scheme that took into account three basic requirements: firstly to guarantee long-term domestic needs, secondly to achieve optimum NGLs recovery from the wet gas fields, and thirdly to ensure a timely development of a number of existing gas fields (discovered but not yet developed) in order to avoid too rapid a depletion of the super-giant Hassi R'Mel field.

In keeping with past resolutions on energy policy, the first requirement was addressed through the concept of 'strategic hydrocarbon reserves'. Restricting these reserves to natural gas stems from two fundamental factors. Firstly, proven gas reserves, re-estimated at some 3000 bcm of non-associated gas,[15] amounted to 70 per cent of global hydrocarbon reserves, as against 15 per cent for oil, and represented a reserve/production ratio of sixty years, as against twenty years for oil. In addition, the ratio of remaining to initial reserves was 90 per cent for gas, but only 40 per cent for oil. This meant that proven gas reserves constituted the bulk of hydrocarbon reserves and were the least depleted primary source of energy. Estimates of additional gas reserves were also substantial, and considered at that time to be more important than those of oil from a long-term perspective.

3.1.2 Domestic Requirements

Gas production capacity and the rate of gross output are disproportionate with regard to domestic requirements and exports. Indeed, the gas supply system implies a cycling process aimed at optimal recovery of the liquids contained in the wet gas fields. Gas in excess of commercial needs is re-injected to maintain the internal pressure of the reservoirs and avoid any loss of liquids that would result from retrograde condensation. Consequently, more than two-fifths of the gross production is re-injected. Table 3 illustrates the 1997 gas balance and Table 4 shows the consumption.

The evolution of the disposition of gas production since commercial gas first flowed in 1961 is illustrated in Figure 2. Gas re-injected, which is plotted in the negative half of the figure, affects the remaining reserves only to the extent of the 'shrinkage' in volume resulting from the extraction of NGLs. The bulk of the re-injection takes place in Hassi R'Mel. It is worth noting that the super-giant gas field has witnessed three phases in its development. In the early 1960s the

Table 3:   Algeria: 1997 Gas Balance

	Bcm
Gross production	155.7
Flared	6.9
Shrunk	5.9
Re-injected	67.1
Commercial production	75.8
Exports	49.3
Resulting domestic requirements	26.5

Source: *OPEC Annual Statistical Bulletin*, 1997

Table 4:   Algeria: Gas Consumption in 1997

		Bcm
Domestic requirements (net production minus exports)		26.5
Energy sector (excluding power generation)		11.9
Upstream	5.1	
Transportation	2.6	
LNG plants	4.2	
Other sectors		11.6
Power generation	6.1	
Petrochemical feedstock	1.4	
Industrial, commercial and domestic sectors	4.1	
Unaccounted for		3.0

Source: Author's compilations, using statistics from the OPEC Secretariat (as
communicated by the Algerian Ministry of Energy). Other data are based on
statistics released by Sonatrach, Sonelgaz and Enip. The figure of 3 bcm
(unaccounted for) is the result of discrepancies in such statistics, which include
losses.

French companies exploited it as a liquid (condensate) reservoir, flaring
all surplus gas. Once Sonatrach took over the gas business, the Algerian
government forbade any flaring and, as the reservoir was exploited for
gas production only, NGLs were forfeited. After the 1971 nationalization, Sonatrach invested heavily in cycling processes and the reservoir
began to be exploited with an NGLs optimal recovery scheme.

Algeria shifted its consumption pattern away from oil early on. By
systematically promoting domestic use of natural gas, it limited the

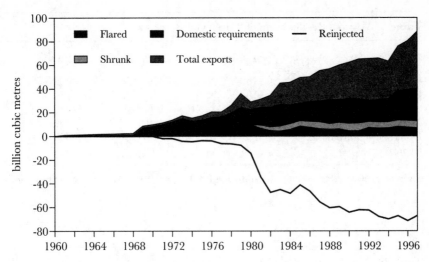

Sources: OPEC, Sonatrach

Figure 2: Disposition of Algerian Gas Production

role of much higher value oil products, releasing them for export. As a result, gas represents 95 per cent of the fuel input of the power generation sector and 60 to 65 per cent of total primary energy requirements.[16]

3.1.3 Export Profile

By fixing a time span of 45 years (1990–2035) to cover future domestic requirements, it was calculated that up to 45 per cent of the proven, non-associated, gas reserves could be dedicated to exports. The resulting cumulative exports of 1350 bcm (Table 5) would correspond to a profile of 30 bcm per year in 1990, building up to 60 bcm in 2000 (Table 6) and sustained at that level until 2015, that is 25 years of export commitments (Bouhafs 1996).

Having revived and completely redesigned two American contracts, and also renegotiated the basics of four existing ones in Europe, as pointed out in the first section of this chapter, Sonatrach embarked on negotiations for several new contracts. It also opened discussions with additional potential customers, including Ruhrgas, with which the company had severed relations in the early 1980s.

With a new ambitious objective of doubling exports, and the realization of strong competition from Russia and Norway in the Mediterranean market, Sonatrach was compelled to offer more flexibility, both in terms of 'take-or-pay' requirements and price mechanisms (see Table 2). Indeed as pipelines offer more flexibility in

Table 5:   Algeria: Re-allocation of Proven Gas Reserves

	1960–1989	*1990–2015*	*2015–2035*
Gross production	1160	2320	680
Flared gas	162	130	40
Shrinkage	40	130	40
Net production	464	2060	600
Domestic requirements	232	710	600
Exports	231	1350	-

Source: 1960–1989: Sonatrach's statistics; 1990–2015–2035: Author's own simulations

Table 6:   Sonatrach's Total Commitments in 2000

Importers	*LNG* Plants	*TRANS-MED* Pipeline	*GME* Pipeline	*TOTAL* Imports
Western Europe				
GDF/France	10.3			10.3
DISTRIGAZ/Belgium	4.5			4.5
BOTAS/Turkey	4.0			4.0
DEPA/Greece	0.7			0.7
SNAM/Italy	1.8	19.3		21.1
ENEL/Italy		4.0		4.0
PETROL/ Slovenia		0.6		0.6
ENEGAS/Spain	3.8		6.0	9.8
TRANSGAS/Portugal			2.5	2.5
USA				
DISTRIGAS/Boston	1.3			1.3
DUKE ENERGY/Louisiana	1.0*			1.0
Transit Countries				
ETAP/Tunisia		0.4		0.4
SGG/Morocco			na	na
TOTAL Exports	27.4	24.3	8.5	60.2

* Maximum envelope: 4.5 bcm per year

Source: Sonatrach, *MEES*, Barrows (various issues)

terms of load modulation than the LNG plants, the take-or-pay ratio has been lowered to as much as 85 per cent in recent years. Also some of the 'pass through' factors, that is the extent to which a change in the price of the alternative fuel is reflected in the natural gas prices, have been lowered in a move to maintain a competitive edge or even increase Sonatrach's market share.[17]

3.1.4 Limits to the Penetration of the US Market

There was a general belief in the late 1980s that the US gas market was recovering and that the 'bubble' of low cost gas, which arose as a result of deregulation and industry restructuring, was deflating. Indeed, on the supply side, the collapse of domestic drilling activity and the natural depletion of producing fields signalled a pause in supply growth. On the demand side, the trend was upward again after reaching its lowest annual level in 1986. In addition, initiatives such as the Clean Air Act amendments were considered a key determinant for future market growth.

Anticipating announced competition from Norway and Nigeria, and building on its improved links with Boston's Distrigas and Panhandle Eastern Pipeline Company, Sonatrach entered rapidly into talks in order to reposition itself in the US market. The initial export objective of 10 to 12 bcm of LNG per year included sales of 2.4 bcm contracted with Shell, with the possibility of additional volumes, until the Nigerian Bonny project came on stream.[18] However, this prospect was frustrated by the collapse of the negotiations that Shell initiated with its US partner Columbia Gas to reopen the Cove Point terminal in Maryland. Finally, only Distrigas and Trunkline Gas Corporation[19] would provide for 'framework contracts' of up to 1.3 and 4.5 bcm respectively.

Re-entry by Sonatrach into the US market would not have been possible without the company radically adapting its contractual principles and practices. When renegotiating its contracts, Sonatrach had to take into account two fundamental factors pertaining to a deregulated market. Firstly, the company was no longer in a position to transfer market risk to its clients. Indeed in a highly competitive market, buyers unsure of their future market share could not support 'take-or-pay' commitments, requiring instead greater flexibility in contracted volumes over shorter time spans. Secondly, the development of spot markets and, since 1990, of futures markets, facilitated price discovery for prompt deliveries and for future spot gas supplies. As a result, market-based prices replaced the old indexation formula where gas prices had been linked to those of oil products or to other alternative fuels.

The contractual arrangements with Trunkline and Distrigas, though not strictly identical, reflected these developments. The deal with Trunkline called for the buyer to prospect the market and submit sale offers to Sonatrading, the newly established off-shore Sonatrach trading subsidiary. Under the agreement both Sonatrading and Trunkline were required to approve the volumes, terms and selling prices of each offer. To be acceptable to both the seller and the buyer, the anticipated selling price must cover, at a minimum, the cost of production, liquefaction, shipping and regasification.

In the Trunkline contract, gas prices fob correspond to some 63 per cent of the selling price. In the Distrigas contract, the price formula is more elaborate. Basically, prices fob are the highest of two options: an evolving minimum price, or 63 per cent of either the selling price or a reference price indexed to oil products and competing gas delivered by other suppliers. In both cases, there is no purchase obligation and no take-or-pay provision. As a consequence LNG is to be imported on a short-term spot basis, possibly on a cargo-by-cargo basis, only when gas can be sold at a price attractive enough to Sonatrach. For this reason Sonatrach and its clients could not realize the total 5.8 bcm per year agreed upon for the two contracts.

The collapse of the Shell deal and the limited volumes realized with Trunkline and Distrigas, have certainly frustrated Sonatrach's initial objective of diversifying its outlets. In addition, realized prices on the US market have been, on average, disappointing in comparison with initial expectations. Though there is a prospect for Sonatrading to redeploy its trade activity of LNG spot worldwide, Sonatrach should be expected to continue to deliver the bulk of its LNG production to the European market. Beneficially, however, the experience of a deregulated US market should stand the company in good stead when markets in Europe follow suit with liberalization.

3.1.5 Distinctiveness of the Mediterranean Market

The importance of gas in Europe has grown significantly since the end of the 1980s. Key drivers of gas penetration have included the emergence of combined-cycle gas turbines as an economic source of baseload electricity, the growing awareness of environmental problems and commitments to tackle them, as well as the regulatory changes that were taking place in the region. Major shifts of gas policy in Europe included the removal of the 1975 EC 'Gas Burn'[20] which precluded the use of gas for power generation, and the prospect of dismantling coal subsidies.

Stronger demand was developing in the Mediterranean basin. With the exception of France where nuclear energy was maintaining a strong position in the power generation sector, gas was displacing all alternative products in the power generation sector of the key consuming countries. In addition, increasingly perceiving gas as an abundant, viable and secure energy source, countries such as Italy and Spain committed themselves to increase gas penetration, while others such as Greece and Portugal decided to introduce it to their energy market. Such moves helped gas to gain momentum, with little chance of a reversal as had been experienced in the first half of the 1980s.

On the commercial side, Sonatrach introduced additional elements of flexibility in its new contractual arrangements in order to capture additional market share in Italy and Spain and to penetrate new markets. The company admitted that, for gas to compete with alternative fuels such as the heavy fuel oil and gas oil, available in the different end-use segments, gas prices would have to reflect the final consumers' willingness to pay for it. As a result, a new generation of contracts, largely for pipeline gas (second tranche to SNAM through the expanded Trans-Med, and Enagas through the planned GME), were signed in December 1990 and June 1992. In these contracts, prices were indexed to gas oil and heavy fuel oil. As pipelines offered more flexibility than the LNG plants, take-or-pay requirements were also lowered to as little as 85 per cent of contracted volumes.

At the same time as consolidating its traditional markets and securing new outlets, Sonatrach was to face another major challenge – that of funding the huge underlying investment programme.

3.1.6 Capital Investment and Financing Constraints

By the end of the 1980s, only three fields of non-associated gas had been developed (Sonatrach 1996): in addition to the super-giant Hassi R'Mel field, which was brought into commercial stream in 1961 and expanded considerably in the period 1978–80 production from Alrar field since 1983 and from Rhourde Nouss, since 1988, was considered adequate to supply the domestic and export markets. However, to sustain the 60 bcm annual export target beyond the turn of the century, a major investment programme was devised, not only to expand export capacity but also to bring on stream all discovered, as yet undeveloped, gas fields south-east of the Hassi R'Mel hub (Table 7).

The scale of capital investment for the proposed programme is illustrated in Table 8. Gas investments, including associated upstream NGLs processing schemes of the wet gas fields, would amount to more than $12 billion, representing some 60 per cent of Sonatrach's total investment programme for the period 1990–2000. Financing such a

Table 7:   Algeria: Location and Development of Proven (remaining) Gas Reserves.
Distribution based on total proven reserves of 3000 bcm of non-associated
gas

Regions (with main satellites)	Date of discovery	Producing regions (wet gas)	To be developed (wet gas)	To be developed (dry gas)
Hassi R'Mel & Oued Noumer	1956	1740		
Alrar & Stah	1961	210		
Rhourd Nouss, Hamra, Gassi Touil	1962	390		
TFT* & Ohanet	1960		150	
In Amenas	1955–63		320	
In Salah	1955–57			190

* TFT: Tin Fouyé Tabenkort

Source: Compiled from Sonatrach (1996 and 1998).

programme involved seeking the support of EU institutions as well as
further opening to foreign private oil companies.

3.1.7 Strengthening Relations with the EU and its Institutions

The promotion of political and economic relations with the EU was a
major goal of Algeria's foreign policy. Enlargement of the EU to the
Mediterranean countries, and the imminent realization of an Arab
Maghreb Union (a political and economic union involving Algeria,
Libya, Mauritania, Morocco, and Tunisia) was to give a new dimension
and impetus to the relationship. These developments clearly represented an opportunity for Algeria to exploit emerging gas markets.[21]
This prospect was reinforced by a return to political normality between
Algeria and Morocco after a long period of border disputes and
strained relations caused by the Western Sahara issue. The long-
standing concept of linking Algerian gas reserves to the European
markets via a western pipeline, through Morocco, then across the
Strait of Gibraltar into Spain, Portugal and further north, was finally
achievable.

Such a prospect broadened the scope of bilateral talks, initiated in
the mid-1980s between the European Commission and the Algerian
government at ministerial level, aimed at promoting dialogue in the
energy field.[22] The original aim was to discuss energy policy aspects,
which were of mutual interest. Algeria took advantage of the
opportunity to clarify the new direction given to energy policy in the
context of the enactment of the 1986 hydrocarbon legislation and, in
the aftermath of the oil price collapse the same year, the new

Table 8: Algeria: Capital Investment Needed to Double Exports, 1990–2000 (Re-valued in 1996 US dollars)

	Main characteristics	$million	Observations
Refurbishing LNG plants	Rising capacity from 20 to 28bcm/yr	2400	Contracts awarded in 1990. Credit financing, with leading role of US Exim-Bank. Arzew completed in 1996–97. Skikda delayed until the end of 1998
Expanding the Trans-Med pipeline capacity	Raising capacity from 16 to 24 bcm/yr	250	Contract awarded in 1994. Credit financing, with leading role of the EIB. Commissioned in June 1995
Constructing the GME pipeline	520km, 48", one comp. station, 9.5 bcm/yr	850	Idem. Commissioned in October 1996 (compressor station in 2000/2001)
Developing gas fields south-east of Hassi R'Mel	11 wet gas fields with expected total production of 200 million tonnes of NGL (LPG and condensate) and 300 bcm of natural gas over 20 years,	3700	Oued Noumer (1992), Alrar Ouest (1993) and Rhourde Nouss (1994) fields have been developed by Sonatrach (credit financing). Foreign companies involved so far are Total on Hamra field (since1991), Total & Repsol on TFT (since 1996) and Amoco on four fields in In Amenas (since July 1998). Ohanet and Gassi Touil should be sponsored by Sonatrach. Similarly, Hassi R'Mel South is planned to be developed by Sonatrach by 2002
Constructing the second pipeline Alrar-Hassi R'Mel	965km, 42"/48", four comp. stations, 10bcm/yr	2000	Contracts awarded in 1993. Financing on credit, with leading role of the EIB. Commissioned in May 1997
Developing In Salah gas fields (1st phase)	Seven dry fields with expected total production of 200 bcm over 24 years	2000	BP-Sonatrach partnership. Contract awarded in December 1995 (decision of development expected by mid 1999 at the earliest)
Constructing the In Salah pipeline (Krechba-Hassi R'Mel)	500km, 48", 10 bcm/yr (1st phase)	1000	Idem (cost of In Salah gas development may be brought down, depending on the final configuration of the scheme)
Total investments		12200	

[1] So far Sonatrach and its foreign partners have announced the following capital investments: Hamra ($575 million), TFT ($850 million), In Amenas ($900 million), BP ($3000 million).

Source: *MEES, Petroleum Economist* (various issues)

framework negotiations between Sonatrach and its European gas clients. In addition, in a context where Sonatrach was experiencing difficulties in commercializing its gas, the talks focused on future prospects for improving the gas business climate.

However, the end of the 1980s witnessed dramatic changes on the European scene, with the fall of the Berlin Wall and the subsequent collapse of the Soviet Union. Anticipating a major move by the EU to support the political and economic transition of the newly independent states, Prime Minister Lubbers of the Netherlands proposed a 'European Energy Community' initiative combining concern about long-term energy security in Western Europe with that over the political and economic situation in Eastern Europe. In addition to the far-reaching implications of such an initiative, the Algerian authorities were concerned by other political issues stemming in particular from the concept of the Internal Energy Market and its prime objective of liberalizing the internal market for gas. As a consequence, co-operation with the EU and its institutions was raised higher on both the political and energy agenda of Algeria.

In the energy sector, with the new Algerian gas strategy taking shape, the interests of both parties focused on the expansion of gas. The EU was keen to increase and diversify its energy supplies, and to facilitate the introduction of natural gas to the emerging markets of the Mediterranean. However, the EU institutions limited their involvement to the gas delivery pipelines only, within the Trans-European Network (TEN) programme.[23] As a key contributing factor to the Internal Energy Market, the TEN was a geopolitical and economic framework, which involved Russia, Algeria, Norway, and the UK as major incremental suppliers to the EU. As a result, EU support was extended simultaneously to the Belarus–Poland new corridor, to the expansion of the Trans-Med and construction of the GME pipeline, to the new Norwegian pipelines, as well as to the UK–Belgium Interconnector.

In the case of Algeria, financing was extended through the European Investment Bank (EIB) as part of the 'horizontal financial co-operation' policy, a component of the EU's 'Redirected Mediterranean Policy'. Such loans were dedicated to financing projects of mutual benefit to the Union and Mediterranean Partner Countries, especially in the energy sector. In addition, as the political crisis deepened in Algeria from 1992 the European institutions played a key role in mitigating the perception of increasingly high risks, and acted as a catalyst in helping to secure other sources of funds for Sonatrach's projects.

Although the EIB was subsequently to extend its financial support to the second phase of the development of the Rhourde Nouss gas field, financing the investment programme upstream was considered more the preserve of private international oil companies. Their involvement supposed a radical change in the upstream policy and the introduction of specific incentives for gas development.

3.2   'Denationalization' of Gas

The 1986 hydrocarbon legislation had restricted foreign participation in the gas industry and had ruled out association on any hydrocarbon field discovered before 1986, which was the case with most of the fields, as shown in Table 7. While relaxing the fiscal terms provided for by the law would not have posed fundamental problems (the 1986 legislation was conceived in 1982–85 and approved by the parliament in 1986 when oil prices collapsed), extending participation to the gas sector and in fields already discovered was politically too risky to consider. Indeed, since the complete nationalization of the gas industry in 1971 (by contrast nationalization of the oil industry was initially aimed at 51 per cent participation only), gas, in the face of persistent dogmatic attitudes and ideological barriers, was an emotive subject for debate. Referring to his later proposal to amend the 1986 hydrocarbon law, Minister Aït-Laoussine, provocatively said that he 'proposed to the parliament to "denationalize" Algeria's gas reserves'. Such changes and the prospect of participation in existing oil fields provoked a deep emotional response in the country. Subsequently Aït-Laoussine explained:

> Twenty years ago the foreign companies had so much control over Algeria's natural resources that they could suffocate the national interest. Furthermore, our national company was not experienced enough to play, with no handicap, in the league of the international oil companies. So nationalisation seemed the proper course. Now the situation has changed. Algeria has ownership and Sonatrach has become a mature player. But we recognise that we lack the financial means and we do not have the sort of technical and human resources required to fulfil our ambitious plan (Aït-Laoussine 1992:7).

3.2.1 By-passing the Law
Until such legislative changes occurred in November 1991, Sonatrach was urged to seek other forms of partnership and alliances to expand its gas business. The first move came in November 1989, with a Gas Co-operation Agreement signed with Shell to explore possible joint-venture prospects in the gas industry. Although the agreement was aimed at broader co-operation across the gas chain, it collapsed with

the failure of Shell to execute its contract to buy Algerian LNG for the American market, without the opening of the Cove Point terminal.

A more significant move, though not much noticed, was the agreement achieved with Total of France in May 1991 to develop the already discovered, but not yet developed, Hamra gas field. To get around the prevailing restrictions imposed by the 1986 law on discovered yet undeveloped fields, Total agreed to finance the development of the field and be reimbursed and remunerated only from anticipated proceeds of LPG and condensates (Faïd 1994). At the same time the two partners agreed to create a jointly-owned marketing company to sell LPG from the Hamra field.[24] This 'quite novel' and 'unusual' arrangement, as the energy trade press qualified it, provided the seminal structure for future developments.

As laws are first by-passed then modified, the necessary changes to the 1986 law came in amendments promulgated in November 1991, amid deteriorating economic and financial conditions and major political uncertainties. It is worth noting, indeed, that it was an FLN-dominated parliament on the verge of losing the general elections to the ironically more 'resource-nationalist' Islamists, which enacted the radical changes. The changes included a more competitive fiscal package based on a production-sharing type agreement, the possibility for participation in discovered or producing fields, the right to share in natural gas discoveries, the right to invest in transportation activities, and a provision for international arbitration for the settlement of disputes between Sonatrach and its partners.

3.2.2 The New Gas Regime

To understand the radical nature of the changes related to gas, it is worth remembering that, by a decree dating back to the nationalization period of 1971, the discovery of gas by a foreign company was, until 1986, considered purely and simply as a 'dry well'. The 1986 legislation opened a new possibility: in the case of a commercial discovery, a foreign oil company may be reimbursed for its exploration investments and eventually granted a bonus. The company may also be called upon to form a joint marketing company to export the newly discovered gas. In all cases the foreign company had no right to any share of gas production, which remained in Sonatrach's ownership.

The provisions of the 1986 legislation were far from stimulating investments in the gas sector. Indeed, as reserves are the main focus of the industry, foreign companies would be more interested in acquiring the right to production than solely engaging in trading activities. On the other hand, the financial burden of developing any commercial discovery would rest with Sonatrach alone, at a moment when lack of funds, combined with limited technical and human resources, was hindering a challenging gas export programme.

Taking into account the number of undeveloped gas fields and the gas-prone nature of many prospective areas in the country, the 1991 amendments introduced a key incentive in granting the right to share in natural gas discoveries and allowing investment in the transportation sector. Basically, the amended legislation made applicable to gas the provisions already applicable to hydrocarbon liquids. Therefore, under a production-sharing agreement, a foreign company obtains the right to share in gas production.

However, to avoid competition in its core markets, Sonatrach has been given authority to control the terms of the marketing arrangements. This restriction has induced Sonatrach and its partners to engage in joint marketing and to substitute the concept of production sharing by that of revenue sharing. Sonatrach may also market both shares of produced gas and share back revenues from the sale of gas. This option allows it to integrate gas produced in association into its export profile, rendering economically viable smaller gas accumulations. Similarly, in the case of a wet gas field, gas provisions provide for the possibility of substituting a share of NGLs (condensate and LPG) for that of gas, which reverts to Sonatrach. As a result, forms of partnership based on sharing risks, costs and earnings, hitherto unknown in Algeria were possible.

3.3   New Alliances: The Examples of BP and Amoco

Since the gas sector was opened in 1991, Sonatrach has entered into deals with BP covering seven core dry gas fields in In Salah area (1995), with Total/Repsol on the wet gas field of Tin Fouye Tabenkort (1996), and with Amoco on four wet fields in the In Amenas area (1998).[25] Taking into account broader objectives announced by BP and Amoco, which include downstream and trading activities, it is expected that their recent merger will have far-reaching effects on the Algerian gas scene.

3.3.1 The Sonatrach-BP Deal
The In Salah gas contract was signed in December 1995 after two years of formal negotiations. The process started in 1991, when the two companies sought to extend their co-operation beyond the oil exploration agreement they were negotiating on Sour El Guelta (Northern Algeria). The framework agreement of July 1992 states both

parties' interest to extend their cooperation to the development of the gas resources located in the south west of Algeria. Similar interest manifested by other foreign companies did not match BP's strategic resolve to mobilize the financial and technical resources required by the project. Indeed, BP's move came as part of its 1989 gas strategy to establish a significant supply position in southern Europe.

In spite of limited geological risk, the economic position of the In Salah gas is marginal. The gas is dry, hence there is no additional revenue from NGLs as for the wet gas fields in the south east, to strengthen the economic viability of the project. The gas is also remote, requiring the construction of a 550-km pipeline to link the fields to the Hassi R'Mel hub. However, the economy of the project is enhanced by much more favourable fiscal terms. In addition, the economic risk taken by the two partners upstream should be mitigated by the readily available export infrastructures, as well as the proximity of the southern European markets.

One of the major features of the contract is that it covers the entire gas chain. The contract not only provides for the joint development and production of gas by a joint operating body, but also for the construction and exploitation of pipelines, as well as for the joint marketing of the gas produced. The joint marketing company, In Salah Gas Services, allocates revenues from the sale of gas to each partner as reimbursement of their investments and profits, after deduction of royalties.

The most significant feature is that In Salah gas is expected to enter the European market in 2002/2003, as it approaches full liberalization. Having secured a first gas deal with Enel for 4 bcm per year, through the Trans-Med pipeline (as a result of assignment of the contract between Sonatrach and Enel to In Salah gas[26]), the question is where to take the following tranche of gas of some 5 bcm per year. This speculative issue will be examined in Section 4 of this chapter.

3.3.2 The Sonatrach-Amoco Deal

Amoco reached an agreement with Sonatrach in June 1998 for the joint development, under a production-sharing agreement, of four wet gas fields in In Amenas, south-east of Hassi R'Mel. Under the terms of the agreement, Sonatrach is committed to take the entire gas production from the In Amenas fields. The reimbursement of Amoco's costs and its share of profits under the agreement will include shares in either the liquids or both the liquids and the gas revenues sold by Sonatrach.[27] Therefore, contrary to the BP deal, Amoco will not be involved in the commercialization of gas.

In spite of restrictive access to the gas in the case of In Amenas, the Sonatrach-BP-Amoco deals may act as a major incentive for further exploration and development in neighbouring gas-prone areas.[28] Such a prospect would bring new reserves and broaden the scope of future contributions to the European gas business. What one BP team leader noted about BP involvement in Algeria can be extended to the merged BP Amoco: '[the project] takes the story of Algerian exports into the next phase, and brings new reserves into the picture, together with new forms of partnership and possibly new ways of selling the gas' (Drury 1996:1). Sonatrach's attitude to such an expectation will be discussed in the next section.

4.   The Options Ahead

So far Sonatrach has reinforced its 'gas dimension' along such lines as consolidating outlets, developing export facilities and expanding the upstream. Faced with new opportunities and challenges, the company is now at a critical turning point in its development.

Indeed, it may begin to question the emphasis on its gas business upstream, as it is likely to be tempted to shift its focus towards the resurgent domestic oil sector. In the market place, its strategy will depend on the understanding of the changes taking place in Europe and the threat such changes could pose to its global market share position. While the company is expected to build on its strengths in terms of expanded export infrastructures and contractual arrangements, and draw from its experience of the deregulated American gas market, the main options forward include: moving mid- and downstream, breaking out of the Mediterranean market, and reviving the domestic gas downstream sector.

The company's ability to make quick decisions in a tougher competitive environment will be crucial in this regard and will depend on the newly implemented institutional and energy policy framework. Furthermore, the extent to which the new organizational setting can keep politics out of business will be critical to Sonatrach's success and destiny.

4.1   Reassessing Gas Expansion Upstream

Having consolidated its gas business around the target of 60 bcm per year set ten years ago, Sonatrach's present objective appears to be the expansion of exports to at least the potential extra capacity of the existing pipelines. With additional compressor stations, such potential may translate into up to 6 bcm per year via the Trans-Med pipeline to Italy, and up to 9 bcm per year via the Maghreb–Europe pipeline to the Iberian Peninsula (Bouhafs 1994a). While the present proven reserves may sustain an export profile of 65 bcm per year beyond the initial horizon of 2015, any further increase of exports will require both the expansion of its gas resource base and a higher market share.

It is worth remembering that the target of 60 bcm of annual exports was determined on the basis of allocating proven, non-associated gas reserves, with the priority objective of meeting long-term domestic requirements. It is now understood that the estimation of such gas reserves, some 3000 bcm, was rather conservative. On the other hand, the economic recession witnessed during the 1990s will inflect the trend of future domestic requirements. The combination of these two determinants may allow an upward revision of exports to possibly 65 bcm per year from 2002/2003. Such a view is corroborated by the fact that the expected production from In Salah,[29] 9 bcm from 2002/2003, will cover the existing supply contract between Sonatrach and Enel for 4 bcm per year, leaving only an additional 5 bcm to be exported. Therefore, with only a modest increment coming from the In Salah venture with BP, Sonatrach should not be expected to increase dramatically its exports in the medium term.

Amoco's recent involvement in the upstream gas business in Algeria, which preceded its announced merger with BP, will not affect such a medium-term perspective. As explained earlier, by investing in wet gas fields, Amoco is to be granted only a share of revenues, and will not be involved in the commercialization of gas, which is to be transferred to Sonatrach in order to sustain its gas supply commitments. However, BP Amoco may consider the Algerian upstream as a 'long-term play' and use its new strength to make a greater contribution to the exploration and development in neighbouring areas.[30] Sonatrach's attitude to such a prospect will depend on how the company reassesses the development of its oil industry and whether such reassessment would shift the emphasis of its strategy from gas to oil.

The gas strategy, established ten years ago amid a general pessimism about the prospects for oil, did not take into account a possible revival of the oil sector. Now, as a result of the recent boom in the prolific region of Berkine, oil production is expected to double from the 1995 base when production began in partnership, to some 1.5 million barrels per day in 2005. Therefore, developing gas reserves further afield and from costly reservoirs may not be the best option from the point of view of both the government (lower taxes) and the company (lower returns on investment). Instead, the company could consider the potentially superior option of looking for low-cost assets domestically, or possibly outside the country.

While the latter option remains a 'major strategic objective for Sonatrach' (Preure 1998), the company is well aware of its limited capability and its disadvantages relative to established firms, in terms of financial and technological resources, as well as in terms of economies of scale. This would be why Sonatrach seems to have adopted a tactical 'sequencing' of its deployments that has led it to moderate its international ambitions and shelve all projects involving high barriers to entry.[31] The other option for Sonatrach is to allow BP Amoco to expand its business upstream in Algeria, within a much broader alliance. In this case, Sonatrach would be allowed to combine its expertise with those of its much stronger associates in other parts of the world, fulfilling its international ambitions.

4.2 Awakening to the New Challenges

In considering the issue of adaptation to changing gas market structure and prices, the share of natural gas in overall exports and its destination are certainly important factors for Sonatrach. By 2000, as 60 bcm of gas exports are reached, natural gas will represent 45 to 50 per cent of the total volume of exports and, at present price structure, some 35 to 40 per cent of their value. Therefore, natural gas will be the country's single most valuable export item, and a major factor in determining Algeria's economic outlook.[32] Exports to the USA have ultimately been disappointing, and the prospects for any further penetration are now extremely limited. As a consequence, Sonatrach is expected to rely heavily on the present markets of Western Europe, especially its southern flank (see Table 6).

For Sonatrach, what is at stake is its market share position, the outcome of which has been decided so far by reliability, supply flexibility and relative costs. Indeed, the company has had a long track-record as an important and reliable gas supplier that neither the dogmatic stance of the early 1980s, nor the present tragic internal situation of the country, have affected. The cost advantage obtained by its proximity to the market, its easy transit routes, and its diversified, readily expandable, export infrastructures have also added to its strong competitive advantages in the southern part of Europe.

However, as market developments unfold and pressure on prices increases, Sonatrach has to find fresh ways to differentiate itself, take advantage of new opportunities and add value to its gas business.

4.2.1 Understanding the Changing Nature of the Market

In spite of limited involvement overseas,[33] Sonatrach's experience of the deregulated American gas market should enable it to foresee the changes taking place in Europe and their ultimate implications. Prior to the adoption of the EU gas directive, significant changes in the national legislation of client countries such as Spain put the company on the alert. However, Sonatrach has been slow to admit the ineluctability of such a move.

What Sonatrach has probably failed to foresee clearly is the nature of the politically driven UK–Belgium Interconnector, which has been devised as a means of facilitating further deregulation of the British gas market and also as an additional tool to liberalize the European market and promote the single European market for gas. This pipeline, linking Bacton in England to Zeebrugge in Belgium, was commissioned in October 1998. As the capacity of the pipeline has not been fully contracted on a long-term basis, the excess supply at the borders of North-west Europe will be a key driver of both prices and new, short-term, contractual arrangements. In addition, it is expected that gas trading through the Interconnector will greatly influence the gas business in that part of the European market (Stoppard 1996; Weston 1998). For reasons developed more fully below, Sonatrach's business in Belgium may be the first casualty of the Interconnector.

Because of greater emphasis on security of supply, liberalization and competition do not necessarily mean the end of long-term contracts with take-or-pay clauses. However, they may render Sonatrach's contracts portfolio, negotiated in an era of monopoly and managed markets, untenable. The first contract that may well come under pressure is the LNG supply contract between Sonatrach and Distrigaz. Since 1996, Sonatrach has embarked on routine 'price re-opening' discussions with its clients in order to bring its gas prices in line with those of its competitors. Delays in settling the Distrigaz case only underline the complexity of the new situation created in North-western Europe. While it is still unclear what impact the Interconnector will have on the Belgian market, industrial consumers will certainly try to take advantage of the normally cheap gas from the UK.[34] In addition, with the likely development of a spot market at Zeebrugge, they would favour a more market-related price formula in the form of a Zeebrugge gas index (Weston 1998). This would increase pressure on the Belgian government for an open access regime, ultimately undermining Distrigaz's monopoly.[35] This perspective must have prompted Sonatrach to 'rethink its strategy' (Preure 1998). In fact the company's attitude betrays a dual stance: defensive and offensive.

In the aftermath of the adoption of the EU Gas Directive, the company's senior management have taken advantage of international forums to warn against the 'regulatory risks imposed by consuming countries' (Hamel 1998:2), pointing to the impact of 'a hasty implementation of the Directive [which] could jeopardise the dynamics of the gas industry and the investment willingness of both the exporting and importing gas companies' (Hached 1998:19). These arguments were further emphasized in an important, though little publicized, conference in Algiers on 3 December 1998. The conference, which involved the key gas-exporting companies and gas-importing utilities in Europe, expressed concern about the impact on the gas industry of the new economic environment. Although the initiative was triggered by the prevailing oil price crisis, the Algiers conference also expressed concern about the likely effect of the forthcoming liberalization of gas markets in Continental Europe. However, it failed to foresee the different policy directions signalled by the two phenomena (Aïssaoui 1999).

With its competitors adopting a much more aggressive export drive into the market, Gazprom's movement downstream into Germany, and Abu Dhabi, Australia, and more recently Qatar increasing LNG spot sales into the Mediterranean, Sonatrach is at the same time adopting a more offensive stance. Having realized the threat such changes could pose, they also realize the opportunities they could offer. Aït-Laoussine, who successfully implemented the concepts at the origin of the opening up and expansion of partnership in the gas sector in the early 1990s, emphasizes the need henceforth to move downstream:

> If under the 'seller's market' conditions of the past, downstream integration gave the producers a mere economic edge (which enabled them to access a welcome but by no means crucial additional margin), in today's 'buyer's market' conditions it has become a necessity not only to achieve a fair value for their gas but also to protect their market share.[36]

4.2.2 Moving Mid- and Downstream

In spite of lower institutional barriers to entry, the company aspiration to move mid- and downstream may be frustrated by its financial constraints. Therefore pooling its resources with those of its partners, in the financial, technical and marketing fields, is likely to be a major component of its strategy. In the words of the CEO, Sonatrach intends to use these partnerships as a lever to move mid- and downstream:

> We consider that natural gas producers should be able to have access to consumers' markets and, under alliances with oil companies or distributors,

find new diversification opportunities, either in the distribution system or in power generation. Partnerships, similar to the one we concluded with BP, can be considered to this effect (Attar 1997).

This strategy may complement that formulated by BP. The British company, whose aspiration since the end of the 1980s is to grow and build an integrated gas business, sees liberalization of the market as a unique opportunity to expand into Europe. Although BP's knowledge of operating in deregulated markets is rather limited, it has been developing a whole range of business skills in the liberalized British gas market, including selling gas downstream to power generators and large industrial users. In the aftermath of their merger, BP and Amoco will certainly add another dimension to such an experience, which may stand In Salah gas in good stead when new tranches of gas are sold (Quinn 1998). Nevertheless, substantial hurdles have to be overcome.

4.2.3 *The GME Option*

As examined earlier, partnership with BP to jointly develop and produce gas from the In Salah region provides for the joint marketing of gas produced. This gas is expected to enter the European market in 2002/2003 at the second stage of its opening. The BP-Sonatrach joint marketing team has been exploring for potential market opportunities in Portugal, Spain, Italy, Turkey, and other southern European markets. While traditional arrangements will continue to be part of the scene for the foreseeable future, other options, including selling gas mid- and even downstream, are carefully considered. Having secured a first gas deal with Enel for 4 bcm per year, through the Trans-Med pipeline, the next least-cost, highest-revenue, option would be shipping some of the additional gas through the GME to supply the markets of Morocco, Spain and Portugal, where power generators and large industrial users will soon be in a position to buy gas directly. However, Sonatrach and BP Amoco must be aware of the complexity of access to the transit section through Morocco and the Strait of Gibraltar (Aïssaoui 1997).

Like the Trans-Med pipeline, the GME was conceived, from the Algerian perspective, to maximize the netback value of gas, while minimizing the political and economic leverage of the transit countries. Thus, having ruled out any 'unitized' option (a shared pipeline from Hassi R'Mel to Cordoba), the project was finally designed as a juxtaposition of independent sections with different ownership, as well as different institutional, financial and commercial frameworks. Shipping In Salah gas mid-stream requires adhering to the Transit

Convention with Morocco, embarking on a joint-expansion scheme with EMPL Ltd, as well as entering into long-term gas transportation agreements.[37]

Although EMPL should be able to enhance the system, possible evolution of the commercial framework to accommodate new shippers may be problematic. Solutions can be transposed from the Interconnector legal framework, where links between capacity and shareholder participation have been severed, allowing shares in the pipeline to be transferred without corresponding change in capacity right.

While the GME option has been under consideration, the merger between BP and Amoco is now raising the question of whether partnership with the new company can lead to better access to the Spanish market and more generally to the European market.

4.2.4 *Sonatrach vs. BP Amoco: Allies or Competitors in the Market?*

Before BP and Amoco announced their merger, it was believed that the combination of Sonatrach and BP's skills and experience would 'provide a uniquely competitive presence in the European gas market' (Rushby 1996). However, contrary to the upstream sector where Sonatrach can build on the partnership already created with BP and Amoco, the move to market In Salah gas jointly and possibly to expand partnership across the gas value chain may prove problematic. Indeed, Sonatrach will have to face increased competition from the two partners as they merge. Limiting the scope to the Mediterranean basin, the following developments should be carefully assessed:

(i) Amoco is the main shareholder and feedstock supplier of Atlantic LNG (Trinidad and Tobago). Enagas will receive 1.6 bcm per year from 1999 from the plant, corresponding to 40 per cent of the initial output. As the capacity of the plant is set to double, Amoco and shareholder Repsol, in a cross-partnership, are seeking to supply a greater volume to Spain, as well as increase their direct involvement in the power generation sector. An alliance, centred on the construction of a regasification plant and a combined-cycle gas turbine near Bilbao was approved in August 1998 by the European Commission. It involves Amoco, Repsol, Iberdrola and the Basque energy holding company EVE. Ultimately, the Spanish market could absorb as much as 75 per cent of the expanded LNG plant.

(ii) Continued success in Egypt has made Amoco the country's leading gas partner. The 'new world-class' natural gas reserves, discovered with ENI in the Nile Delta have increased Egypt's resource base and made a long-term gas export project viable. Partnership with Egyptian Petroleum Corporation is currently aimed at both expanding the domestic gas market and embarking on an LNG export scheme, of up to 10 bcm per year, to Turkey and other eastern Mediterranean countries, early next decade. In the longer run, various other pipeline proposals should complement the LNG project.

These developments are significant in terms of the newly merged BP Amoco's desire to secure new sources of gas and to fulfil its strategy for deeper market penetration in southern Europe. Such developments add a new dimension to the competition ahead, in markets which Sonatrach has so far considered to be captive.

4.2.5 *Breaking out of the Mediterranean Markets*
As already pointed out, the bulk of exports is destined to Western Europe, with Belgium being the only non-Mediterranean country. Jonathan Stern detected this quite early, pointing to the small sales of spot gas to Ruhrgas in the late 1980s as 'poor substitutes for the contractual arrangements which were in place during the 1970s' (Stern 1990:47).

Sonatrach may well try again to reverse its confinement to the Mediterranean Basin and consider breaking again into North European markets. With the prospect of a nuclear moratorium, new gas developments in the German market may offer a rare opportunity for the company to resolutely capture back the market share it unfortunately gave up in the early 1980s. This new window of opportunity is critical to Sonatrach to prepare for the prospect of GdF and Distrigaz of Belgium not extending part or all of the LNG contracts, which expire in 2002 and 2006 respectively (see Table 9). In addition, there is no guarantee that the volumes covered by contracts will be lifted in their totality as the price re-opener clause provides an opportunity for its clients to renegotiate volume flexibility as well. In addition, the company should also prepare for the eventual expansion of its exports beyond the target of 65 bcm per year at the turn of the century.

Should Sonatrach miss such opportunities, it would run the risk of not being able to protect its market share let alone to expand sales to the European market.

4.2.6 *Reviving the Domestic Gas Downstream Sector*
In addition to strengthening its position in the market place, the creation of more value from its gas business constitutes another pressing

Table 9:   Sonatrach's Portfolio of Operational Gas Supply Contracts

Client	Country	Date of signature	First delivery	Volume bcm/yr	End of contract	Observations
1 LNG						
GdF1	France	1964	1965	0.5	2002	Last revised: 1991
GdF2		1971	1973	3.5	2013	Idem
GdF3		1976	1982	5.2	2013	Idem
GdF4		1991	1992	1.1	2002	
Enagas1	Spain	1975	1978	3.8	2013	Original volume: 4.8 bcm
Distrigaz	Belgium	1975	1982	4.5	2006	Original volume: 5.2 bcm
Distrigas	USA	1976	1978	1.3	2013	Last revised: 1989
Duke Energy		1976	1982	*1.0	2009	Last revised: 1987
Botas	Turkey	1988	1994	4	2014	Original volume: 2 bcm
Depa	Greece	1988	1998	0.7	2008	Original schedule: 1991
Snam 3	Italy	1994	1996	1.8	2016	
Total LNG				27.4		
2 Pipeline gas						
Snam1	Italy	1977	1983	10.3	2019	Last revised: 1990
Snam2		1990	1991	9	2019	Build-up:1991-1996
Etap	Tunisia	1989	1990	0.4	2020	Last revised: 1997
Petrol	Slovenia	1985	1992	0.6	2007	
Enel	Italy	1992	1994	4	2014	Build-up:1992-1996
Enagas2	Spain	1992	1996	6	2015	Build-up:1996-2000
Transgas	Portugal	1994	1997	2.5	2020	Build-up:1997-2002
Total pipeline gas				32.8		
LNG and pipeline gas				60.2		

• Maximum envelope: 4.5 bcm per year

Source: Sonatrach Press Releases; Barrows and *MEES* (various issues)

question for the company. Following a fundamental restructuring which will be examined in the next section, Sonatrach is devising what seems to be a major expansion in the petrochemical, fertilizer and, possibly, the power generation sectors. In a move to involve private investments, it organized a series of presentations during the second half of 1998 and early 1999 around the world to outline its plan, which includes the rehabilitation of both base and derivative downstream plants.

The use of natural gas and NGLs (ethane, butane, propane, and condensate) as feedstock in the chemical and nitrogen-based fertilizer industry were among the priority Algerian hydrocarbon projects at the end of the 1960s (Chesny 1969). However, expansion of the initial programme was frustrated following the industrial and energy policy revision of the late 1970s and early 1980s. With the exception of the expansion of the ammonia plant at Arzew in the late 1980s, the industry has not developed at all for the last fifteen years. Therefore, the current potential of the gas-based industry is limited to three main complexes: an ethylene (120,000 tonne per year) and derivatives complex at Skikda producing thermoplastic products; a methanol (100,000 tonne per year) and synthetic resins complex at Arzew, producing methanol and thermosetting products; and one nitrogen complex at Arzew, providing ammonia (330,000 tonne per year), urea and nitrates.[38]

Contrary to the other segments of the oil and gas industry, Sonatrach had to follow a steep learning curve in this sector for it started the whole process from scratch (Mekideche 1983). As a result, tremendous engineering and technological problems translated into very low capacity utilization, much lower than that of the LNG industry in the 1980s. This meant that the chemical and fertilizer industry could hardly meet the objective of satisfying domestic needs, not to mention exporting to regional markets.

Rehabilitation of the existing plants and the announced expansion suggest that Sonatrach is opting for a 'strong strategic option' (Preure 1998). The option of allowing downstream private investments dates back to the end of the 1980s and early 1990s. At that time, Sonatrach and ENIP, the Algerian petrochemical company, embarked on a number of joint-venture projects with mixed fortunes:

1. Sonatrach with Air Liquide and Air Products & Chemicals to produce 16 million cubic metres of liquid helium from LNG in Arzew. This project, which was announced in July 1990 was brought in production in February 1995 by subsidiary Helios.
2. ENIP with Repsol-Quimica to produce 130,000 tonne per year of high density polyethylene (HDPE) at Skikda. This project, which dates back to December 1990, is finally expected to be started in 1999 by subsidiary Polymed.
3. Sonatrach with Total and Ecofuel to build a 600,000 tonne per year MTBE (Methyl tertiary-butyl ether) plant at Arzew. This project, which dates back to July 1991, has been cancelled due to reservations about its economic viability.

The new projects offered for 'evaluation' to potential partners have been in maturation for some time. The increase of the initial size of most of these projects suggests that Sonatrach is now seeking to build the critical mass necessary to enter the export market competitively (Table 10).

Table 10: Basic Petrochemical Projects using Natural Gas/NGLs as Feedstock

Project	Capacity (tonne/year)	Feedstock	Planned year	Alternative sites
Ethylene	650,000	Ethane	2002	Skikda
Methanol	800,000	Natural gas	2002	Arzew/Issers/Djen-Djen
MTBE	400,000	Butane	2002	Arzew/Issers/Djen-Djen
Ammonia	2x610,000	Natural gas	2003/04	Arzew/Djen-Djen
Propylene	300,000	Propane	2004	Arzew/Skikda

Source: Excerpts from Sonatrach (1998). Excludes derived products and corresponding plants

In addition to this domestically focused programme, which includes gas-powered desalination plants on the industrial sites of Arzew and Skikda, Sonatrach is seeking downstream integration in the buyers' markets as well. An example of such a move is the joint venture between Sonatrach and BASF to build a 350,000 tonne per year propane dehydrogenation plant at a BASF affiliate site in Spain. The plant will produce about 350,000 tonnes of propylene per year using Algerian feedstock in the form of LNG and propane from Arzew.

Sonatrach seems to have great faith in its new downstream orientation. It is expected that the 'validation of this policy by the highest energy institutional body, the National Energy Council, combined with reintegration of the relevant activities within Sonatrach will make a very sound business strategy' (Hamrour 1998:4). In the framework of a revised investment code and other legal and fiscal arrangements offering major incentives to private capital, Sonatrach is focusing its programme on a line of business in which it enjoys competitive advantage, particularly in terms of industrial facilities, low-cost labour, and a full range of fine feedstock products procured by the gas chain (natural gas, ethane, LPGs, and condensate). Although such a programme is open to private domestic capital, it is believed that the strategy will only succeed if Sonatrach involves partners enjoying creditworthiness, technological leadership and a strong market position. Also, a clear feedstock pricing policy, which takes into account their opportunity cost, will be central to investment decisions.

4.3   Changes in Sonatrach's Organization

Faced with a much tougher competitive environment, both abroad and domestically, Sonatrach has embarked on an internal process of modernization (Bouhafs 1994b), with the objective of improving its decision-making and implementation process. In that vein it has been seeking to secure new statutes, to extend its mission, to clarify its relationship with the government and its main institutions and to shelter its management from excessive political interference.

As a major step in this direction, the National Energy Council approved a fundamental restructuring of Sonatrach in early 1998. Consequently, the company has been given new legal statutes, and several measures have been taken to assign it a whole range of activities which it lost in the early 1980s. Sonatrach now has complete control of NAFTEC, NAFTAL and ENIP, respectively the refining, distribution and petrochemical companies, and 51 per cent interest in the main petroleum service companies. This arrangement is part of a larger portfolio of 'subsidiaries and interests', which include activities within the country and abroad. They are organized under the umbrella of holding companies and supervised by a new branch within Sonatrach, the so-called FIP (Filiales et Participations).[39]

This is the third major transformation Sonatrach has gone through since it was established in 1963. In 1966, in a move to accelerate governmental control over the hydrocarbon sector, the company's mission was extended to include all aspects of hydrocarbon activities. Later, as a result of the massive inflow of capital during the petroleum boom of the 1970s, the company grew rapidly and its expansion was accelerated. By 1978, it was employing some hundred thousand workers, accounting for up to 40 per cent of public investments and 35 per cent of total output.

Its dismantling, in the early 1980s, came as a result of the recasting of the political landscape and the resulting reassessment of economic priorities conducted in 1979, following which the government had embarked on a radical restructuring of the big state-owned companies. Sonatrach was then severed from such activities as refining, distribution, petrochemicals, and other related petroleum services, which were organized through more autonomous enterprises. However, contrary to all the other mammoth state companies, which were split along functional and geographic lines, the core, rent-generating, functions of Sonatrach were preserved intact. Consequently, it remained an important economic instrument under stronger state control (Entelis 1999).

The company has always been sheltered from any transformation that would have undermined government leadership and role. During the socialist orientation of the 1970s, in spite of pressure from the powerful and demanding trade union, the company escaped the new 'socialist rules of management imposed on all other state-owned enterprises (Mekideche 1983). Later, the company was also sheltered from the liberal reforms of the end of the 1980s, which transformed the state enterprises into commercial entities with increasing managerial autonomy.

Although the 1990s have witnessed, so far, a remarkable progression in terms of free-market reforms and the implementation of structural adjustment programmes leading the government to withdraw from micro-economic management and ultimately to privatize state companies, Sonatrach continues to remain immune from any such restructuring. While the new legal statutes confirmed Sonatrach as a joint stock company, its capital is held in its entirety by the state.[40] However, as examined in the preceding section, its downstream subsidiaries could be open soon to private participation in a move to modernize existing plants and expand the refinery and petrochemical business (Hamrour 1998).

4.3.1 *The New Institutional and Energy Policy Framework*
Beyond the merging of companies engaged in refining, petrochemicals and distribution, as well as shareholding in petroleum service companies, the 1998 articles of association of Sonatrach are a major building block in establishing a new institutional and energy policy framework. Sonatrach has now four statutory bodies: the General Assembly, a twelve-member Board of Directors, the Chairman and Managing Director and the Executive Committee (Sonatrach's management body). This new corporate structure is part of a larger energy policy framework, which comprises the National Energy Council (NEC) whose mission, composition and prerogatives were redefined in April 1995 (see Table 2), and the Ministry of Energy (Figure 3). While the Ministry of Energy is normally concerned with the formulation and implementation of sector policy, the NEC sanctions broader policy issues, including alliances with foreign partners as well as long-term deals deemed to be of strategic importance to the country.

Sonatrach's ability to formulate a new agenda, and its capacity for ready adaptation to changes, depend on the degree of autonomy and flexibility such mechanism will provide and how the normal function of policy direction, shareholder, board and management are performed.

From the composition and prerogatives of the new statutory bodies, as provided for by the articles, it could be argued that:
(i)   The general assembly, which performs the state role of ownership and comprises three leading ministers, the governor of the central bank and a representative of the Presidency, runs the risk of inconsistency associated with changes in government;

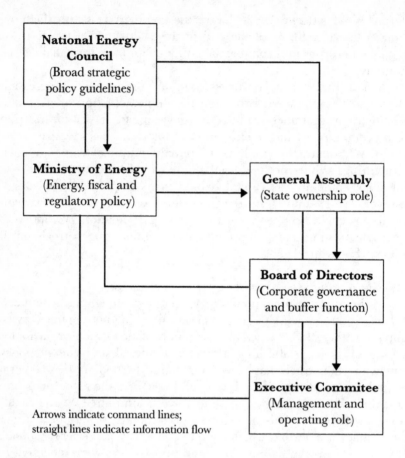

Figure 3: The New Institutional and Energy Policy Framework

(ii) The involvement of government institutions within the board of directors (with representatives from the above leading ministries as well as the central bank) may introduce a beneficial element of scrutiny, which has so far been lacking. However, their inwardness and the restriction of participation of external industry leaders to one person, could limit the Board's external vision. Its capacity to provide Sonatrach with much needed strategic guidance, therefore, depends very much on the disposition and attitude of the four senior management members, together with that of the CMD (Chairman and Managing Director).

(iii) The sweeping powers allocated to the Minister of Energy who sets the agenda for, convenes, and chairs the General Assembly, nominates the CMD and gives prior approval of the appointment of the Executive Committee by the CMD, is a further factor weakening the Board. It may result in a permanent temptation for excessive interference.

(iv) Finally, the involvement of the National Energy Council as a recipient of the general assembly's reports, may add to the confusion about the roles of the different bodies.

Despite these limitations, the new institutional framework offers a clear demarcation of the responsibilities of all those involved in the decision-making process. In spite of possible discontinuity in decision-making associated with changes in government, such framework offers enough guarantee to avoid a situation where 'a new government, possibly with a new management team at Sonatrach, could be ill prepared for dramatic changes in export markets' (Stern 1998:53).

4.3.2 Sonatrach's Achievements and Challenges

Sonatrach has achieved much and has the potential to achieve considerably more. However, the motivations to improve performance and competitiveness have been hindered by political struggles in the course of deeper reforms of the company's role and objective.

In the 1988 edition of PIW's 'Ranking the World's Top Oil Companies', Sonatrach was classified twelfth amid the 'Top 100 companies', between its two main partners BP and Amoco, before they merged. In the ranking of the top gas producers, the company fared even better, coming fourth after Gazprom, Shell and Exxon, thanks to its enormous gas production. Although Sonatrach did much less in terms of 'downstream performance', it has improved its reputation in the market place. Indeed, it tends to be regarded in European gas markets as 'a professional and business-minded company, as opposed to in the mid 1980s when its market image was that of a hard-liner and an unpredictable gas supplier' (Estrada et al. 1995:275).

Recognition should also be made of the company's achievements in the late 1980s and early 1990s to meet the challenge of doubling gas exports and reviving the oil sector (Khadduri 1995). In the oil sector, the ground was laid for increasing the participation of foreign companies, with the result that oil production is expected to double between 1995 and 2005. In the gas sector, the expansion of the capacity of the Trans-Med pipeline, the building of the Maghreb–Europe pipeline, the rehabilitation of the LNG plants to their original capacity, and of course the gas agreements with Total, Repsol, Amoco, and most importantly with BP, to develop gas reserves further afield are among its main accomplishments. In the period of difficult economic conditions, social unrest and political turmoil since 1992, these are outstanding performances and fully deserve to be acknowledged by the gas industry.

Indeed, the achievements and the ability of Sonatrach to maintain a secure flow of gas to its clients in spite of recent disruptions to its export pipelines through terrorist activity, largely mitigate the perceived 'uncertainty associated with the country's political instability' (Stern 1998:53). In the producing areas of the southern part of the country, the security problems have been dealt with with some success, largely through the establishment in April 1995 of four exclusion zones around the producing centres of the Saharan regions, within which traffic and shipments are regulated by security units. Upstream operations have thus been virtually untouched by current troubles. BP for example reported that 'security problems to the south in the region of the major oil and gas installations have been very few and almost invariably related to banditry rather than more organised activity' (Rushby 1996).[41]

Playing in the big league of oil and gas companies, achieving good investment performances, and maintaining its track record as a reliable gas supplier are matters of great pride for Sonatrach and a good source of self-promotion. However, in spite of repeated efforts to modernize, the company can hardly be praised today for its management skills and technological advances. Deficiencies in this area are most notable in what the company describes as one of its core businesses, namely exploration. While Sonatrach had been undertaking a considerable amount of exploration work on its own account, without any tangible success, its foreign partners have made a surprisingly large number of 'world class' discoveries, particularly in the Berkine basin. This has understandably produced mixed feelings among Sonatrach senior management: on the one hand they have recognized half-heartedly the failure of the company's own exploration programme; on the other hand they have derived some pride from the success of the new hydrocarbon strategy, which hinges around greater deployment of the financial and technological resources of international oil companies.

Partnership with foreign oil companies is increasingly seen as a useful complement to the company's strategy of accelerating the development of the hydrocarbon sector to meet government objectives in terms of foreign exchange earnings and fiscal revenues. The quid pro quo is that Sonatrach is dealing with its partners in a constrained manner. This may stem from the fact that, acting as the 'guardian of the state's resource', Sonatrach has to face unacceptable risks: the risk that the foreign partners become dominant in the country and, because of the post 1992 political risk reassessment, the risk that foreign partners take an inappropriate portion of the rent. One solution would be to transfer the contracting activities and corresponding 'management of the rent' to a governmental agency and put Sonatrach on a par with the foreign oil companies. The agency, whose objective would be to foster competition in the upstream sector and liberalization in the downstream sector, would be in charge of regulation, taxation, contracting and monitoring, as well as collection and dissemination of geological and geophysical data. In this case Sonatrach would run its operation, solely or in association, and carry the normal risks associated with oil company operations, namely the geological, investment and market risks. This option was initially considered by the reform-minded Hamrouche government in 1990–91 in a move to modernize Sonatrach and turn it into a commercial company with separate subsidiaries, facing competition but still owned by the state.[42] Such a move was also intended to discover Sonatrach's costs, so far hidden by high resource rents.

As a transition to this ultimate solution, Sonatrach may be compelled to shift its objective function, which has consisted in maximizing the 'upstream hydrocarbon rent'. Indeed, now that the normal functions of a corporate structure are being restored, and the role of both the state, as the resource owner and shareholder, and the company are being clarified, it would be easier for Sonatrach to adopt a 'maximizing value' objective instead. Such a shift will have far-reaching implications for the management, which should be expected to move the company beyond its traditional means of managing national resources.

This likely shift in the company's role and objective is championed by the younger members of staff. Less obsessed by the 'resource ownership' of its post-nationalization elders, this younger generation is more aware that as the rent moves downstream, being the 'guardian of the state's resource' matters less and that the skills, culture and values, which were at the origin of Sonatrach's relative success so far (Sonatrach 1996), have to adapt to the new commercial and competitive environment.

In this regard, the most pressing and critical issue is the ability of the company to adapt to the global changes affecting its role as an important player in the world market place. Whether the new institutional and energy policy framework, analysed in the previous section, will free the company from the shackles of government control and bureaucracy and allow it to move rapidly in this direction remains to be seen. What is certain is that the new organizational framework cannot drive the process of change forward in the absence of changes in attitudes towards a more competitive environment. Attitudes towards privatization are as important, since the company is expected to promote and attract local and foreign private participation in the capital of its new downstream subsidiaries (Hamrour 1998).

Political interference, magnified in the present period of traumatic transition, has greatly impacted on Sonatrach. As a result, attitudes have been influenced by the ongoing struggle between rent-seekers and reformers, which has lain at the heart of Algeria's politics since the end of the 1980s. Therefore, the extent to which the new institutional and organizational setting can keep politics out of business, will be critical to the company's success and destiny.

5.   Conclusions

The perspective provided in this chapter derives from a retrospective analysis of how Algerian gas policies have evolved, of what economic and social imperatives have driven these policies, of how ideological and political considerations have constrained them, and of the main concepts and determinants of the ongoing strategy. Consideration was also given to the new institutional and energy policy framework as well as to the changing perceptions and attitudes, as driving factors of the company destiny.

Affirmation in the early 1970s of sovereignty over hydrocarbon resources and state ownership of the industry came as a logical result of a consensual revolutionary commitment and was therefore predictable. However, there is no evidence since then of a smooth historical trend from which to extrapolate. The first change in government attitudes towards energy policy occurred in the late 1970s and early 1980s, with changing circumstances and political leadership. By the end of the 1980s and early 1990s, an opposite, more radical, change came as a response to immense economic and social pressures, and was favoured by fundamental political and ideological developments.

This process of change left Sonatrach in an invidious position. The company had to adjust its strategy to conform to successive governments' depletion policies while coping with the uncertainties of the market place. In the 1980s, Sonatrach had little room for manoeuvre in expanding its business and protecting its market share. If there is a lesson to be learned from that period, it is that the shrinkage of Sonatrach's export trade was more the result of a widening gap between dogmatic attitudes and reality than of a failure to foresee the changes and adapt accordingly.

With its main market concentrating in Western Europe, the company was fortunate to embark on a new strategy at the end of the 1980s, at the time when auspicious changes were taking place in EU energy policy and new gas markets and segments were emerging. In addition, as the EU was keen to support the deliverability of incremental supplies, both politically and financially, Sonatrach was able to successfully implement its investment programme aimed at doubling its exports in the 1990s.

With the 1990s coming to a close, Sonatrach has positioned itself as a key supplier of gas to Europe for decades to come. It has long-term contracts in place to export 60 bcm per year – some 57 of which is bound for Western Europe – diversified export infrastructures, as well as the advantage of easy transit routes and proximity to its main markets in the Mediterranean. In addition, in spite of difficulties stemming from the present domestic environment, the company has proved to be a reliable gas supplier.

Although Algeria's gas reserves appear to be relatively large, its gas-dominated economy and subsequent long-term domestic requirements have tempered its export ambitions. However, to maintain the long-term viability of the country's internal and external economic balances, the Algerian government is putting pressure on Sonatrach to expand its exports. Sonatrach's main difficulty will be deciding whether it should expand gas exports, or shift its focus on the comparatively much higher rent generating oil exports. Should the In Salah gas project receive the go ahead signal,[43] the next tranche of gas, that is 9 bcm per year in 2002–2003, will be traded by In Salah Gas Services, the Sonatrach-BP joint-marketing company. As 4 bcm per year have already been assigned to Enel to cover an existing contract with Sonatrach, only 5 bcm per year are left for additional exports.

Any further expansion above 65 bcm will require additional low-cost gas reserves. As there is still considerable potential for new gas discoveries, the involvement of major oil and gas companies upstream is expected to give a new impetus to gas development. In particular, a merged BP Amoco could provide tremendous synergy and make a major contribution in exploring further the gas-prone regions where the company is involved. While the non-commercial risks, stemming particularly from long-term investment possibilities and their financing, will be mitigated by such partnerships, the extent to which new supplies can be brought on stream depends on the shorter-term commercial risks resulting from changing market structures and prices in continental Europe.

With such risks looming on the horizon, Sonatrach has a much more immediate concern. Gas is becoming one of Algeria's most valuable export items and Sonatrach is urged to protect both its market share and the value of its exports. Hence its apparently dual stance, partly defensive and partly offensive. One should expect Sonatrach to resist any move that would undermine the value of its existing contracts, but how much help can it expect from its trading allies, the present buyers? They are themselves unsure of their future market, risk losing their monopoly and will be no longer in a position to shoulder take-or-pay commitments.

Faced with tougher competition to contract incremental gas from In Salah, Sonatrach may be pressured by BP Amoco to consider more flexible terms and to find fresh ways to adapt its traditional modes of supplies. The next move could be selling gas through the GME into the Spanish market. In a strategic move mid-stream, In Salah Gas Services could become a potential user of the different sections of the GME pipeline, beyond the Algerian–Moroccan borders. As market developments unfold and pressure on price increases, Sonatrach is expected to take advantage of further opportunities down-stream that could add value to its gas business. Ensuring access to the end-users, through different aggregation routes than those currently available, will be crucial in this regard.

Such a prospect assumes flexibility and rapidity in the decision-making process and poses the fundamental problem of Sonatrach's autonomy or, conversely, the extent of government involvement in its gas business. Even if the government has been keen in recent years to withdraw from micro-economic management of public enterprises, factors such as the huge macro-economic impact of the hydrocarbon sector (Aïssaoui, 1998; Nashashibi et al., 1998) greatly affects the organizational design of the company and its relationship with the energy policy makers. The institutional and energy policy framework put in place in 1998 reflects such limits. While the new setting would help shelter the company from political interference, it remains to be seen whether it may be conducive to more autonomy. What is certain is that the government and Sonatrach's senior management have had the time and the commitment to focus on the best way forward for the company. In a time of rapid changes moving fast enough will be of vital importance.

Notes

1. Prorationing may be defined as a co-operative policy aimed at controlling supply in order to prevent it from exceeding demand at prevailing prices.
2. After implementation of the Evian Accord, the Algerian government and France's BRP each held 40.51 per cent interest in SN Repal. The Algerian equity was raised to parity following the 1965 Agreement revising the Accord.
3. According to *Middle East Economic Survey* the initial idea was to retain 51 per cent of the shares of the national company and offer the remaining 49 per cent to foreign firms: *MEES* 6 (37), 19 July 1963.
4. The economics of the two deals differed substantially. While CAMEL was to receive sale revenues from its contract with British Methane, it only acted as a processing contractor to Gaz de France, which financed the expansion of the plant, after having cancelled an earlier plan to build a liquefaction plant of its own.
5. Jarjour states that CAMEL's gas (1 bcm per year over fifteen years, chartered by British Methane and delivered to Canvey Island in England), was priced at a base of 53.8 cents/MBtu fob and 76.1 cents/MBtu cif. This corresponds to the rough figure of 7.0 to 7.5 old pence per therm cif reported by *Platt's Oilgram* (30 June 1964). At the time Algerian gas was competing with town gas, which was priced at 11 to 12 old pence per therm for carbonized coal gas and 9 to 10 old pence per therm for gas made from light petroleum distillates. Therefore the argument that CAMEL's gas was priced at parity or above fob oil prices, which was used by the Algerian authorities in the early 1980s (Nabi 1991), misses the fundamental point of gas priced to compete with alternative fuels.
6. Index numbers of posted prices of refined products for all ports are detailed in *OPEC Annual Statistical Bulletin, 1971,* Table 77, p.122.
7. The 1976 Charter follows the Charter of Tripoli (1962) and the Charter of Algiers (1964). Contrary to the earlier two, that of 1976 was submitted to a referendum following a broad public and party debate in an attempt to involve the people directly in the political, ideological and economic transformation of the country.
8. The direct link was sponsored by Sonatrach, Enagas and GdF who created SEGAMO (Société d'Etude du Gazoduc Maghreb-Europe) to supervise it. Bechtel was commissioned to undertake a feasibility study and in 1982 it announced that in its judgement the link was technically and economically feasible (*Platt's*, 11 May 1982).
9. Dutch gas policy was never made explicit. Gasunie commented on this move as follows: 'As part of the reconsideration of Holland's natural gas policy, a debate has been initiated on the desirability and feasibility of additional sales, including the possibility of expansion of exports' (Gasunie Annual Report 1982:25).
10. On 18 June 1982, using the pretext of the coup in Poland, the Reagan

administration announced increased economic sanctions against Soviet gas export pipeline projects, banned the transfer of relevant US technology, and involved both US subsidiaries abroad and foreign companies working under American licence.

11. The Algerian move on prices was quite natural. Indeed, the new oil context made the base prices of around $1.30/MBtu negotiated in the mid-1970s, much less attractive than other available contractual price arrangements. For instance, Abu Dhabi, the other OPEC gas exporter, succeeded without much fuss in increasing its LNG prices in December 1979 to a cif level price of $4.00/MBtu effective 1 January, compared to the previous price of $2.36/MBtu (*MEES*, 23 (16), 4 February 1980).

12. This was the subject of an enquiry by a special commission of the Algerian Parliament. In its later finding, the Commission recognized the particular circumstances in which Sonatrach was forced to accept such an agreement, and also the real loss relating to the exploitation of the LNG shipped by El Paso since early 1978. (*MEES*, 24(13), 12 January 1981).

13. Algeria had tried to secure OPEC support at the meeting in Algiers in June 1980 when the Organisation adopted the following declaration: 'The Conference reiterates OPEC Member Countries' determination to set gas prices in line with those of crude oil, in order to achieve a coherent marketing policy for their hydrocarbons. Therefore, the major gas importing countries should consider the oil-gas price equivalency as a necessary incentive to develop gas resources economically and thus to allow gas to contribute substantially to the satisfaction of world energy needs.' (OPEC Press Release 4-80, Algiers, 11 June 1980).

Although expressing strong backing for the principle of pricing parity between crude oil and natural gas, the declaration failed to mention whether parity should be on an fob or cif basis. This reflected a compromise between the stance of Algeria and Libya on one hand and Indonesia on the other, supporting the more moderate position adopted by the UAE, which had just renegotiated its contracts for LNG exports to Japan on an oil parity cif basis. Taking into account the heavy freight component for long-haul LNG, such distinction was indeed important.

14. Jacques Attali relates the ins and outs of the discussions which took place in 1981 between Jean-Marcel Jeanneney, Mitterand's special advisor on Algerian political and economic affairs, and M'Hamed Yala, the Algerian Minister of Finance in the first Chadli cabinet. Discussions involved such ideas as an indexation of gas prices to both oil prices and the terms of trade between France and Algeria. The difference between 'paid for' prices and 'market' prices would be entrusted to a jointly-managed Fund, which would *inter alia* remunerate imports from France (Attali 1993).

15. Algerian official gas reserves are those of non-associated gas in field already developed or planned to be developed.

16. Domestic requirements are defined as the gas needed in the hydrocarbon sector (to power the re-injection either for EOR or NGLs production

through the cycling process, production processing, transportation and liquefaction), as a feedstock for the petrochemical industry, in the power generation sector, and as final consumption of the industrial, commercial and domestic sectors.

17. In an absolute indexation, every change in the price of the alternative fuel is fully reflected in the price of gas. This is known as a 100 per cent 'pass through' formula. However, it is understood that in face of strong competition, companies have lowered some of the pass through factors to ensure that they maintain their competitive edge or even increase their market share (ECE-UN 1996).

18. Disagreement between Columbia and Shell (which is an equity shareholder of the Nigerian project), led to renunciation by Shell to acquire the Cove Point regasification plant.

19. This contract replaces the one signed in September 1975 between Sonatrach and Panhandle Eastern Pipeline Company. Trunkline Gas Co. is a subsidiary of PanEnergy, which is now part of a new company, Duke Energy Corporation, following its purchase by North Carolina's Duke Power.

20. In October 1990 the European Energy Council agreed unanimously to the proposal by the Commission to revoke the existing Council Directive 75/404/EEC, dating from February 1975, related to the limitation of the use of natural gas in power plants.

21. Algeria also explored the possibility of gas sales to Central and Eastern Europe via Italy. Discussions at ministerial and expert level were held with representatives of the so-called 'Pentagonal Energy Group' comprising Austria, Czechoslovakia, Hungary, Italy and Yugoslavia.

22. These talks took place between May 1985, on the occasion of the Third Arab Energy Conference in Algiers, and March 1992. They were reported in corresponding issues of the monthly EC publication, 'Energy in Europe'.

23. The TEN priority project was agreed by the European Council in Essen, in December 1994.

24. SOTAL (50 per cent Sonatrach and 50 per cent Total) is involved in LPG trading.

25. The seven core dry gas fields in the In Salah area are Krechba, Taguentour, Reg, Garet El Befinat, Hassi-Moumene, In Salah and Gour Mahmoud. The four wet gas fields in the Timimoun area are: Tiguentourine, Hassi Frida, Ouan Taredert and Hassi Ouan Abachou.

26. Delivery under this contract started towards the end of 1996 and will continue to be met by Sonatrach up to the date of first gas production from In Salah. The take-over by In Salah gas does not affect the terms and conditions. Gas will continue to be delivered through the Trans-Med pipeline at the Algerian–Tunisian border, on a long-term, take-or-pay basis, with the price of gas linked to those of crude oil and oil products.

27. Derman and Yassine (1997:6) who suggest that the Sonatrach-Amoco deal on In Amenas is similar to the Sonatrach-Total-Repsol deal on TFT, explain the sharing device as follows: 'To determine the share reverting to the

partner, the entire amount of liquid and gaseous hydrocarbons extracted from the deposit is expressed in tonne oil equivalent. Hydrocarbons produced, whether liquids or gas, are converted to their inherent energy value. The oil company [foreign partner] is allocated an overall energy value to recover its costs and profit from the available liquids (LPG and condensate), either as a share of liquid hydrocarbons extracted from produced set gas quantities or a share of liquid hydrocarbons and a share of the gas revenues, sold by Sonatrach.'

28. Speculative gas reserves (probable and possible) have been estimated at 1400 bcm (Bouhafs 1994a). These reserves are mostly located in the In Amenas and In Salah region where BP and Amoco are respectively involved.

29. The In Salah gas project is in two broad phases. The first is a further appraisal of the seven core fields and exploration for additional reserves. This will enable the partners to decide on the scale of development that would include a 550 km, 48" pipeline link to Hassi R'Mel and the existing Algerian export system. Such a link would allow the transit of some 9 bcm per year during the plateau phase.

30. Current indications suggest that while remaining proven reserves amount to 2990 bcm, probable and possible reserves may amount to 1400 bcm. On the other hand, non-official sources put associated proven gas reserves at 1800 bcm, which may be considered as deferred gas. Consideration of these additional reserves may impact on the ceiling as well as the ultimate time horizon for exports.

31. Sonatrach is keen to be awarded a block or two in Iraq. However, it remains to be seen whether Sonatrach intends to take exploration risks in other countries or simply wants to get concessions abroad and farm out to international firms.

32. Products of the gas chain, i.e. natural gas and NGLs (LPG, condensate and ethane) will generate some 60 per cent of Algerian foreign exchange revenues in 2000.

33. The bulk of oil and gas is exported fob or at the Algerian borders. However, Sonatrach owns two marketing companies. Sonatrach Petroleum Company (SPC), based in London, is specialized in the trading and shipping of liquid hydrocarbons. Sonatrading BV, based in Amsterdam, is specialized in LNG trading on the US market. More recently, In Salah Gas company, a joint venture between Sonatrach and BP, based in Amsterdam, is in charge of bringing the next tranche of Algerian gas to the European market.

34. In the winter of 1998–9, as a result of low cost oil-indexed continental gas, the Interconnector unexpectedly went into reverse flow to allow for the import of cheaper gas in Britain. This led to a convergence of prices between the two markets.

35. Further uncertainty about the future of the Belgian gas utility also stems from a possible merger with its parent company Tractebel, the world's third biggest independent power producer, and the more domestically oriented Electrabel, to form a new energy group straddling both gas and electricity

businesses (*Financial Times*, 25 February 1999). Such a move may herald a wave of concentrations and consolidations of the European utilities, in face of the tougher environment of the newly liberalized energy markets.

36. Personal communication from Nordine Aït-Laoussine, October 1998.
37. EMPL, a subsidiary of Enagas of Spain and Transgas of Portugal, is the financing company and exclusive concessionaire of the transit section. Hence, it finances and supports all the costs, possesses the transportation rights and, in turn, sells transportation services to the shippers involved. Enagas and Transgas (and any future shipper) have their long-term transportation contracts with EMPL, and it is the one that pays royalties (transit fees) to the Moroccan Treasury.
38. The fertilizer industry in Algeria includes also a complex for the production of phosphate at Annaba of 495,000 tonne per year.
39. The new branch is in charge of co-ordination, control and strategic development of 'Subsidiaries & Interests'. It oversees five holding companies in Algeria, as well as Sonatrach's affiliates abroad.
40. Sonatrach capital amounts to 245 billion Algerian dinars, corresponding to some $4.15 billion (1998).
41. Nevertheless, a spate of pipeline bombings at the end of 1997 and early 1998 were reported. Although these did disrupt supplies, their effect was limited and short-lived (see for example *Energy Compass*, Faxfile 13 November 1997).
42. Discussion with Abderrahmane Hadj-Nacer, former Governor of the Bank of Algeria, December 1998. Sadek Boussena, the minister of energy at the time, revealed part of such a plan in early 1990, announcing the formation of five major subsidiaries: exploration; production and marketing; transportation; refining; and international operations. *PIW* (15 January 1990) commented that 'hopes are for a more dynamic state Sonatrach following the current wave of reform sweeping the country'.
43. At the time of writing, the Sonatrach-BP agreement on In Salah was still not concluded. The two companies were due to finish the exploration and appraisal phase by the end of 1998. They planned to submit their findings and recommendations to their respective boards in February 1999. A decision to proceed with full-scale development may be affected by a persistent low oil price environment. According to *MEES* (vol.42, no.14, 5 April 1999) the decision is expected in autumn 1999.

References

Abdesselam, B. (1989), *Le Gaz algérien: stratégies et enjeux*, Algiers: Bouchène.
Aïssaoui, A. (1999), ' Lower Gas Prices: Have Producers Got the Right Signals?', Monthly comment of the web site page of the Oxford Institute for Energy Studies [http://associnst.ox.ac.uk/energy], March 1999.
— (1998), ' Lower Oil Prices: Can Algeria Mitigate the New Crisis?', *Middle*

East Economic Survey, 41(22), June 1998.

— (1997), 'Moving Midstream Along the Maghreb-Europe Gas Pipeline: Institutional, Financial and Commercial Barriers', Unpublished report.

Aït-Laoussine, N. (1992), 'Changing Relationships Between Governments and Private Oil Companies: The Case of Algeria', Washington, PIW and PFC Conference. See 'Aït-Laoussine: New Course for Troubled Algeria', *PIW* 31 (10), 9 March 1992.

— (1990), 'Le Débat sur le gaz algérien: bilan d'une décennie', Unpublished Report).

— (1979), 'Developments in the Natural Gas Industry of Algeria', *OPEC Review*, 3 (2), Summer 1979.

Algerian Energy Committee (1985*), Assyassa wal baramij attaqawiya al jazairya [Algerian Energy Policy and Programmes]*, Algiers: Third Arab Energy Conference.

Attar, A. (1997), 'The European Gas Market: Future Prospects, Uncertainties and New Opportunities for Algerian Gas', Offshore Europe '97 Conference, Aberdeen.

Belguedj, M. (1977), 'Algerian Natural Gas: The Political Economy of Diversification', Doctoral Dissertation, The Fletcher School of Law and Diplomacy, Tufts University.

— (1978), ' Marketing of Algerian Gas', *Petroleum Economist*, 55 (12), December 1978.

Bouhafs A. (1996), 'Le Gaz naturel algérien et la coopération méditerranéenne', Tlemcen: ADESC Conference, published in *El Watan*, 31 July.

— (1994a), 'Le Gaz algérien: situation et perspectives', Milan: 19th World Gas Congress.

— (1994b), 'Stratégie de modernisation de Sonatrach', in Cahiers de l'ISMEA, Série Economie et Energie no.6 (*L'Avenir des sociétés nationales des pays exportateurs d'hydrocarbures*).

Boussena S. (1989 and 1991), Interview with Walid Khadduri and Ian Seymour, *Middle East Economic Survey*, 33 (2), October 1989, and 34 (14), January 1991.

Chesny, C. (1969), 'Le Gaz naturel en Algérie: le rôle privilégié des engrais dans la future pétrochimie algérienne', Thèse de doctorat, Université de Grenoble.

DeGolyer and MacNaughton (1977), *Report on the Oil, Gas, Condensate and LPG Reserves of Algeria*, January.

Derman, A. and H. Yassine (1997), 'Gas Clauses in Algerian E&P Contracts', Kuala Lumpur: AIPN Conference, September, published by Barrows, Petroleum Taxation/Legislation Report, September–October.

Djaroud, M. (1991), *Processus de transfert de savoir-faire et organisation: description et analyse de cas de la pétrochimie, du GNL et du raffinage à Sonatrach*, Algiers: OPU.

Drury, D. (1996), 'The In Salah Gas Project', unpublished paper.

ECE-UN (UN Economic Commission for Europe) (1996), *Gas Contracting: Principles and Practices*, New York and Geneva: UN.

El-Zaim, I. (1984), *International Gas Market Restructuring and Algeria's Natural Gas Policy and Marketing Strategy*, The International Research Centre for Energy and Economic Development. Boulder, University of Colorado.

Entelis, J.P. (1999), 'Sonatrach: The Political Economy of an Algerian State Institution', *Middle East Journal*, 53 (1).

Estrada, J. et al. (1995), *The Development of European Gas Markets: Environmental, Economic and Political Perspectives*, John Wiley & Sons.

Faïd, M.K. (1994), 'Le Gaz naturel: tendances et perspectives – La contribution de l'Algérie', Milan: 19th World Gas Congress.

Fergani, Y.M.B. (1983), 'The Role of Natural Gas in Algeria's Energy Policy', A Presentation to the Ninth (Informal) Meeting of the Chief Executives of the OPEC National Oil Companies, Hassi R'Mel.

Ferroukhi, R. (1995), 'Algeria's Energy Sector: A Quantitative Analysis', Doctoral Dissertation, Washington: The American University.

FLN (Front de Libération Nationale) (1980), 'Resolution de politique énergétique adoptée par le Comité central du FLN', Algiers: FLN.

Ghozali, S.A. (1975), 'Le Pétrole et le nouvel ordre économique international', published by Les Cahiers du Club du 'Nouvel Observateur' no. 6, under the title: 'Les Mensonges de la coopération', *Nouvel Observateur*, Hors Série, Spécial Economie, Paris.

Hached, A. (1998), 'Implications of Structural Changes in the European Gas Market: Sonatrach's Perspective as an LNG Supplier', Stavanger: ONS Conference.

Hamel, M. (1998), 'Algerian Oil and Gas Policies', London: CGES Conference.

Hamrour, A. (1998), 'Strategies for the Effective Restructuring of the Oil Refining and Petrochemical Industry in Algeria', London: SMi Conference.

INESG (Institut National des Etudes Stratégiques Globales) (1996), 'La Nouvelle place des hydrocarbures' in *Economie algérienne: Les enjeux et les choix à moyen terme*, Algiers: unpublished report.

Jarjour, G. (1990), 'Commercialisation du gaz naturel algérien: analyse retrospective des accords d'exportation, 1962–1989', GREEN Research Report, Cahier 90-06, Québec: Université Laval.

Khadduri, W. (1995), 'Algeria: Oil, Gas and Politics', *Middle East Economic Survey*, 38 (37), June 1995.

— (1989), 'Algeria's Oil and Gas Industry at the Crossroads', *Middle East Economic Survey*, 33 (2).

Khelil, C. and Harouaka, A. (1979), 'Algeria's $33.4 Billion Program to Develop Hydrocarbon Reserves', *Pipe Line Industry*, 54-58.

Løchstøer, C. (1990), 'Algeria 1980–90: Political Changes and Implications for Gas Developments', Lysaker: The Fridtjof Nansen Institute.

Mazri, H. (1975), *Les Hydrocarbures dans l'économie algérienne*, Algiers: SNED.

Mekideche, M. (1983), *Le Secteur des hydrocarbures [en Algérie]*, Algiers: OPU.

Nabi, B. (1991), *Où va l'Algérie? Indépendance-Hydrocarbures-Dépendance*, Algiers: Dahlab.

Nashashibi, K. et al. (1998), ' Algeria's Hydrocarbon Sector: Evolution and Prospect' in *Algeria: Stabilisation and Transition to the Market*, Washington: IMF, Occasional Paper.

Pauwels, J.-P. (1983), 'Une nouvelle politique gazière' in *Réflexions sur les nouvelles orientations économiques et énergétiques du plan quinquénnal 1980–1984 et sur l'organisation de l'économie algérienne.* Algiers: ENAL.

Pawera, J. C. (1964), *Algeria's Infrastructure: An Economic Survey of Transportation, Communication, and Energy Resources*, New York, London: Praeger, Special Studies in International Economics.

Pelletreau, P. D. (1987), 'Revolution and Evolution: The Liquefied Natural Gas Contracts Between the United States and Algeria', Doctoral Dissertation, Washington: The George Washington University.

Preure, M. (1998), 'Réalisations et perspectives d'une compagnie pétrolière d'un pays producteur: Sonatrach', Paris: IFP Panorama.

Quinn, A. C. (1998), Developing and Marketing New Tranches of Algerian Gas: The In Salah Gas Project', Gastech '98 Conference, Dubai.

Rushby, I. (1996), BP Exploration Speech to CBI Algeria Conference, London.

Sonatrach (1998), 'Partnership in Petrochemical, Refining, Mining, and Fertilisers Activities in Algeria', London: Sonatrach's Road Show.

— (1996), *1963–1993, SONATRACH a trente ans: Des défis et des hommes*, Paris: AIRE.

— (1994), *SONATRACH: Un groupe pétrolier international*, Algiers: Régie Sud Méditerranée.

— (1977), *The Hydrocarbon Development Plan of Algeria: Financial Projections 1976–2005*, International Bechtel Incorporated.

Stern, J.P. (1998), *Competition and Liberalisation in European Gas Markets: A Diversity of Models*, London: The Royal Institute for International Affairs.

— (1990), *European Gas Market: Challenges and Opportunities in the 1990s*, London: The Royal Institute for International Affairs.

Stoppard, M. (1996), *A New Order for Gas in Europe?*, Oxford Institute for Energy Studies.

Weston, Peter (1998), *Natural Gas Trading in Europe: Liberalisation and its Impact on Long-term Contracts*, London: EJC Energy.

Yousfi, Y. (1984), 'La Politique algérienne d'exportations des hydrocarbures', Annual Meeting of the World Energy Conference, National Energy Day, Algiers.

— (1982), 'Evolution of the Natural Gas Market and International Prices', *OPEC Review*, vol. VI, no. 2.

Zartman, I. W. and A. Bassani (1987), *The Algerian Gas Negotiations. FPI Case Studies*, Washington: Foreign Policy Institute of Advanced International Studies, The Johns Hopkins University.

CHAPTER 3

DUTCH GAS: ITS ROLE IN THE WESTERN EUROPEAN GAS MARKET

Malcolm Peebles

1. Introduction

This chapter endeavours to recount the development of Dutch gas since the discovery of the Groningen gas field in 1959 through to December 1998, and to assess the developments affecting the outlook of the Dutch gas market following the EU Gas Directive.

The history of Dutch natural gas and the role it has played in Western Europe's energy scene is really all about the discovery and development of the Groningen gas field – the largest field ever found in the area – complemented by the subsequent development of other smaller fields onshore and offshore the Netherlands. Groningen has had a profound effect on Europe's energy portfolio, including, not least of all, the revitalization of mainland Europe's high-cost manufactured gas industry which after the Second World War and prior to the discovery of Groningen had entered into a period of progressive decline in the face of severe and increasing competition from cheap oil and for some applications electricity as well.

For the purposes of this chapter, Western Europe is defined as comprising the countries listed below, recognizing that since the collapse of the Soviet Union in 1991 a number of other countries in the so-called Eastern Europe have now been 'added' to Europe as a whole. However, these latter countries have been largely ignored in this chapter as their gas industries were founded mainly on Soviet

Western European Countries				
Austria	Belgium	Denmark	France	Germany
Ireland	Italy	Luxembourg	Netherlands	Norway
Portugal	Spain	Sweden	Switzerland	United Kingdom

(Russian) gas and thus did not play a part in the Dutch gas story (although this is beginning to change as will be touched on briefly later).

In discussing the role of Dutch gas it is necessary to go back in time, in fact to the late 1950s when Groningen was discovered, and to review how the Dutch government and N.V. Nederlandse Aardolie Maatschappij (NAM) set about its exploitation both in the Netherlands and export markets.

Before doing so, two further comments are necessary. Unlike the oil industry which uses a barrel of oil as its universal international unit of measurement, the gas industry has no comparable unit. Gas statistics are variously quoted in cubic feet, cubic metres, petajoules, kilowatt hours, tonnes of oil equivalent, and so on. However, many gas statistics, but not all, are now given in cubic metres, in particular in billions (10 to the 9th) cubic metres (bcm) and this unit will be used in this chapter.[1] There is a further complication. Many gas statistics do not quote the calorific value of the gas. In the case of Groningen this is important as the gas as distributed has an untypical calorific value of approximately 8,400 kcal/m^3 (or 35.17MJ) due, inter alia, to its 14 per cent nitrogen content which is not extracted before sale, whereas most other gases have an average calorific value after treatment of around 9,400 kcal/m^3 (about 39 MJ). Thus for most practical purposes, one cubic metre of Groningen gas is equivalent to 0.88 cubic metres of conventional quality natural gas. However, as the calorific values of some of the figures quoted in this chapter are not specified by their originators, they are not necessarily consistent and should therefore be regarded as orders of magnitude rather than precise comparable numbers. As the saying goes: 'there are lies, damn lies and statistics'!

2.   Historical Background

2.1   Pre-Groningen Years

A brief review of the evolution of the gas industry in the Netherlands may be helpful in setting the scene before discussing in greater detail how the business developed following the discovery of Groningen.

The first recorded use of manufactured gas for lighting purposes was in The Hague in 1820. The first privately-owned gas company was established in Amsterdam in 1825 and the second in Rotterdam in 1826. Initially, and in common with the gas industry in many other countries at that time, the principal use of manufactured gas was for lighting public buildings and streets, and as distribution systems were built, for home lighting as well. By 1876, manufactured gas enterprises existed in virtually all Dutch cities and large towns. By 1920 there were 195 gas companies. As time passed gas lighting increasingly lost ground to electric lighting, to be replaced by growth in the use of gas for water heating and cooking and some industrial applications.

By the end of the Second World War only 150 gasworks remained and gas lighting had almost died out; many gasworks had been badly damaged or poorly maintained during the war and had to be rebuilt. During the post-war period conventional supplies of low calorific value manufactured gas were supplemented by reformed refinery gases and coke-oven gas from the steel industry together with some imports from Germany. Limited quantities of associated natural gas also became available from oil producing fields.

In 1962, the year before the start of Groningen gas supplies, total consumption of all types of gas amounted to about 1,000 million cubic metres of natural gas equivalent. About one-quarter of this was associated natural gas of which approximately one-half was reformed to manufactured gas quality. Reformed refinery gases constituted about 20 per cent of total gas supply. Most of the balance was coke-oven gas. The total number of gas consumers at that time amounted to nearly 2.5 million, mostly residential consumers using gas for cooking and water heating, of which less than 400,000 had been converted to natural gas. Sales to industrial consumers were small in number and quantity.

2.2   The Mining Act of 1810

The general framework of the search for hydrocarbons was provided by the Netherlands Mining Act of 1810, founded on French legislation inspired by Napoleon. In essence, this Act allowed exploration without licence subject only to the consent of the surface owner. A Deed of Concession by the Crown to the surface owner and finder was, however, necessary before any discovery could be mined. The Act also stated that if the right to mine was not granted by the Crown to the finder, the latter was entitled to certain payments to reimburse him for the costs he had incurred, plus a small reward. The surface owner also received a lump-sum payment, and if and when actual mining took place, he then became entitled to payment for the use of his land.

This Act still forms the basis of Dutch mining legislation, although it has, of course, been considerably expanded and altered in many respects since 1810.

2.3   The Discovery of Groningen

The first indication of the existence of the Groningen gas field came on 22 July 1959, when as a result of exploration drilling near the village of Slochteren in the province of Groningen, NAM announced the discovery of a gas-bearing formation. Initially, reserves were assessed to be fairly modest at about 60 bcm, but these were increased progressively as more drilling was carried out. In July 1962 the government announced that reserves were at least 150 bcm, and in October that year this was raised to 500 bcm. In October 1963 the figure was raised again to 1,100 bcm, and subsequent revisions increased reserves to over 1,700 bcm by 1976 with the probability of further increases including, by that time, past production. Indeed by 1998 Groningen's ultimate recoverable reserves were assessed to be about 2,800 bcm.

By any standards, Groningen is a major non-associated gas field. Where it stands in a world league table is of little or no consequence as various countries/companies have different standards and methods of measuring so-called proven, probable and possible reserves. Also gas composition, and hence the gas's calorific value, is another factor to be taken into account when comparing one field with another. Furthermore, it is only when a particular gas reservoir is nearing the end of its useful productive life that it is possible to determine the full extent of the reservoir's ultimate recoverable reserves.

Leaving such considerations to one side, what is not in dispute is that the Netherlands had found a major gas field located on land in an industrialized country within close proximity of the major industrial conurbations of Belgium, Germany, France and the UK, indeed within striking distance of southern Europe as well.

2.4   Arrangements for the Exploitation of Groningen Gas

When searching for the most appropriate way to organize the exploitation and marketing of Groningen gas, the government kept the following two objectives in mind. First, that the gas should be sold on a commercial basis consistent with the greatest possible benefit to the national economy; and secondly, that the gas should be introduced as smoothly as possible, without violent dislocation of the existing energy market.

To achieve these aims, the government decided to end the existing public monopoly of the bulk supply of (manufactured) gas enjoyed by the State Gas Board (SGB) but to maintain nevertheless a large measure of direct state participation. In view of the fact that N.V. Nederlandse Staatsmijnen (DSM) as the largest producer and distributor of solid fuels and manufactured gas in the Netherlands would be adversely affected by the introduction of Groningen gas, the obvious course was to employ DSM as the instrument of state participation in the marketing of this gas. In view of the considerable technical and commercial problems envisaged, it was agreed that Shell and Esso, the shareholders of NAM, would play a large part not only in production but also in the wholesale marketing sector, hitherto 100 per cent state-owned, so that full benefit could be derived from their know-how, experience and financial resources. This was welcomed by Shell and Esso, who after drawing upon their earlier experiences in the United States concluded that they did not wish to be confined to selling gas ex-field but to participate as far downstream as was politically feasible and economically desirable. At the same time the state, via DSM, would participate in the cost of and proceeds from the production of Groningen gas (but not for non-Groningen gases) through a new unincorporated financing partnership known as the 'Maatschap' comprising NAM 60 per cent and DSM 40 per cent which, inter alia, is responsible for setting joint economic policies for the exploration and exploitation by NAM of Groningen gas.

For the transportation and wholesale marketing of gas within the Netherlands a new corporate entity, N.V. Nederlandse Gasunie, was set up on 6 April 1963 with the ownership of Shell 25 per cent, Esso 25 per cent, DSM 40 per cent with, in this instance, the state having a direct 10 per cent stake, giving the government an effective 50 per cent holding. In subsequent years DSM was replaced by Energie Beheer Nederland B.V. (EBN) which is the holding company for the state's interests in oil and natural gas reserves and production. These arrangements are shown schematically in Figure 1.

In May 1963 a concession for the exploitation of hydrocarbons in the province of Groningen was granted to NAM, as part of the overall development plan. Their first delivery of Groningen gas to Gasunie took place on 9 December 1963.

As far as exports were concerned, these were to be carried out by NAM for the account of Gasunie and for this purpose a separate division of NAM was set up known as NAM/Gas Export. In addition, Internationale Gas Transport Maatschappij N.V. (IGTM) was created in April 1963, owned 50/50 Shell/Esso, to provide technical advice and develop gas transport and/or distribution ventures outside the Netherlands. This led subsequently to the creation in Germany of three pipeline companies, NETG, METG and SETG, to transport

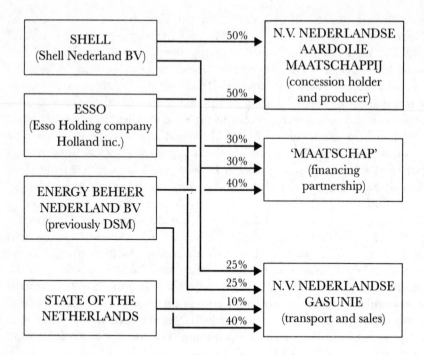

Figure 1: Corporate Arrangements for Groningen Gas

Groningen gas from the Dutch/German border onwards. And as a consequence of various manufactured gas utilities deciding to purchase Groningen gas, Shell and Esso acquired varying percentage interests in Ruhrgas, Thyssengas and DETG of Germany and Distrigaz of Belgium, as well as in the aforementioned ETGs. Here again this participation was not driven solely by the desire to add value downstream of production, although that was important, but also to help stimulate the companies concerned with the injection of money and commercial and technical expertise. Participation was politically impossible in the case of state-owned Gaz de France and SNAM of Italy, while the prospect of exporting Dutch gas to the UK, which at that time was Europe's largest gas market, disappeared with the discovery of gas in the British southern sector of the North Sea in 1965. Export contracts were, however, concluded with Gaz de France and SNAM for the supply and sale of Groningen gas at their national borders. For completeness sake, exports to Austria were also considered but the idea was abandoned following objections from the Soviet Union which regarded Austria as its 'territory'.

   The activities of IGTM, which at an earlier date had been merged with those of NAM/Gas Export, resulted in IGTM being disbanded in 1971. And in April 1975, Gasunie took over the activities of NAM/ Gas Export in respect of Dutch gas exports on the same contractual terms and conditions as were then applicable to such sales. However, Gasunie did not acquire the shareholding interests of Shell and Esso in Germany and Belgium which remained as they were, except for the subsequent independent sale by Esso of its shareholding in Distrigaz in the 1970s.
   The development of exports is discussed in more detail in Section 5.

2.5   Ministerial Discretions

While the above events were taking place, the then Minister of Economic Affairs, J.W. de Pous, reserved to himself the following powers in view of the importance of Groningen gas to the Dutch economy:

i)   the right of approval of the transfer price between the Maatschap and Gasunie;
ii)   the right of approval of the gas sales plan;
iii) the right of approval of conditions and tariffs for the delivery of gas by Gasunie to Public Distribution companies in the Nether-lands, as well as the right to approve the price level for other customers;
iv)   the right of approval for the construction of transmission lines and other facilities for the transportation and storage of gas;
v)   the right of approval of Dutch border prices for export sales; and,
vi)   the right to have a limited quantity of gas supplied by and for the account of Gasunie at prices and conditions as stipulated by him, if he should consider this desirable to promote industrial develop-ment in certain parts of the country.

Although Gasunie was formed specifically for the purpose of bringing Groningen gas to market, it also had the right to purchase, transport and sell all refinery gas, manufactured gas and natural gas produced in the Netherlands outside the Groningen concession in so far as such gases were supplied to third parties by the shareholders of Gasunie including their affiliated companies.
   It is clear from the foregoing that although the wholly state-owned gas industry responsible for the bulk supply and transport of gas in the Netherlands was the first to have been partly privatized – long before Margaret Thatcher had 'invented' the concept – the government still

retained a firm hand on how the industry would be developed through its various 'rights of approval' and direct or indirect shareholding interests in certain of the newly created entities.

The so-called 'De Pous Memorandum' which set out the government's objectives and ministerial discretions continues to form the foundation stone for gas policy in the Netherlands, albeit with various changes of emphasis by later governments to better reflect the market conditions then prevailing. Nevertheless, in broad terms, the conclusion of this memorandum is still valid today, namely: 'The Minister expects the development of natural gas to be undertaken with the utmost energy and in such a manner as to ensure the maximum profit is obtained from this natural resource for our economy as a whole.'

2.6   *Revenue Flow and Sharing*

In simple terms, Gasunie receives all revenues from the transport and sale of Groningen gas. It purchases the gas at the wellhead from NAM at a 'transfer price' related to expected yearly realizations, calculated to give Gasunie an annual return or dividend of 20 per cent (i.e D.Fls 80 million) on its share capital of D.Fls 400 million after allowing for operating and other costs, corporation taxes, and so on. Prior to 1972, this resulted through the partnership arrangements in Gasunie and the Maatschap in a profit split of approximately 70/30 in the government's favour.

As a result of changes in Gasunie's prices to PD companies and industrial customers, a new so-called 85/15 agreement was introduced with effect from 1 January 1972. This related to the additional proceeds from sales of Groningen gas within the Netherlands defined as being the difference between actual prices and indexed reference prices. This gave a split on additional proceeds of 85/15 in the government's favour. The arrangement did not apply to exports. Neither this nor subsequent agreements applied to non-Groningen gas. In 1974, effective 1 January 1975, a new agreement was reached with the government applicable to Gasunie's annual weighted average prices for both inland and export sales. This resulted in a split of 95/5 in the government's favour for sales above a certain average unit price level after allowing for Gasunie's operating and other costs but before deducting corporation tax.

In summary, and ignoring many detailed provisions and subsequent changes, the state receives 70 per cent of the revenues from Groningen gas up to a specified average unit price, 85 per cent on the next tranche of prices, and 95 per cent above that. The balances of 30, 15 and 5 per cent respectively flow from Gasunie via the Maatschap to the private shareholder, NAM, subject to certain constraints on the total revenues, net of revenue fiscal charges, it can receive. What these agreements mean in practice is that the state bears the brunt of any downturns in annual sales volumes and/or average unit wholesale prices, and is the main beneficiary when sales and/or prices are high. To illustrate the point, Table 1 shows estimated state revenues in money-of-the-day from both inland and export sales, the volumes involved, and average yearly wholesale prices for selected years. None of these figures is precise and should be regarded as orders of magnitude only.

Table 1: State Revenues, 1975–90

	1975	*1980*	*1985*	*1990*
Sales bcm	95	90	80	70
Wholesale prices D.ct/m^3	10	25	40	20
State revenues D.Fl.billion	5	15	25	10

Source: Author's own estimates

Put another way, as a rule of thumb a rise or fall in oil prices (to which gas prices are linked) of US$1.00/barrel represents a gain or loss of about D.Fl 500 million in state revenues from gas. The high annual state revenues from gas in the late 1970s and the first half of the 1980s, contributing in some years more than 10 per cent of GDP, were at a time when although the overall Dutch economy was performing dismally and worse than most other European countries, spending rates were high. Against this background, the impact of significant revenues from Dutch gas on the economy led to the development of an economic theory known as 'The Dutch Disease', a term which was given wide currency by the media.

Such information as is revealed on the government's and its partners' total takes from Groningen gas and related matters is normally confined to statements made by the Minister of Economic Affairs to Parliament. Gasunie as an incorporated company does, of course, publish annual accounts, but the unincorporated Maatschap does not.

Gasunie's 1998 results were as follows. Gross revenue (turnover) in 1998 at D.Fl 17.1 billion was 11 per cent down on 1997 at D.Fl 19.2 billion. This reduction was due mainly to lower sales and lower oil product related gas prices which fell by nearly 7 per cent to an average of Dct 21.4/m^3.

Total gas sales in 1998 were 79.7 bcm (inland market 43.3 bcm, exports 36.4 bcm) compared with 83.9 bcm in 1997. Exports to Germany and Italy were down, which in the case of Italy was of a temporary nature while the pipeline through Switzerland to Italy was being upgraded. Ambient temperatures also adversely affected sales with 1998 being the warmest year on record. As a result of competition in the Netherlands and the arrival of British gas via the Interconnector, Gasunie lost more than 10 per cent of its local sales.

3.   Supply

3.1   *The Transmission System, Conversion and Gas Quality Considerations*

Once formed, Gasunie acquired the gas transmission systems of SGB and DSM amounting to nearly 3,000km. These systems had to be adapted and reinforced to accept higher pressure 'dry' natural gas and extended in order to bring supplies to all parts of the Netherlands (see Map 1). By 1998, the total length of the main transmission system had reached about 11,630km complemented by a distribution network of 100,000km. A construction programme of this magnitude in one of the world's most densely populated countries has been a major operation and has presented a number of unique problems. These included the crossing of many large rivers and canals, and the need to avoid any lasting interference to the country's immense and vital system of drainage canals. Another difficulty was the nature of the subsoil, largely sand or peat, combined with a very high water table. The latter necessitated the sinking of drainage wells up to 6 metres in depth at distances of a few metres apart. Water then had to be pumped out for many days before the water table had been sufficiently lowered and the sand had become dry enough to prevent the trench from caving in before the pipes could be laid.

The transmission system was designed to operate at a pressure of around 65 bar equivalent to about 950 psi. With initial gas pressures at the wellhead of more than 200 bar (say 2,900 psi), the pressure has to be let down before the gas is fed into the transmission system at 65 bar. However, as gas is produced the wellhead pressure will gradually decline over time to the point where it may need to be boosted by compressors back up to 65 bar. A further consideration is that as gas flows through the pipeline its pressure will drop due to friction.

At periods of low demand in the summer the pressure drop at low gas velocities is minimal. But when demand in the winter is high,

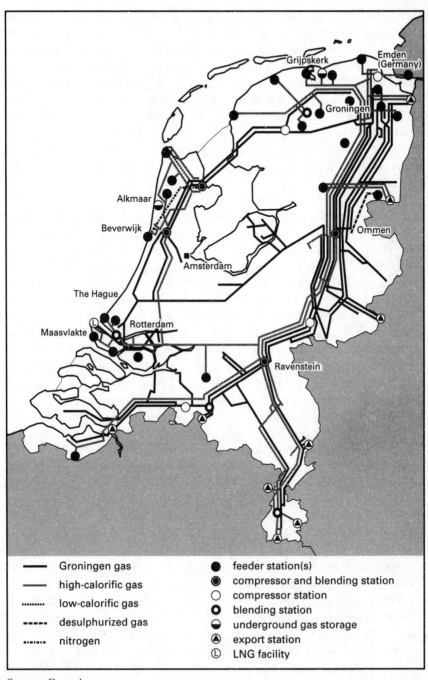

——	Groningen gas	●	feeder station(s)
——	high-calorific gas	◉	compressor and blending station
··········	low-calorific gas	○	compressor station
- - - - -	desulphurized gas	◉	blending station
·······	nitrogen	◓	underground gas storage
		◬	export station
		Ⓛ	LNG facility

Source: Gasunie

Map 1: The Dutch Gas Transmission System

pressures will fall due to high gas velocities because of the greater friction between the rapidly flowing gas and the pipeline wall. To maintain the necessary pressures for both internal supplies and exports, Gasunie has built eight compressor stations at Alphen, Beverwijk, Oldeboom, Ommen, Ravenstein, Spijk, Wieringermeer and Zweekhorst which are controlled from a central station at Groningen.

Deliveries by Gasunie to public distribution companies and large consumers are made through 1,114 Custody Transfer Stations where the gas pressure is dropped to 8 bar (115 psi). Pressure is further reduced to 25 mbar before it is delivered to residential and other small consumers.

At the outset the decision was taken to distribute Groningen quality gas throughout the country, i.e. it was decided not to extract the 14 per cent inert nitrogen gas that Groningen gas contains. At that time Groningen was the only source of natural gas of any consequence, it was only in later years that other gas fields with different gas qualities were discovered and developed onshore and offshore the Netherlands.

This decision meant that the appliances (about 5 million) of the existing 2 million customers were converted over the five-year period 1964 to 1968 from low calorific value manufactured gas to higher calorific value Groningen gas. The die was set. With the benefit of hindsight it would probably have been more cost-effective over the long term to have extracted Groningen's nitrogen content at the point of production given that nitrogen has no heating value.

In most developed natural gas markets, gases from different fields with differing gas qualities are processed at or close to the points of production to provide a common nation-wide gas quality before transmission and distribution to end-consumers. Exceptionally, and where logistically convenient, some gas of an original and different quality may be delivered directly through a dedicated pipeline to a large consumer, e.g. a power station, where gas quality considerations are not normally vital. But in the Netherlands as more fields were discovered, Gasunie was obliged to build two main transmission systems, one for Groningen quality gas and the other for so-called high calorific value gas. These are complemented by smaller pipeline systems dedicated to low calorific value gas (i.e. lower than Groningen), desulphurized gas and nitrogen. These systems are in turn supported by nine blending stations to ensure that the equivalent of Groningen quality gas is distributed to residential and other small consumers whose appliances can only operate efficiently and safely with a gas of a consistent quality and pressure. However, for many larger consumers, burners can be adjusted at point of use to operate satisfactorily with gases of higher or lower calorific values. Both Groningen quality and high calorific gas are exported through fourteen export and metering stations.

During the 1990s, Groningen gas has comprised between 40 and 50 per cent of Gasunie's total sales (internal and exports), other fields on the Dutch mainland 15 to 20 per cent, the Dutch sector of the North Sea 27 to 37 per cent, and imports from Norway and the UK 3 to 4 per cent – whereas in the early years Groningen comprised over 90 per cent of Gasunie's total sales.

3.2 Small Fields Policy

Prior to the first oil crisis of 1973 the government's policy in broad terms (de Pous's Natural Gas Bill of 1962) was to develop markets quickly as energy (gas) was abundant. This crisis underlined the need for a change in policy. It led to Lubber's Energy Bill of 1974 with its theme of energy scarcity, conservation and restrictive sales policies with the intention of conserving Groningen gas as a buffer stock for the long term and as the swing supply source in winter months when demand was high in both the Netherlands and export markets.

At that time Gasunie was given responsibility for purchasing gas from other Dutch fields which were all small in relation to Groningen, hence the term 'small fields policy'. The choice of Gasunie for this task was obvious and not contested. Although Gasunie did not have a statutory monopoly on gas purchases, it did have the right and obligation of first refusal and gave priority to such purchases on a take-or-pay basis. The price basis under the small fields policy was not a problem as end-user prices were high – which after deducting Gasunie's margin gave an acceptable 'base purchase price' or net-back to the producers. This encouraged them to produce at the lowest possible cost as they, the producers, carried the price risk.

Other incentives to develop small fields, particularly offshore fields, included a fast annual depletion rate of 7.2 per cent (equivalent to thirteen years) for offshore fields compared with 5 per cent (twenty years) for onland fields other than Groningen. And as unit production costs offshore are normally greater than onland, the swing factor for the former at 1.1 was lower than that for onland fields at 2. The swing factor is the required deliverability capacity, i.e. the quantity of gas that can be physically delivered per field per day. At a swing factor of 1.1 this means that the producer has to install sufficient capacity to be able to deliver 1.1 times the capacity required to deliver the annual contracted volume at a constant rate if called upon to deliver additional supplies during periods of high demand.

This 'small fields policy' has resulted in the development of many small deposits of gas which otherwise may have been uneconomic for the producers and thus left in the ground. The policy has been very successful for all concerned and has added to the Netherlands overall producible reserves portfolio and helped, therefore, to extend the ultimate depletion of Groningen. There are currently over ninety small field and similar purchase contracts and in recent years these fields have collectively contributed on average more than half of Gasunie's total supplies.

Finally, following the enactment of the EC's Hydrocarbon Directive in 1995, producers are no longer obliged to sell their gas to Gasunie, although the government has retained the right of approval as to depletion rates and prices.

3.3   Technology

In addition to the beneficial effects of the small fields policy, advances in technology in recent years have also been important in adding to the reserves portfolio. In particular, the development of three dimensional (3D) seismic, combined with evermore powerful computing facilities and resolution, have led to the identification of a significant number of new prospects, many of which were not possible to identify in the past with two dimensional (2D) seismic. For example, NAM has made discoveries approaching 10 bcm in blocks which have been producing for 25 years.

Another advancement is horizontal drilling which enables the well bore to be exposed to a much longer section of the reservoir than is possible with vertical or inclined wells. With horizontal wells the inflow potential and hence recovery rates per well are increased more than compensating for the higher drilling costs involved.

These and other examples of how technology has helped in the discovery and recovery of new reserves, and in reducing unit capital and operating costs, are not, of course, unique to the Netherlands. However, it is fair to say that the Netherlands is one of the countries at the leading edge of technological exploration and production advancement.

3.4   The Resource Base

At the end of 1998, total expected gas reserves in proven fields onland and offshore the Netherlands, after conversion to Groningen gas quality, were assessed by Gasunie at 1,875 bcm. Of this total, Groningen gas, after allowing for past production, amounted to 1,150 bcm. The balance of 725 bcm is distributed over a large number of relatively small fields, some of which have yet to be brought into production. In addition to these reserves, Gasunie expect that a further 325 bcm will be discovered in new Dutch fields over the next 25 years. This estimate is in line with estimates published by the Netherlands Institute for Applied Geosciences.

In assessing the future supply potential, account is also taken of the 250 bcm to be imported under existing and planned contracts with Norway, the UK, Germany (the German sector of the North Sea) and Russia giving a total resource base for long-term planning purposes of 2,450 bcm. The breakdown of this figure is given in Table 2 together with the two previous year's estimates for comparison purposes.

Table 2:   Total Gas Resources. Billion Cubic Metres Groningen Gas Quality

	1998	1997	1996
Groningen field after past production	1,150	1,220	1,250
Non-Groningen fields after past production	725	640	650
Expected new Dutch discoveries	325	340	350
Existing and planned import contracts	250	270	300
Totals	**2,450**	**2,470**	**2,550**
Total demand including exports	2,215	2,040	2,130
Balance remaining after 25 years	**235**	**430**	**420**

Source: Gasunie

Current government policy is to ensure that there is an adequate resource base to meet annual demand over the next 25 years, and that delivery capacity, based on the likely maximum hourly demand, is also sufficient in the years ahead. Present planning assumes that most of the non-Groningen fields, new discoveries and imports will be utilized over the 25-year period, and when these sources are unable to meet daily/hourly demand, typically during winter time, Groningen supplies would make up the balance. The latter is complemented by Gasunie's LNG storage and peak shaving facility at Maasvlakte, near Rotterdam, and underground storages at Grijpskerk (NAM, operational 1996), Norg (NAM 1997) and Alkmaar (Amoco 1997). And as the pressure of the Groningen reservoir inevitably continues to fall, compressors will need to be installed and/or further storage capacity will be required if Gasunie is to meet its currently foreseen delivery capacity obligations.

As a matter of interest, there have been times when every well in the Groningen field has been shut down and others when every flow valve has been fully open. On 2 January 1997, a record daily output (all sources) of 558 million m³ was registered. The ability of Gasunie to offer its customers at home and abroad a highly variable offtake has, of course, a commercial value.

It is not without justification that Dutch gas, in particular Groningen gas, has over the years come to be regarded as N.W. Europe's swing supplier, a role that no other European supplier has yet been able to match in volumetric and variable load factor terms.

4.   Domestic Market

4.1   *Gasunie's Gas Marketing Plans*

Every year since 1963 Gasunie has prepared and published a Gas Marketing Plan (Plan van Gasafzet) which takes a 25-year forward look at the demand for gas in the Netherlands by main market sector, export sales and the resource base, including imports, to meet these demands. These Plans require the approval of the Minister of Economic Affairs before publication and should be viewed against Gasunie's principal objectives which are:

(i)   to maintain the required delivery capacity and safeguard gas supplies in the longer term;

(ii) to maximize the revenue from natural gas on the basis of its market value and related services, while operating at the lowest possible cost; and,

(iii) to promote the safe and efficient use of natural gas.

In preparing these Plans and forecasts Gasunie takes due account of government policy directives and the views of such bodies as EnergieNed, SEP (the association of Dutch electricity generators), Ministry of Housing, National Geological Service, Central Bureau of Statistics, gas producers and major customers and various other entities. Much of the data in the following sections have been taken from Gasunie's recent Plans.

Hitherto Gasunie's Plans have been regarded as the representative and authoritative view of the outlook for natural gas in the Netherlands given its dominant role as the country's principal trader and transporter and, until recently, sole exporter and importer of gas. But following the Dutch government and EU's recent moves towards liberalization of the gas (and electricity) markets, Gasunie's dominant position will undoubtedly be eroded. This was acknowledged by George Verberg, the managing director, who indicated that Gasunie could lose about 20 per cent of its business particularly after British gas arrives on the Continent through the Interconnector which commenced commercial operations on 1 October 1998. What this 20 per cent may comprise was not defined. It remains to be seen how Gasunie's future Plans will accommodate and report imports, local sales and/or exports by third parties in which they will have little, if any, direct involvement other than allowing access to its transportation system.

4.2 *Public Distribution Companies and the Residential Sector*

In 1963 there were 170 Public Distribution (PD) companies united in six regional organizations which in turn founded the Commissie Samenwerking Regional Organen Gasvoorziening (SROG) to negotiate with Gasunie on their behalf arrangements for gas supplies and related conditions. In that year it was agreed, inter alia, between Gasunie and SROG a price formula for gas supplies to PD companies, and that Gasunie would supply large users with an annual consumption in excess of 2 million cubic metres direct. As to pricing, the approach was to establish uniform consumer tariffs throughout the country to assist rapid gas penetration. This was set at Dutch cents (Dct) 12 to 14/m³ according to quality.

As would be expected, prices have risen over the years reflecting the effects of inflation, oil product price movements, and the imposition of taxes such as VAT. By the second half of 1998 the average small consumers' tariff had reached Dct 40.7/m³ excluding VAT, surcharges and the standing charge. Changes up or down now basically reflect changes in the price of domestic gas oil to which gas prices, with a time lag, are linked.

Other changes have been the replacement of SROG by VEGIN in 1972, which in turn was subsequently superseded by EnergieNed. This was not just a change of name but a merger of VEGIN with VEEN, which represented electricity interests, and VESTIN, district heating interests. This reflected the fact that as a result of mergers and take-overs the number of PD companies had declined by 1997 to thirty energy utilities, i.e. companies concerned not only with the distribution of gas but also with electricity and/or district heating. In 1997 these energy utilities decided they no longer wanted EnergieNed to negotiate prices and conditions of supply with Gasunie on their behalf. Instead, in future they will conduct their own negotiations with Gasunie or other suppliers. Some commentators predict that within a few years there will be fewer than ten utilities. What hitherto was often regarded as a rather staid segment of the business is now undergoing rapid and fundamental changes not only in the Netherlands but in several other European countries as well. It remains to be seen if companies selling both gas and electricity are even-handed in their sales tactics or favour, perhaps for historical reasons, one fuel over the other.

Putting such considerations to one side, the outlook for the residential/small consumers market is likely to be one of modest growth given that natural gas has already achieved over 90 per cent penetration of the household market, the highest percentage of any country in the world. Future growth will depend, inter alia, on increases in the housing stock (estimated to be about 3,000 new homes per year), switches from point heating to central heating and the demand for higher comfort levels. These will be partly offset by improved insulation in existing homes, more efficient appliances as old appliances are replaced, and the loss of some of the cooking load to electricity. Overall Gasunie's 1998 Gas Marketing Plan forecasts that sales to the residential market will increase from 12.8 bcm in 1998 – of which 78 per cent was used for space heating, 19 per cent for water heating and 3 per cent for cooking – to about 13.4 bcm in 2024. This represents a total consumption over the next 25 years of about 325 bcm. However, given the very high percentage of gas used for space heating, these estimates are very dependent on the duration and severity or otherwise of winter temperatures which are, of course, impossible to forecast. Finally, recent contracts with Edon and Enercom have secured for Gasunie about half of the total market volume of the public distribution sector over the next few years at agreed prices until end 2001.

4.3   Commercial Sector

This comprises the sale of gas by PD companies to offices, schools, hospitals, hotels, restaurants and similar commercial and social enterprises. Sales in 1998 at 6.0 bcm are forecast to rise to 6.7 bcm in 2024 representing a total demand of about 150 bcm over this period. These estimates are temperature sensitive as space heating is a major part of the gas used by many customers in this sector.

4.4   Greenhouse Growers Sector

As this is an important use of gas in the Netherlands it merits separate mention. Temperature-corrected gas demand in 1998 at 4.9 bcm at an average price of Dct 25/m³ is expected to fall to 4.7 bcm in 2024, representing a total of 125 bcm over the period. This relatively modest decline in future annual consumption rates reflects increasingly stringent environmental requirements, i.e. 4 per cent improvement in energy efficiency per year. This may cause some small greenhouse growers to go out of business and others to resort to higher efficiency combined heat and power (CHP) projects for their energy needs.

Increased use of CHP is foreseen not just in this sector but also for commercial and industrial sector applications as a means for achieving reductions in emissions and energy saving. Moreover, any electricity generated which is surplus to local requirements can be fed into the electricity grid, thus helping to reduce the need for new power station capacity. Similarly, any surplus heat can be used locally for other heating purposes. Installed CHP capacity is expected to rise to over 1,000 MW by 2000 and to grow at around 130 MW a year thereafter. Gasunie's Gas Marketing Plans take into account the growth in CHP in assessing the future growth in demand for natural gas.

4.5 *Industrial Sector*

The arrangements agreed between Gasunie and SROG in 1963 were that PD companies would supply small industrial customers, while Gasunie would supply direct industrial customers whose annual consumption exceeded about 2 million cubic metres. From modest beginnings, sales by Gasunie in 1969 to industry, including at that time power stations and chemical plants, at 7 bcm equalled sales to PD companies. Sales for power generation were boosted by the introduction of interruptible supply contracts in 1967, also an industrial pricing system linked and adjusted quarterly to the price of heavy fuel oil with fixed annual charges and variable commodity prices related to three ranges of annual consumption. In this way it was possible to ensure that gas prices did not get unduly out of line for any length of time with competitive oil prices. Although adjustments have, of course, been made over the years, the basic concept of indexing industrial gas prices to oil product prices with a time lag has been maintained. The average price in 1998 for customers with an annual consumption of 10 to 50 million m³ was Dct 20/m³ excluding VAT. In 1996 and 1997 it was 20 and 22 respectively. By January 1998 the price for an annual consumption of 10 million m³ was Dct 26/m³ falling to Dct 22/m³ in December following the downward trend in oil prices (see Table 7).

Gas consumption by the industrial sector in 1998 amounted to nearly 14.4 bcm. Future demand will be conditioned by the rates of economic growth achieved, the extent to which the use of CHP grows beyond its present capacity of 3,010 MW, and the success realized in energy savings by increased efficiency; as always competition from oil cannot be ignored. Current planning assumes annual consumption will grow to some 26 bcm representing a total of about 550 bcm over the next 25 years.

4.6   Power Sector

Electricity generation is the remaining sector of consequence. First sales of natural gas for power generation were made in 1965. With the introduction of interruptible supply contracts in 1967 sales expanded rapidly thereafter to the extent that by end 1969 over 30 per cent of the country's total installed power generation capacity was equipped to utilize natural gas. By the mid 1970s sales were averaging about 10 bcm a year, or around 25 per cent of Gasunie's total inland sales. However, during the 1990s sales by Gasunie to power plants declined progressively to 4.8 bcm in 1998. This adverse trend reflects a combination of the continuing rapid growth of decentralized CHP generating capacity among industrial users and greenhouse growers, offset to some extent by increased gas sales to these market sectors as a fuel for CHP plants, and increased use of Norwegian gas imported by Samenwerkende Elektriciteits – Produktiebedrijven (SEP) for the Eemshaven power station, some 30km from Emden, Germany, the landing point of Norpipe.

SEP's contract for the import of approximately 2 bcm a year at a load factor of 6,000 to 8,000 hours over the period 1996 to 2015, was a ground-breaker in two main respects. By way of background, prior to the EU's Electricity Directive of 1996, i.e. liberalization of Europe's electricity industry, SEP as the co-operative of the Dutch electricity generators, was responsible for the purchase of all fuels for all Dutch power stations and had a monopoly on the country's imports and exports of electricity.

The first feature was that this was the first import of gas not undertaken directly by Gasunie. The second feature was that the price agreed with the Norwegian Troll partners was largely coal rather than oil related. In essence, the base price was related to the price of imported coal in N.W. Europe, which at that time was about $40 per metric tonne, indexed as to 75 per cent with coal price changes and 25 per cent with inflation rates. At an assumed constant $40/tonne coal price, the contract would result in a higher gas price than average Norwegian oil indexed gas prices up to the equivalent of about $20/

barrel crude oil. Above about $24/barrel the price to SEP would be lower. The $20–$24 range was intended to cover changes in exchange rates, crude oil/oil products ratios and time lag effects. As a consequence of the subsequent demerging and restructuring of SEP, doubts have been expressed by the Norwegian suppliers whether this contract can continue to be fulfilled. On 23 October 1998, Statoil, as the operator of Troll, applied to a Dutch court for an injunction against SEP for guarantees in this respect. At the time of writing the outcome is not known as discussions between Statoil and SEP continue.

In 1997 the country's total electricity consumption, including transmission losses, was about 97 TWh. This comprised electricity generated from coal, natural gas and blast furnace gas, nuclear, due to be phased out by 2004, decentralized CHP (24.5 TWh in total), renewables (2.8 TWh) and imported electricity. Reliable data for 1998 are not yet available.

According to Gasunie's 1997 and 1998 Plans, future electricity demand is expected to be met by existing capacity and imports until about 2004 when new capacity will be required with the phasing out of nuclear and the growth in demand. Long-term demand is assumed to be satisfied by existing coal-fired plants, which would contribute some 25 per cent of total generating capacity in 2004, declining thereafter, blast furnace gas at around 750 MW, imported electricity rising to 1,000 MW, and more decentralized CHP, renewables and natural gas-fired capacity.

As far as natural gas is concerned, current consumption at about 15 bcm, split between power stations and decentralized CHP, is expected to grow to around 30 bcm per year by the end of the next 25 years representing a total of some 250 bcm over the period.

4.7 Total Netherlands Demand

Based on the foregoing, total Netherlands cumulative inland demand plus export commitments, which are discussed later, as assessed in Gasunie's 1998 Plan amounts to 2,215 bcm. For comparison purposes the estimates in the two previous 25 year Plans are given in Table 3.

Although generalizations can be misleading, nevertheless it is reasonable to conclude that in recent years and over the forthcoming medium term, total demand has and is expected to continue to average about 80 bcm per year split very approximately 50/50 between inland demand and exports. Annual variations around these averages, excluding the effects of market liberalization, tend to reflect mainly changes in economic activity and ambient temperatures in both the

Netherlands and export markets acknowledging that there are other influences on demand as one would expect. Details of actual demand by main market sector are given in Table 4.

Natural gas's share of the Netherlands total energy consumption at 44 bcm in 1997 was somewhere in excess of 42 per cent as shown in Table 5.

If nothing else, and in the absence of any qualifying comments, these figures highlight the perennial problem of how published statistics from different sources can and do vary quite significantly. Be that as it may, it is nevertheless reasonable to conclude that excluding the transportation market where natural gas does not yet compete with gasoline, diesel and LPG, gas's share of energy consumption is probably in excess of 60 per cent.

Table 3:   Estimated Cumulative Demand Over Next Twenty-five Years. Billion Cubic Metres Groningen Gas Quality

	1996	*1997*	*1998*
Public Distribution sector	325	330	325
Commercial sector	175	150	150
Greenhouse Growers sector	125	120	125
Industrial sector	500	500	550
Power Generation sector	165	150	250
Total inland demand	**1,290**	**1,250**	**1,400**
Exports	840	790	815
Total demand	**2,130**	**2,040**	**2,215**

Source: Gasunie

Table 4:   Actual Demand by Main Market Sector. Billion Cubic Metres Groningen Gas Quality

	1992	*1993*	*1994*	*1995*	*1996*	*1997*	*1998*
Small consumers	15.7	16.4	15.3	15.9	18.8	15.5	15.4
Large consumers	3.3	3.4	3.5	3.6	4.2	4.5	4.6
Greenhouse Growers sector	3.9	4.6	4.4	4.4	4.8	4.1	4.1
Industrial sector	11.9	11.9	12.5	13.3	14.0	14.5	14.4
Power Generation sector	8.8	8.7	8.1	7.5	6.1	5.2	4.8
Total inland demand	**43.6**	**45.0**	**43.8**	**44.7**	**47.9**	**43.8**	**43.3**
Exports	40.6	41.4	38.3	38.4	45.9	40.1	36.4
Total demand	**84.2**	**86.4**	**82.1**	**83.1**	**93.8**	**83.9**	**79.7**

Source: Gasunie

Table 5:   Primary Energy Consumption in 1997

	BP mtoe	*BP* %	*Gasunie* %
Oil	39.5	46.6	32
Natural Gas	35.2	41.5	52
Coal	9.5	11.2	12
Nuclear/others	0.6	0.7	4
Totals	84.8	100.0	100

Source: BP and Gasunie

5.   International Trade and Prices

5.1   *Imports and Transit Gas*

Although there is no law regarding imports (or exports) of gas, nevertheless Gasunie is obliged to seek governmental approval before concluding any deals. On the face of it, it is rather surprising that a small country like the Netherlands – population circa 15.5 million, area 15,770 square miles – with huge indigenous gas reserves should wish to import gas, which it has been doing since 1977 from Norway and more recently from the UK as well. The main reasons for this were to reduce the country's dependence on indigenous reserves over the longer term, and to have a foothold and gain practical experience of the international gas business from an importer's perspective. In 1997, Gasunie imported about 3.5 bcm via Germany from Norway, while SEP imported for its own account some 2 bcm, also from Norway, for the Eemshaven power plant. Imports from two fields in the British sector of the North Sea are relatively small at around 0.3 bcm in 1997. Gasunie's total imports in 1998 were about 5 bcm but as yet no breakdown by source is available.

Imports from Britain via Belgium are expected to increase now that the Interconnector is operational and the necessary pipeline links are available from Zeebrugge, the landfall of the Interconnector pipeline. One example of this is the purchase by Gasunie from Conoco of over 8 bcm of British gas over 8.5 years commencing 1999. Others include 7 bcm by Norsk Hydro from Mobil over fifteen years, 8 bcm by Elsta from Centrica over eight years, and 6 bcm by EnTrade and Delta from Centrica over eight years; the latter are energy utilities.

In May 1996, an agreement was signed by Gasunie with Gazprom for the supply of at least 80 bcm of Russian gas over a period of twenty years starting in 2001. Undoubtedly, more import deals will be concluded by Gasunie and/or by energy utilities and other large volume consumers for their own account in the coming years as the market is increasingly liberalized.

Apart from enhancing long-term security of supply, associated with these import deals is Gasunie's intention to become a major European 'gas banker', that is to say to provide a range of services including transmission, storage, gas quality and load factor management, also gas swap arrangements and the like. Needless to say, there are a number of other companies/countries keen to provide similar services in what will become a very competitive area of activity as liberalization advances.

As far as transit gas is concerned, for many years Gasunie has provided a transit service through the Netherlands for Norwegian gas landed at Emden, N.W. Germany, destined principally for Belgium and France. It also provides a similar service for small quantities of British gas en route to Germany. In 1998, total transit volumes under separate contracts with third parties declined to 9.0 bcm compared with 10.8 bcm in 1997 due to production restrictions in the supply of Norwegian gas to Belgium and France via the Netherlands.

5.2   *Exports*

In earlier sections of this chapter details were given of the corporate arrangements for the export of Dutch gas, initially by NAM/Gas Export and from 1975 by Gasunie. What was not mentioned was that prior to 1963 the State Gas Board had signed a contract with the German company, Energieversorgung Weser-Ems (EWE), for the supply of small quantities of associated natural gas from the Schoonebeek concession which was switched to gas from Groningen in 1963. First exports of Groningen gas to Thyssengas (Germany) and to Distrigaz (Belgium) were made in 1966, to Ruhrgas (Germany) and Gaz de France in 1967, and to SNAM (Italy) and Switzerland in 1974. By 1970, total exports amounted to 11.3 bcm reaching a peak of 51 bcm in 1976. In recent years (see Table 6) they have averaged 40 bcm per year with annual variations mainly reflecting changes in economic activity and ambient temperatures in the export countries concerned.

In recent years – 1998 was not typical for various reasons – total exports of Dutch gas have been of the same order of magnitude as Norwegian gas exports, with Russia being the major exporter to Europe at nearly 120 bcm in 1997. However, the latter includes Finland, Turkey and several so-called Eastern European countries, e.g. Bulgaria,

Table 6: Dutch Gas Exports. Billion Cubic Metres Groningen Gas Quality

	1992	1993	1994	1995	1996	1997	1998
Belgium/Lux	4.5	5.0	5.4	4.8	6.0	5.0	5.6
Germany	23.7	25.1	22.6	23.9	28.3	23.6	21.1
France	5.7	4.7	4.8	5.1	6.0	5.4	5.7
Italy	6.1	6.0	4.9	4.0	4.9	5.5	3.3
Switzerland	0.6	0.6	0.6	0.6	0.7	0.6	0.7
Totals	40.6	41.4	38.3	38.4	45.9	40.1	36.4

Source: Gasunie

Poland, Romania and others, so the figures are not strictly comparable. For completeness sake, Algerian gas exports to Italy, Spain, Portugal and the former Yugoslavia by pipeline at 23 bcm, and as LNG to France, Belgium, Italy, Turkey and Spain also at 23 bcm totalled around 46 bcm in 1997.

To avoid any misunderstanding, not all of the gas exported from the Netherlands has come from Groningen, far from it, but it was the discovery of the Groningen gas field above all else that enabled exports on this scale to be contemplated and realized. Published data do not give a breakdown of exports between Groningen gas and other gases.

Whereas virtually all British North Sea contracts up to the 1990s were depletion type contracts, all Dutch gas export contracts are supply type contracts of a stated volume and duration. Both types of contract have their advantages and drawbacks, but given the magnitude of Groningen and the multiplicity of buyers involved, depletion contracts were obviously impracticable.

Periodically, Gasunie and its customers come together to review the terms and conditions of their supply contracts to better reflect current market circumstances; the next round of renegotiations is due to take place in 1999. These renegotiations may centre on, for example, the ability of Gasunie to extend the duration and/or volume of supply or, perhaps, the customer's desire to have greater offtake flexibility; inevitably pricing arrangements are an issue for renegotiation. Back in 1980, exports were due to terminate in the late 1990s/2000. Since then the Dutch government's willingness to increase the volumes available for export has enabled Gasunie to extend some of its contracts to 2021. To illustrate the point, in 1996 the government approved the export by Gasunie of a further 240 bcm (and the import of 120 bcm) with the result that in 1997 Gasunie concluded a new contract with SNAM for the supply at the Dutch border of an additional 80 bcm over the period 2001 to 2020. At the same time the existing contract for 6 bcm a year which was due to expire in 2009 was extended to 2015. This will raise total exports to Italy from 6 to 10 bcm per year in the early years of the next century. It also agreed a Letter of Intent to supply Poland with 2 bcm a year over fifteen years, and discussed possible exports with potential customers in the Czech Republic, Austria and Slovakia without, as yet, any success.

Interestingly, Gasunie's historic de facto monopoly of gas exports was broken in 1997 with the conclusion of a contract by Mobil to supply its German affiliate, Mobil Erdgas Erdol, with 100 million m^3 a year from the Munnekezijl concession, operated by NAM, in which Mobil has an interest. Admittedly, the quantity involved in this instance is very small, but is nevertheless indicative of the export competition that Gasunie can expect from producers in the coming years. Be that as it may, the financial importance of Dutch gas exports to the national economy at an estimated state revenue of some Guilders 10 billion a year in recent years remains. Actual revenues vary, of course, from year to year reflecting the combined interaction of volumes, prices and exchange rate fluctuations.

As to pricing, in line with most European long-term wholesale contracts, no details have been published so far of Gasunie's pricing arrangements with its export customers. As such it is only possible to make some generalizations which may not be precise in all respects. Up until the first oil shocks of 1973, Dutch border prices comprised a base price indexed as to 95 per cent with fuel oil or crude oil prices and inflation. This was at a time when inflation rates were low and oil prices were relatively stable. Thereafter, as contracts were renegotiated, indexation with fuel oil prices was reduced and gas oil introduced to better reflect the mix of oils with which gas was competing. In broad terms, a typical border price could comprise a base price (e.g. Dct 30/m^3) indexed as to 90 per cent with LSFO prices for say 40 per cent of the total volume and 80 per cent with gas oil prices for say 60 per cent of the total volume, at a load factor of 33 per cent or nearly 3,000 hours (one year equals 8,760 hours). Typically, Continental European gas companies define load factors in hours whereas elsewhere percentages are usually preferred. Quite often part of the price was also indexed to inflation, e.g. wholesale price indices. To this would be added a capacity charge. Price adjustments would be made monthly based on a rolling average of fuel oil and gas oil prices over say a nine-month period to help smooth out the effect of abrupt changes up or down in oil prices. Over time more complicated price arrangements have been introduced, but the basic concept of indexing the base border price with oil prices, with a time lag, has prevailed. To further complicate matters, some buyers have different pricing arrangements for different tranches of their overall supplies.

For many years prices for Dutch gas exports tended to be the 'marker' prices for other major gas imports from outside Europe. Indeed it was the Dutch who first introduced the concept of linking and indexing gas prices with competitive oil product prices which subsequently was adopted by all other major suppliers. It now remains to be seen how pricing will evolve in mainland Europe as markets become more liberalized and with an increasing number of players selling and buying smaller volumes of gas over short- to medium-term periods. However, unlike North America and Britain which have ample gas supplies and spot trading, substantial European buyers with their high degree of dependence on imported gas, will need to be mindful that if new long-term major supply projects are to be encouraged, a sufficient degree of pricing stability will need to be maintained to justify the huge investments required for future long distance gas supplies. This is not to say that future pricing arrangements need necessarily continue to be oil related as in the past. It could well be that gas prices may eventually decouple from oil prices and live a life of their own as has long been the case with international coal prices, and is increasingly becoming so with wholesale gas prices in North America and Britain. Much will depend on the future level of oil prices and the degree to which gas can secure a premium over less environmentally friendly competing fuels.

5.3   *Dutch Gas and Oil Prices in 1998*

In addition to the price indications quoted in previous sections of this chapter, Table 7 details the monthly average gas prices in Dct/m^3 applicable by customer category for three selected months of 1998. Also shown are comparable oil prices in D.Fl per tonne to which gas prices are indexed in variable proportions, and equivalent gas and oil prices converted to US dollars per million Btu ($/MMBtu) at the exchange rates applicable for the months in question.

All local Dutch gas prices include national, local environment and ecological taxes but exclude VAT at 17.5 per cent. Oil prices include duties but likewise exclude VAT.

As far as Dutch gas exports are concerned, several journals regularly publish their best estimates of Dutch gas border prices in US$/MMBtu. In practice Gasunie has invoiced its customers in various currencies, e.g. German customers in marks, Gaz de France in ECU (the

Table 7:   Gas and Oil Prices in 1998

Gas Prices

	January		June		December	
Annual Consumption	Dct/m3	$/MMBtu	Dct/m3	$/MMBtu	Dct/m3	$/MMBtu
100,000 m³	56	8.14	56	8.29	53	8.45
1 million m³	33	4.86	32	4.78	29	4.68
10 million m³	26	3.86	25	3.74	22	3.58
50 million m³	23	3.40	22	3.28	19	3.08

Oil Prices

	D.Fl/ tonne	$/MMBtu	D.Fl/ tonne	$/MMBtu	D.Fl/ tonne	$/MMBtu
Fuel Oil	331	4.14	320	4.06	288	3.93
Gas Oil	657	7.82	599	7.23	553	7.17

Source: *World Gas Intelligence*

forerunner of the Euro), Distrigaz in a combination of guilders and Belgian francs, and so on. Thus the accuracy or otherwise of these published prices in dollar terms will reflect, inter alia, the exchange rates chosen and any other applicable contractual terms and conditions including indexation with oil prices mainly in dollars. While the overall trends of these published prices are reasonably consistent, absolute numbers can and do vary by some 10 US cents/MMBtu or more. In order to be consistent and comparable with Table 7, the author has selected those estimated prices published by *World Gas Intelligence* recognizing that their data may not necessarily be any more or less precise than that published by others. Table 8 also shows average export prices for Algerian, Norwegian and Russian gas.

Readers, however, should not assume from the foregoing data that any one supply source is necessarily cheaper or more expensive than any other as unit prices will be affected by such matters as the quantities involved, point(s) of delivery, load factors, indexation provisions, exchange rates, gas quality considerations, and so on – they are not strictly comparable.

As to the future, there is the question of accommodating the EU's new single currency, the Euro, which was introduced in eleven out of the fifteen EU countries on 1 January 1999. Sooner or later it is likely that all of Gasunie's export sales will be invoiced in Euros, and if other international gas suppliers follow suit, it should then be easier to compare wholesale (border) prices in Euros without the complication of adjusting prices in national currencies to reflect fluctuations in

Table 8: Published Dutch Gas Export Prices in 1998. US$/MMBtu

	January	*June*	*December*
Exports to			
Belgium	3.10	2.85	2.58
France	2.67	2.55	2.09
Germany	2.65	2.53	2.07
Italy	2.67	2.55	2.09
Average Dutch Export Prices	2.77	2.62	2.21
Average Algerian Export Prices	2.68	2.43	2.13
Average Norwegian Export Prices	2.72	2.58	2.15
Average Russian Export Prices	2.49	2.37	1.91

Source: *World Gas Intelligence*

exchange rates with the dollar. But to the extent that gas prices continue to be indexed, where appropriate, with dollar denominated oil product or crude oil prices, exchange rates will still have an influence on resultant prices.

6. Politics and Policies

6.1 Significant Political Policies

It is appropriate at this point to summarize the significant political policies, some of which have already been mentioned, affecting the development of Dutch gas. Many of these are identified by the name of the incumbent Minister of Economic Affairs.

The de Pous Memorandum of 1963 was the first indication of government policy and its general approach still holds good today. In brief, the message was to develop gas markets quickly for the maximum benefit of the country, with the Minister reserving to himself various rights of approval on prices, infrastructure requirements and export sales.

The Lubbers Energy Bill of 1974 following the oil price shocks of 1973, adopted a more cautious policy focused on a perceived energy shortage, a common view of many governments and most oil companies at that time, with the need to conserve Groningen gas and restrict sales, which by then were substantial, for the longer term.

Following the second oil crisis of 1979, the government decided to tighten its export commitments in terms of volume and prices and for this they appointed Spierenburg, a senior civil servant, to lead a series of renegotiations with all Gasunie's export customers.

Policies changed with van Aardene's Review of 1983, when once again energy was seen to be abundant, with the adoption of a more liberal approach to sales, except for power stations, and the need to defend export markets against increasing competition from other sources.

In de Korte's Energy Bill of 1989, further increases in nuclear power were postponed indefinitely, and restrictions on the use of gas for power generation were removed. At the same time, it was decided that the basic structure of the Dutch gas industry as set up in the early 1960s still served its purpose and should, therefore, be maintained.

There then followed several government White Papers of which the most significant was the Third White Paper on Energy Policy of 1996. This was initially directed at the electricity industry to which gas was added as the then Minister, Hans Wijers (who was succeeded by Jorritsma in 1998) was a strong advocate of radical liberalization of both the electricity and gas industries. This Paper is discussed later, but it should be noted that while liberalization was of prime concern to the gas industry, the focus of the White Paper was really on sustainability and the country's response to climate change.

There have been several other important policy statements and legislation not mentioned above or elsewhere since the 1960s, but the above summarizes those of most significance to the gas industry. Variations in policy by different governments were essentially reactions to events in the overall energy scene, and their degree of change reflected the views of the governments of the day and the aspirations and forcefulness, or otherwise, of the incumbent Ministers of Economic Affairs. In general, Dutch governments have been willing to adopt new policies, or to reconfirm existing policies, as and when necessary. Although conscious of national needs, they have also had the foresight to try and anticipate future events outside their control.

An interesting feature of the Dutch gas scene compared with many other European countries is the surprising lack of formal legislation, in that few laws have been enacted that directly relate to the gas business. However, it should be noted that important gas legislation is being put to parliament for consideration in 1999.

6.2   EU Gas Liberalization

Getting fifteen member countries of the European Union to agree on the steps to be taken to liberalize European gas markets has been a very difficult and protracted process. There are significant differences in the structure, ownership and stage of development of various national markets. For instance, Great Britain, the Netherlands and Denmark are largely self-sufficient in gas and are also exporters, whereas Belgium, Luxembourg, Finland and Sweden rely entirely on imports. Germany, Italy, France and Austria have limited reserves and have to import the major part of their requirements. Spain, Sweden and Ireland have been concerned about the unequal development of their regional markets. New markets like Portugal and Greece, with, as yet, no large consumers, have sought protection while they create their necessary infrastructures based on imported gas. In Finland over 90 per cent of gas is used for power generation, in France only negligible amounts. In some countries the gas business is still largely or wholly in the hands of state-owned monopolies, while in others the industry is fully privatized. There are hardly any European gas markets alike in all essential respects.

On the political front, some national governments have been pro-liberalization, e.g. Great Britain, while others, e.g. France, have been against it, and yet others, e.g. the Netherlands, have changed their stance over time. And progress towards liberalization has been speeded up or slowed down depending on which government has had the Presidency of the EU for its six-month term of office.

In these circumstances it is hardly surprising that it has taken nearly a decade to agree a rather watered-down EU Gas Directive more or less acceptable to all. The Directive was approved by the EU on 8 December 1997 and came into force on 10 August 1998 with member countries having two years in which to implement it.

As far as the Netherlands is concerned, in the early years it was opposed to liberalization, but subsequently it became active promoters of the concept. Indeed, following the publication of the government's Third White Paper on Energy Policy in 1996, the Netherlands has come to be regarded as the leading supporter – after Great Britain where it was already well advanced – of liberalization of Europe's gas (and electricity) industries.

Among the many features of the Directive, it provides for consumers with an annual consumption of more than 25 million m^3 per year to contract directly for their own supplies if they so wish. After five years this threshold will be lowered to 15 million m^3 a year, and after ten years to 5 million m^3 a year. At the same time targets were set for that minimum proportion of each national market which will be open to competition, namely 20 per cent of a country's total consumption in the first stage, 28 per cent by 2003, and 33 per cent by 2008. There are exceptions to these rules, e.g. Portugal and Greece because of the early stage of their development of gas markets; and there are qualifications such as, if the consumption levels criteria should result in higher minimum percentage levels of total consumption, member states are allowed to change their consumption levels criteria if they so wish. There are also many other rules regarding third-party access to transmission systems and storage, safety and environmental issues, unbundling and transparency of accounts, non-discriminatory licensing of companies to build and operate gas facilities, the handling of cross-border and other disputes, dealing with take-or-pay provisions in gas contracts, and many more. However, as this chapter is concerned with Dutch gas they will not be elaborated on here.

Suffice it to say that as this Directive has to be enacted into national legislation, the story is far from being over and one may yet see some issues being reappraised before all is set in tablets of stone.

6.3   *Liberalization of the Dutch Gas Industry*

As mentioned above, the Netherlands has changed from being an implacable opponent to a vigorous proponent of liberalization in the space of a few years. That's fine, governments change and so can their policies – as was the case with the pro-liberalization government elected in 1994 which perceived that that was the way ahead. In this regard, the Christian Democratic party, in one guise or another, has governed the country without interruption, except during the war, from 1917 until 1994. Under the Dutch system of proportional representation, these have been Christian Democratic led coalition governments since 1976, during which time the basic structure of the Dutch gas industry as set up in the early 1960s has remained largely untouched. However, the government elected in 1994 (which was re-elected in 1998) comprising a coalition of VVD, a right of centre Liberal party, D'66, a left of centre reforming party, and PvdA, a moderately inclined Labour party, has pursued radical social and economic policies. The days of compromise and consensus politics were over to be replaced with liberalization and competition as far as the gas industry is concerned reflecting, inter alia, the government's concern about the possibility of lower prices and the declining role of Dutch gas relative to the growing competition from Norwegian, Russian and Algerian gas. Admittedly, this is an over simplification of a far more complex situation.

The government's Third White Paper on Energy Policy (Derde Energienota) published in 1996 has several main themes which for gas can be summarized as:

(i)   sustainability and climate change;
(ii) first liberalization, then privatization;
(iii) competition in place of regulation and consensus politics;
(iv) market where possible, government (regulation) where necessary;
(v)   change market from supply-driven to demand-driven, and from plans to contracts; and,
(vi) non-discriminatory negotiated access.

Like the EU Directive, only more rapidly, the Dutch market is to be opened up progressively to consumers and suppliers as follows: from 1 January 1999 to consumers using more than 10 million m^3/year; from 1 January 2000 to consumers using more than 1 million m^3/year; from 1 January 2002 to consumers using more than 170,000 m^3/year; from 1 January 2007 to all consumers.

The latter implies that residential and other small consumers will be able to contract with any supplier if they so wish, as is already the case in Great Britain since 23 May 1998. However, in order to protect small, captive consumers and achieve a more gradual liberalization, the Ministry of Economic Affairs (through a licensing system) will authorize supplies to small consumers until end 2006 and maintain close monitoring thereafter as the transition to liberalization proceeds.

The volumetric thresholds indicate that by 2000 some 45 per cent of the total inland market would be open to competition, by 2002 about 65 per cent, and, of course, 100 per cent after 2007.

In Great Britain the pace and extent of liberalization has been forced along by a government-appointed independent Regulator against a background of enabling legislation. Two crucial features have been the obligation on British Gas, as it then was, to make over part of its contracted supplies on commercial terms to third parties to give them in effect an immediate access into the large consumers market. This, reinforced by third parties' own supplies and the requirement (until 1997) for BG to publish its price schedules, made it relatively easy for BG's competitors to undercut its prices and gain market share. From 1990, when competition really began, to end 1995, BG lost 65 per cent of its commercial and industrial business. In 1997 its share was 24 per cent of a larger market. And by August 1998, more than 3 million out of a total of 19 million residential consumers had switched from BG to other gas marketers. By 1 May 1999, the storage of gas will change from a monopoly to a competitive business. Purchasers will be able to buy from BG capacity rights for up to five years, but with no entity being able to buy more than 20 per cent of total capacity.

The second feature was the separation of BG's gas transportation network which, as in the Netherlands, is a natural monopoly. This followed immediately after the demerger on 17 February 1997 of British Gas plc into two independent listed companies. BG plc and Centrica plc, with Transco, as part of BG plc, being responsible for transportation and storage with tariffs being strictly controlled by the Regulator.

In the Netherlands a rather different approach has been adopted. There will not be an independent regulator. Under the Competition Law which came into effect in January 1998, the Monopolies Commission will deal with any disputes on third-party access and other matters as specified in the EU Gas Directive. And unlike British Gas in Great Britain, Gasunie will not be obliged to surrender any part of its existing business, or to separate out its transportation system which will be available to others on a negotiated access and revenue neutral, for Gasunie, basis.

From 1 January 1999, Gasunie's transportation tariffs will be distance related based on five entry points to the system at Groningen, den Helder, Rotterdam, Zelzate and Aachen, plus a load factor element calculated from 8,000 hours/year. Other aspects of the tariff include an entry charge, hourly balancing, duration premia or discounts, indexing with a percentage of the rate of inflation, gas volume, pressure and quality considerations, and so on. The tariff will also apply to Gasunie's own sales which in future will itemize the transport charge separately from the commodity charge.

At this very early stage of liberalization of the Dutch gas market one can be almost certain that changes will need to be made to the 'ground rules' in the light of actual experience, as has been the case with the much larger and more advanced, in terms of liberalization, British market. One interesting common feature is that Great Britain and the Netherlands are, as yet, the only two markets in the world where competition will extend nationwide right down to the residential market, although there are some areas of the United States and Canada where this also applies.

To conclude this section, one example of the advent and effects of liberalization is EnTrade, a subsidiary of Pnem and Mega which merged in 1997. Reputed to be the largest Dutch energy distribution company selling and buying gas and electricity, EnTrade operates in the southern half of the country. In September 1998 it completed construction of its own 60km pipeline from Eindhoven to the Belgian border to facilitate the import of its purchase from Centrica of 600 million cubic metres a year of British gas via the Interconnector, thus avoiding reliance upon Gasunie's pipeline system. To this end, it has also co-built with Delta, another Dutch utility, a pipeline which links EnTrade's pipeline with the Interconnector. Pnem-Mega is now planning to build its own distribution systems to serve several major cities and is contemplating extending its activities to countries like Germany, France, Belgium and Switzerland as and when suitable opportunities arise.

7.   An Assessment

7.1   Missed Opportunities

Even well-managed enterprises miss out on some good business opportunities from time to time, for that is the nature of business. As regards Dutch gas, the following are personal perceptions with the benefit of hindsight – they are not facts. But it is, of course, conceivable that some of these possible strategies may indeed have been considered at the time and then rejected as being premature, unnecessary, too difficult, politically undesirable or impossible, overtaken by events or whatever.

In no particular order of importance or chronology, one can question whether Gasunie realized the full value from export buyers for the swing capability it had to offer, particularly in the 1970s and 1980s when most other major suppliers were only able to deliver high load factor gas and before much storage capacity existed in the countries concerned.

Second, would it have been possible for the Norwegians and the Dutch to have combined their interests in some way so as to offer export customers the benefits of larger volumes of both base load and swing gas? This would have been a formidable combination and would have made it that much more difficult for competitors to make inroads into the European market. However, as Soviet and Algerian gas were in the market place before Norwegian gas became available in significant quantities, perhaps this was never a real possibility if only for timing reasons. To some, the thought of the Dutch and Norwegians as bedfellows is not easy to comprehend, but there are many strange relationships and alliances in the gas business! The recently announced merger of Exxon and Mobil is a very good example, given their radically different approaches to the gas business, but this is only one facet of the merger.

In the early 1960s, exports to the UK were frustrated by the discovery of southern North Sea gas. But later on there was an opportunity for a relatively cheap and quick linking of the Dutch and British offshore systems which could then have created a gas hub at say Den Helder or Bacton and reduced or negated the need for the Interconnector. In all fairness it should be noted that linking the Dutch and British systems is now being seriously considered. Alternatively, and with an eye to the future, Gasunie, or NAM, could have acquired a stake in the Interconnector as, for example, Gazprom did to become a 10 per cent shareholder. One suspects that Shell may have been more willing to do so than Esso, but given their joint gas and oil producing interests in the UK, the Netherlands and Germany, it was presumably a question of both in or both out – if only to maintain harmony with their various existing joint venture interests. But it is not too late, as evidenced by SNAM's recent acquisition of a 5 per cent interest in the Interconnector from BG's original 40 per cent shareholding.

It is somewhat surprising that Gasunie has not, so far, attempted to integrate downstream in export markets although, of course, Shell and Esso did so in the 1960s. Presumably Gasunie with its 50 per cent state interest would have found it difficult for political reasons, although state-owned Gazprom has had no such inhibitions with Wintershall (Wingas) in Germany.

7.2   *The Future, Perhaps?*

As a one-time professional planner, the author cannot resist the temptation to speculate about the future. In the good bad old days, one of the roles of a gas planner was to try and forecast long-term supply and demand balances, price trends and the like. Job retention hinged more on having plausible explanations of why one got things wrong, as it was generally only by happenstance that forecasts were right. Today it is a much more sophisticated activity of 'what if, then …' otherwise known as scenario planning.

Dutch gas, indeed European gas as a whole, is now entering a new era of liberalization which will result in various radical changes leading to an industry which will have little resemblance to the one that has existed for several decades. Imagining that we are already in the future, the following are some tentative speculations on what we might find..

In the case of Dutch gas, the hitherto dominant role of Gasunie is increasingly eroded as other suppliers penetrate the market, selling directly to large consumers and energy utilities which in turn market both gas and electricity. Competition forces down wholesale and retail prices to the point where some marketers are obliged to withdraw and sell out, as has happened in Britain. Gasunie loses 40 per cent or more of its existing inland business within four or five years, perhaps sooner, provided that adequate supplies are available to others at competitive prices.

If the present government remains in office, Gasunie is privatized and restructured. Shell seeks to increase its shareholding interest and gain management control, with partial success. Prior to its merger with Mobil, Esso would have retained its existing share until it received an offer it could not refuse. Likewise it would have sold its share in Thyssengas and the ETGs and generally retreated to its upstream citadel. However, Esso's gas strategy is now uncertain and will be conditioned by the extent to which Mobil's hitherto aggressive approach to downstream opportunities will find favour or not in the newly merged company.

Retention by Gasunie, whether privatized or not, of the country's transport system becomes untenable and is hived off as a separate regulated entity with a fixed rate of return. A privatized Gasunie seeks to acquire a variety of interests outside the Netherlands in an endeavour to replace business lost at home. It will no longer be restricted to making a 20 per cent return on its share capital.

Groningen, which for many years provided the essential swing element for N.W. European markets, is subject to increasing competitive pressures as more swing gas becomes available from Norway and Britain and from growth in national storage capacities. Throughout Europe, storage becomes an important and profitable business in its own right.

Any remaining PD companies are absorbed by or merged into large regional multi-energy utilities. After a period of intense competition with some casualties, the inland market settles down with say half a dozen or less energy utilities sharing the small consumers market between them, with competition then largely confined to the peripheries of their regional boundaries and, more generally, to the large consumers market throughout the country. It is worth noting at this point that two of the largest Dutch utilities, PMG and Edon, have recently announced their intention to merge giving them combined annual sales of nearly 6 bcm to 1.6 million customers and 31 billion KWh to 2.3 million customers.

To take advantage of 'cheap' supplies and to 'capture' consumers, some utilities decide to reconvert their residential, commercial and small industrial consumers to conventional high calorific value quality gas. Groningen low calorific value quality gas is increasingly forced back into the large user and power generation market, with export customers also pressing for non-Groningen quality gas. Eventually NAM is obliged to install some nitrogen extraction facilities to retain market outlets.

The continued existence of the unincorporated Maatschap comes into question as pressures mount from all sides for more openness and transparency. Eventually the government is obliged to replace the Maatschap with a new corporate structure. Ways and means are devised to maintain state revenues.

No new coal-fired plants are built and existing capacity is increasingly shut down or converted to gas-firing. Within five years, coal is phased out of the country's energy portfolio except for steel making.

At some suitable export/import location, the Netherlands establishes one of Europe's four or five principal trading hubs as spot, short-term sales and a futures market develop at a faster rate than currently envisaged by many national governments. Gasunie provides a comprehensive range of gas banking and similar services as indeed is already their declared intention.

Throughout the liberalization era, Shell, Gazprom, BG, Elf and some others including local utilities remain alert to any opportunities to add value to their business. Again the strategy of Exxon-Mobil (assuming the merger is approved) is as yet uncertain, as also is that of the newly merged BP-Amoco which became effective on 31 December 1998.

It is unlikely that all or indeed many of the foregoing flights of fancy will happen whatever government(s) may be in office during the coming decade. So be it, these speculations are simply to suggest that in a liberalized world things will be different and that new developments or changes to how business was done in the past can have unexpected consequences. This is not to say that the way in which business is conducted should be taken out of the hands of government, far from it, but in a rapidly changing world some actions taken in all good faith at the time can become largely irreversible and have surprising knock-on effects.

In a sense the energy industry is once again in a crisis situation, this time one of abundant oil supply at very low prices with a static or declining demand. While this has not yet had a marked impact on Europe's gas business, other than a reduction in revenues and profits from oil priced linked gas sales, it has already resulted in the postponement of several major new gas supply projects in the Pacific Basin region. If this situation should prevail for a number of years, then many new gas supply projects aimed at European markets could likewise become uneconomic and call into question the availability of future supplies. The internal problems in Russia and Algeria are another cause for concern. In the appropriate circumstances, this could be an opportunity for low technical cost Dutch gas to increase its market share in export markets if the government so wished. We shall see. As always the future is unpredictable, except in retrospect when we all get it right!

8. Conclusion

The discovery and subsequent rapid development of the huge Groningen gas field gave the Dutch gas industry virtually instant lift-off aided, not least of all, by the existence of over 30 million European households already very familiar and accustomed to using (manu-factured) gas for many years. The size of the reserves was such that it enabled the Netherlands to pioneer and establish N.W. Europe's international pipeline gas trade. In so doing, it helped more than any other country to revitalize what had become a rather moribund manufactured gas industry. For many years from the early 1960s, Dutch gas set the pattern for the development and expansion of international trade from other sources within and outside Europe. Today, some 35 years on, Dutch gas still has a significant influence on the further evolution of Europe's gas business.

Throughout this time successive pragmatic Dutch governments have maintained a light but firm hand, and have steered the development of the local market and export trade by policy directives and through its interests in Gasunie and the Maatschap, rather than by a series of possibly heavy-handed, stultifying, time-consuming legislation. The apparent conflicting objectives of maximizing (gas) resources for the benefit of the country's economy, while at the same time ensuring that sufficient resources will be available for future generations, have, so far, been achieved. And the unique small fields policy has been highly successful and fair to all parties concerned. If nothing else, it has brought forward supplies and extended the resource base which otherwise might have remained undiscovered and/or undeveloped.

In its totality, it is reasonable to conclude that the management of Dutch gas by government and private industry has been a success story, albeit not without some hiccups along the way. For instance, the decision to convert the country to Groningen quality gas when little other gas was thought to exist, may have been sensible at that time. A further motive was to help 'protect' export markets from the inroads of higher quality gas from other sources. But in retrospect, initial benefits have probably long since been overtaken by the extra costs involved in transporting 14 per cent of valueless nitrogen and the complexities of blending-in higher quality gases from non-Groningen sources. Reactions to the oil crises of the 1970s may also have been too big and too quick, but then virtually all governments and the oil industry itself got it wrong and over-reacted.

The key question now is whether the government's approach to liberalization is soundly based – have they got a tiger by its tail? In Europe, the only experience so far is the British market which differs in several important respects from the Dutch and other continental European markets, and thus does not necessarily provide a reliable guide for the Netherlands. However, some changes seem likely. With the already very high penetration of the residential market, little more growth is feasible. Consumers will benefit from lower prices as competition from a fewer number of energy utilities selling both gas and electricity hots up. Gasunie will lose a growing proportion of their direct sales to large consumers and energy utilities to third-party suppliers. How much is anyone's guess, but probably more than either Gasunie and the government now expect. The government and Gasunie will come under increasing pressure to offer more attractive transportation tariffs than those now proposed, and, like Britain, to clearly separate Gasunie's pipeline system from its other activities.

Probably the major battleground will be the power generation market with both Gasunie and coal losing market share. Unlike Britain and Germany, the Netherlands no longer has a local coal mining industry to protect and the government will find it difficult, even if it wanted to, to resist the inroads of environmentally friendly natural gas. As Gasunie is not really a profit centre (only a fixed 20 per cent dividend on its share capital) the government may opt out and devise other means, in addition to the Maatschap for Groningen, for 'controlling' the gas business.

After almost forty years of orderly market development, the Dutch gas industry is now about to depart from a sheltered haven to sail on uncharted, stormy waters. It will be interesting to revisit the scene in five years time.

Selected References

The following are some of the principal references used in writing this chapter. The author has also drawn on his own knowledge and experience of the Dutch gas industry during his professional career.

Annual Reports, British Gas plc (various years).
Annual Reports, N.V. Nederlandse Gasunie (various years).
Blauwdruk, N.V. Nederlandse Gasunie, 1997.
BP Statistical Review of World Energy, The British Petroleum Company plc (various years).
Development of Groningen Gas (1971), Shell International Gas Ltd.
European Gas Markets, PH Energy Analysis Ltd (various issues).
Facts, N.V. Nederlandse Gasunie (various years).
Gas Marketing Plan, N.V. Nederlandse Gasunie (various years).
Gas Matters, EconoMatters Ltd (various issues).
Gas Transportation in Europe, EJC Energy, 1997.
Peebles, M. (1980), *Evolution of the Gas Industry*, Macmillan Press.
Petroleum Intelligence Weekly, Energy Intelligence Group (various issues).
Petroleum Review, The Institute of Petroleum (various issues).
Stern, J. (1998), *Competition and Liberalisation in European Gas Markets*,
The Royal Institute of International Affairs.
World Gas Intelligence, Energy Intelligence Group (various issues).

Note

1. Over the years the metric system of measurement devised by the French in 1798 has increasingly displaced the imperial and other systems of measurement for many purposes. At the invitation of the French government, two Dutchmen, Jean Henri van Swinden and Hendrik Aeneae, defined mathematically the standard metre and kilogram in that year. The Netherlands was the first country to adopt these standards in 1820, twenty years before they were adopted by the French! In 1983, these standards were redefined in terms of the speed of light. The metre is now defined as the distance travelled by light in a vacuum in $1/299, 792, 458$ of a second.

CHAPTER 4

SOVIET AND RUSSIAN GAS: THE ORIGINS AND EVOLUTION OF GAZPROM'S EXPORT STRATEGY

Jonathan P. Stern

1. Introduction

This chapter traces the evolution of Gazprom's export strategy from the Soviet period through 1998 and offers some thoughts on how the company's thinking may develop in the future. It is concerned with export *strategy* rather than export development and for this reason, the details of the actual export projects receive rather less, and the rationale and motive behind the projects rather more, attention.

Section 2 looks at Gazprom as a company and its evolution from a Soviet Ministry to a joint stock company. Section 3 examines the physical and commercial assets which Gazprom inherited at the break-up of the Soviet Union. This section covers the beginning of gas trade – exports and imports – and the events of the Cold War which prevented a more substantial and rapid development of exports to Europe.

Section 4 deals with export strategy in the post-Soviet era and is divided into three sub-sections: the difficulties of developing satisfactory trading relationships with former Soviet republics; the restructuring of trading relationships within Europe away from simple expansion and towards an approach emphasizing value, notably the development of downstream gas marketing, with the creation of 'trading houses', and corporate alliances with major national and international energy companies.

Section 5 summarizes the origins and evolution of Gazprom's export strategy during the three decades 1968–98, in respect of both former republics and European markets. It then looks forward to the institutional evolution of the company and the Russian gas industry in the next century, noting how changes in political leadership and economic policy could have a substantial impact on Gazprom in terms of changing the relative profitability of delivering gas to different markets. These factors could also bring about institutional change, in particular a proliferation of Russian (and possibly also foreign) companies producing and exporting gas, which would have a significant impact on European gas markets.

2.   The Evolution of Gazprom as a Company

2.1   Origins and Ownership[1]

In the former Soviet Union, all industrial activity was carried out by government ministries. For most of its history the gas industry had its own separate Ministry of the Gas Industry, but prior to 1965 – and again just before it became known as 'Gazprom' – it was part of the Ministry of Oil and Gas. In 1989, under the guidance of Victor Chernomyrdin, the gas industry broke away from the Ministry of Oil and Gas and became Gazprom – an independent 'concern'. The period immediately prior to, and following, the break-up of the Soviet Union saw efforts by different parties to carve out different futures for the gas industry:

(i)   Existing management sought to establish Gazprom as a joint stock company, and to hold together all the constituent parts of the Soviet gas industry.

(ii)   Individual republics sought independence from Moscow's control of the industry.

(iii) 'Economic reformers' sought to break up the industry.

However, with the break-up of the Soviet Union at the end of 1991, gas industries in the republics became independent entities, despite the interconnected nature of the network. In 1992, a series of presidential decrees established Gazprom as a joint stock company with a 40 per cent state ownership.[2] Fifty per cent of the shares were given to workers and various sections of the population (including national minorities) and Gazprom itself purchased a 10 per cent shareholding of which 9 per cent were designated for sale to foreign investors.

By the end of 1992, Gazprom 'concern' had become RAO Gazprom – a partly privatized joint stock company. Five years later, its ownership was officially recorded as: foreign investors 1.98 per cent, Russian individuals 21.85 per cent, Russian organizations 35.3 per cent, Russian Federal Property fund 0.87 per cent, Russian government 40 per cent.[3] The governance of the company, in terms of how the government's share should be represented has become controversial. Gazprom Chairman Rem Vyakhirev votes 35 per cent of the government's 40 per cent share and according to a Trust Agreement reached in April 1997, the Chairman is required to make a quarterly report to a ten-person committee headed by the Deputy Prime Minister and the Energy Minister.[4] In July 1998, the government announced that 5 per cent of its shareholding would be sold to foreign investors and although the sale was delayed by financial crises, 2.5 per cent was sold to the German company Ruhrgas (see Section 4).

2.2   Taxation and Payments

Gazprom's relationship with successive Russian governments has been periodically difficult, despite the fact that the company's former chairman – Victor Chernomyrdin - held the position of Prime Minister from 1992 to Spring 1998. There have been perennial disagreements and complaints:

(i)   From the government side, about the amount of tax which Gazprom should pay.

(ii)   From Gazprom, about how payment arrears (particularly those owned by government departments and companies) should be set against taxation.

By late 1998, non-payment of bills by Russian customers had become Gazprom's most serious problem. Non-payment on a large scale began in 1992 and steadily increased as prices were raised massively towards 'market levels'. By the mid-1990s, payment arrears by Russian customers had grown to around 50 per cent of receivables. Since 1996, this picture has been complicated by the widespread appearance (or, to be strictly accurate, reappearance) of barter trade. In 1996, Gazprom's accounts published for the first time according to international accounting standards (IAS), stated that 57 per cent of accounts receivable settled during the calendar year were in the form of barter trade or inter-enterprise transfers.[5] The 1997 IAS Accounts suggested that only 26.6 per cent of gas delivered was paid for, but cash payments by the end of the year accounted for 15 per cent – a considerable increase from the 7 per cent figure at the beginning of the year. However, 58 per cent of payments were made in the form of 'mutual cancellations' (that is inter-company transfers) and barter, of which the latter appears to have accounted for 11–20 per cent, leaving around 30 per cent of deliveries for which no payment at all was received. Nevertheless, the company had some success in reclaiming outstanding payments from previous years, with accumulated indebtedness falling by 59.4 per cent, albeit still leaving a substantial R82 trillion (around $13.5bn at 1997 exchange rates) outstanding.[6]

In 1998, the payments situation worsened sharply with the start of the country's major economic and financial crisis. Debts increased by 24 per cent in the first half of the year; the share of payment was 16 per cent cash and 84 per cent barter, but in July and August the volume of cash payments dropped sharply. At the same time, Gazprom began to use disconnection more widely as a means of debt control. During 1997, only fifty customers were disconnected, but during the first half of 1998, the number was 2,230. This does not mean that those customers necessarily remained disconnected from the system over a long period, but it signalled the beginning of a change in policy on the part of Gazprom.

Dealing with a government desperate to raise its receipts from taxation, has become an increasingly difficult problem for a company the size of Gazprom, which presents a huge target for the government to aim at. Gazprom's total tax bill increased from R60.6bn in 1996 to R62.9bn in 1997 although with the fall in the ruble, the dollar value fell from $11.8bn to $10.9bn. But Gazprom substantially reduced its tax penalties, suggesting that a greater proportion of its 1997 bills were paid on time. By mid-1998, the company's payments to the State Tax Service represented one-quarter of Federal tax receipts (*Interfax Petroleum Report*, 5–11 June 1998:13).

In July 1998, the Russian government – desperate for immediate cash and forced to meet IMF conditions on tax collection so that further substantial loans would be granted – ordered the Federal Tax Service to confiscate property at Gazprom's subsidiaries which owed significant amounts of tax. However, the detail of indebtedness revealed that government organizations owed more to Gazprom in unpaid gas bills than Gazprom owed to the government in taxes.[7] Since that episode, both sides have tried to avoid similar eruptions by carrying out a monthly mutual cancellation procedure between Gazprom's tax bill and the government's gas debt. There are increasing problems between the company and the government regarding export taxes, with Gazprom's Chairman claiming that the proposed 1998 taxation arrangements had made exports to Europe unprofitable, a situation which would have been exacerbated by the imposition of an export tax for the first six months of 1999.[8] The 1998 tax crisis ended with the Russian president appearing to urge Gazprom to cut off customers (particularly industrial ones) who did not pay bills, and by October of that year a 'tax treaty' had been signed between the company and the government. Under this agreement, it appears that Gazprom will pay a guaranteed amount of tax revenue which will be monitored monthly. This will take into account, both the tax which Gazprom owes the government, and the revenues owed by government organizations to Gazprom in payment for gas. This would appear to give the company substantial discretion as to whether it chooses to continue to deliver gas to non-paying, non-government customers. But non-payment is a highly political issue, given the unemployment and social unrest which could result from payment enforcement; and a crucial financial issue, given the sums of money and gas involved. In the post-1993 period, successive governments used non-payment of utilities as a way of reducing direct government subsidies to the industrial and manu-facturing sector. Large-scale disconnections would constitute an important political act, as they could give rise to substantial bank-ruptcies and unemployment. They would also have a huge impact on the gas industry with a significantly reduced production requirement, as bankrupt customers were forced to close, and remaining customers would begin to introduce conservation measures as they felt the real financial impact of gas prices. This author has estimated that, of the 282 bcm[9] gas which was delivered to non-residential/district heating consumers by Gazprom in 1996, around 140–180 bcm would have been necessary to support the same level of economic activity (Stern 1998:44–5).

2.3 Restructuring, Liberalization and Regulation

Gazprom has eight major production subsidiaries. Three of these are located in Siberia and account for around 80 per cent of production, each centred on a single field complex: Nadymgazprom (Medvezhe), Urengoygazprom (Urengoy) and Yamburggazodobycha (Yamburg). Until 1997, the company's fourteen transmission subsidiaries were responsible for transportation *and sales* of gas throughout Russia. In the early part of that year a restructuring of the company was announced whereby all gas sales would be handled by a newly created marketing subsidiary, Mezhregiongaz. This, and other reform measures (see below), suggest that the transmission subsidiaries have become transportation-only companies with no merchant function.[10]

At the beginning of 1997, it was announced that a newly-created Federal Energy Commission (FEC) would set regionally differentiated gas prices for industrial and residential customers. The eventual idea was that the Commission would be responsible for regulating transmission tariffs. Gazprom then announced a corporatization of the company which was accelerated by the April 1997 changes in the Russian government which brought to the fore – once again – younger economic reformers intent on reining in the power of the Russian monopoly utilities and increasing tax receipts from these companies. The reforms envisaged by government suggested a three stage process (*Interfax Petroleum Report*, 2–9 May 1997):

Stage 1, to be completed during 1997 included: regionally differentiated gas prices; a unified system of transmission pricing for independent producers and Gazprom subsidiaries; encouraging new investors (domestic and foreign) to develop new fields and pipelines; transparency of production and transportation costs; accounting and reporting procedures for Gazprom subsidiaries; establishing tariffs and conditions for access to pipelines (including a Commission to look at access for independent producers); tendering for rights to develop gas fields favourably located with respect to existing pipelines.

Stage 2, to be completed during 1998 included: bringing residential prices up to those paid by industrial customers; transferring authority for local transmission tariffs to regional energy commissions.

Stage 3, to be completed during 1999–2000 included: separation of production from transmission with contracts between different subsidiaries; regulation of transmission tariffs.

Implementation of these reforms would amount to Gazprom being transformed into a full open access transportation company before the end of the century. Although it would be unwise to make this assumption too readily, by end-1998, significant institutional and regulatory reform had taken place. A transparent tariff, regulated by the FEC, had been established for access to the pipeline network. While no applications for access had been reported, the existence of these arrangements placed Russia far ahead of the majority of European gas industries in terms of liberalization.

Despite gradual progress towards liberalization there have been periodic suggestions, both from successive Russian economic reformers and their foreign advisers, and from the international financial organizations which are their creditors, that Gazprom should be 'broken up'. The year 1998 demonstrated just how quickly events can drive perceptions:

(i)   At the beginning of the year, conventional wisdom seemed to suggest that Gazprom's leadership had 'seen off' the current group of economic reformers who were the authors of the utility reforms and whose political longevity seemed to be in doubt.

(ii) By the middle of the year, Victor Chernomyrdin – Gazprom's political patron – was no longer Prime Minister, and the company's future in its present form, appeared less assured.

(iii) By the end of the year, economic and political crisis had overwhelmed narrow sectoral reform considerations, and a unified Gazprom was once again seen as an island of stability in a sea of crisis.

Even leaving aside the crisis conditions of late 1998, it has always been difficult for protagonists of radical liberalization and the break-up of Gazprom to get to grips with the difficulties of the payment situation. For as long as payment arrears continue, even at the levels of 1995–7 (let alone what has been seen in 1998), it will be hugely difficult to create solvent companies to produce, transport or sell gas within Russia. Once payment arrears are resolved, or reduced to more manageable proportions, these developments can be discussed more realistically. However, in terms of the focus of this chapter, liberalization and future reform of Gazprom will be extremely important in terms of its impact on exports to European gas markets and we return to this issue in Section 5.

2.4   *The Growing Importance of Finance and Profitability*

The first page of Gazprom's 1997 Annual Report contains a revolutionary statement about the company's strategic development plan:

> the company's previous emphasis on increased gas production as the primary goal has been replaced with a more flexible management of energy resources to enhance the efficiency and profitability of the company.

To a western audience this may only appear to acknowledge the obvious. However, the change in corporate culture associated with the shift in emphasis away from increasing output towards increasing profit, is enormous.

In the post-Soviet era, the financing of the gas industry has undergone dramatic change. The Ministry (and Gazprom in its earliest incarnation) was financed out of the central budget. When all companies were required to become self-financing, the problem of non-payment in the domestic market became acute. Gazprom has become heavily dependent on European export earnings both to achieve profitability, and for loan guarantees. The company's 1997 accounts showed that Gazprom's sales within Russia of more than 300 bcm earned only slightly more than its European sales of 117 bcm.[11] In reality, as already noted, there are serious problems in valuing

Gazprom's sales within Russia because of the high percentage of non-cash receivables.

In August 1998, financial crisis exacerbated Gazprom's already difficult financial situation. Government financial disarray and subsequent political instability precluded the possibility of any significant loans from the international financial community. The fall in the value of the Russian stock market ran the risk of share sales at 'giveaway prices'. Meanwhile, to add to the company's problems, a combination of oil prices at historically low levels and increased competition in European gas markets, had seen 1998 prices fall by around 20 per cent compared with the previous year.

The irony of Gazprom's financial situation is that – because of the non-payment situation in the domestic economy and in the former republics – customers who can be served at lower cost are, at best marginally profitable, while the highest cost customers (at the end of long pipelines) in Europe provide the majority of the revenues. This is the reason why, if the Russian payment situation can be regularized in the future, the effect on export policy could be substantial and we return to this theme in the concluding Section.

3.   Soviet Inheritance and Trade Strategy

3.1   *Resources, Production and Pipeline Infrastructure*

A town gas industry existed in pre-revolutionary Russia from 1819 onwards, but natural gas was relatively slow to be introduced on a large scale, in part due to Stalin's determined efforts to create an energy economy based on coal. In the immediate post-War period, oil and natural gas were relatively neglected and large investments were made in synthetic fuel plants based on coal and shale. According to Campbell (1967:8–10), by the late 1950s, this effort was scaled down in favour of investment in oil and gas fields.[12] However, the foundations of the gas industry had been established with the first long distance (845 km) natural gas pipeline (between Saratov and Moscow) commissioned in 1946. The 1950s were a crucial decade for the Soviet gas industry: at the start, gas production was less than 6 bcm (with indications that even some of these volumes were associated gas which was flared); by 1960 production exceeded 45 bcm, and this figure had more than doubled by 1964 (Ebel 1970:128, Table 45; Orudzhev 1976:26–43). During the same period, 10.4 million dwellings were either converted to natural gas from town gas, or supplied with natural gas (Orudzhev 1976:76).

From these beginnings, 'supergiant' fields were discovered at: Urengoy, Yamburg, and Zapolyarnoye (Western Siberia); Orenburg; Shatlyk (Turkmenistan) in the mid to late 1960s. These were followed in the 1970s by the Yamal Peninsula fields (Bovanenko and Kharasevei) which firmly established the industry's resource base (Peebles 1980:158, Table 6.5; Stern 1980:Ch.2). Despite being shorn of the reserves in the other Soviet republics, proven gas reserves (according to Russian classification), were around 40 trillion cubic metres (tcm) at the time of the break-up of the Union; a figure which has since climbed to nearly 49 tcm. Of this figure, 45 tcm are onshore of which: 10 per cent are in European Russia, 78 per cent are in western Siberia and 4 per cent in eastern Siberia and the Far East (Vyakhirev 1996). Of the reserves in western Siberia, 10 tcm are located in fields on the Yamal Peninsula, including 6.7 tcm in three fields on the western shore of the peninsula.[13]

Gazprom owns 70 per cent of Russian proven reserves and in 1997 the company engaged the well-known American company DeGolyer and McNaughton to re-evaluate the reserves in the most important fields (see Map 1) according to the international classifications 'proven and probable'. Table 1 shows the results from eight fields, evaluated by DeGolyer in 1997, accounting for 51 per cent of the reserves owned by Gazprom; a further eight fields (19 per cent of reserves) were evaluated in 1998. The figures of 14.2 trillion cubic metres (tcm) of gas and 133 mt of oil, for 1997 in Table 1 which are based on a 51 per cent reclassification of the reserves, had risen to 18.8 tcm and 215 mt by the end of 1998 based on a reclassification of 66 per cent of reserves. The Annual Report claims that the western evaluation fully supports Gazprom's estimates using Russian methodology, however on the basis of the reclassified figures for two-thirds of the reserves, one would expect the eventual total to be around 25 tcm, which compares with the figure of 33.4 tcm of explored reserves usually cited in Gazprom sources.

The figures of 3.8 tcm for Yamburg and 3.9 tcm for Urengoy are particularly important. This is the first time that remaining recoverable reserves figures have been published for two out of Gazprom's three major producing fields (see Map 1) allowing an estimate of how many years these fields can produce at current levels: around 18 years for Urengoy and 20 for Yamburg (depending on ultimate recoverability factors). Also interesting in Table 1 is that the figure of 4.9 tcm for 'Yamal' is considerably below the 10 tcm (noted above) usually claimed in Russian sources. It is not clear whether this is because only the

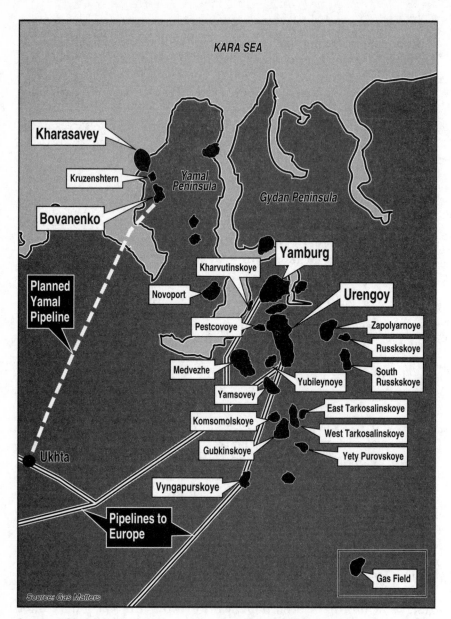

Source: Gas Matters

Map 1: West Siberian Gas Fields and Pipeline Corridors

Table 1:   Gazprom's Proven and Probable Gas and Oil Reserves

	December 31	
	1997	*1996*
GAS (trillions of cubic metres)		
Fields subject to independent evaluation		
Urengoy	3.935	4.144
Yamburg	3.809	3.979
Others	1.014	1.049
Total Western Siberia	8.758	9.172
Urals and Volga Regions	0.506	0.533
Yamal	4.936	4.936
Total	14.200	14.641
Fields not subject to independent evaluation		
Zapolyarnoye	3.074	3.074
Medvezhe	0.693	0.733
Astrakhan	2.195	2.200
Shtokman	2.156	2.156
Other fields not audited	5.790	5.840
Total	13.908	14.003
Total Gas Reserves	28.108	28.644
CONDENSATE AND OIL (million tons)		
Fields evaluated by DeGolyer and McNaughton	132.9	137.0
Fields not subject to independent evaluation	1,639.0	1,598.2
Total condensate and oil reserves	1,771.9	1,735.2

Source: *Gazprom IAS Accounts*, 1997

Bovanenko and Kharasevey fields (see Map 1) have been evaluated.

It is important to stress that the figures in Table 1 are *Gazprom's* reserves, not total *Russian* reserves which include gas associated with oil, and also major fields in Eastern Siberia and the Far East which are the subject of possible export projects in East Asia (see Section 4). It is also important to draw attention to Gazprom's oil reserves, since oil development is a significant area where the company clearly feels that revenues and profits can be expanded. Production of 9mt in 1997 is relatively insignificant given the company's reserve base of 1.8 billion tons and, as we shall see in Section 4, one of the main aims of the company's strategic alliances with Shell and ENI is to develop oil production capacity.

With such a large resource base already established by 1970, the principal task of the 1970s and 80s was to build a pipeline infrastructure in order to deliver these resources to consumers. This was achieved on a scale and at a speed never before witnessed, given the immense difficulties of the terrain. The Unified Gas Supply System (UGSS) – comprising pipelines over 720mm diameter – grew from 21,000 km in 1960 to 67,500 km in 1970 to 94,700 km in 1980, with large diameter pipeline comprising an ever-growing share of the total. At the break-up of the USSR in 1991, the length of the Russian system was 148,600 km, a large part of which was accounted for by Siberian pipeline corridors comprising fourteen pipelines with a diameter of 1220mm (48 inch) and 1420mm (56 inch), stretching thousands of kilometres over permafrost terrain and numerous water and mountain crossings.[14]

During this period, markets for gas were developed throughout the Soviet Union. At the break-up of the Union more than 70 million households were supplied by gas (the majority via district heating) which accounted for more than three quarters of both the rural and the urban population.[15] In addition, the Soviet Union was one of the first countries to recognize the advantages of gas-fired power generation at a time when this was deeply unfashionable in market economies. Major cities such as Moscow are almost totally dependent for their electricity on a 'ring' of gas-fired stations.[16]

Table 2 shows the Russian gas production levels and pipeline assets in 1992 – the first year of existence of an independent Russia – and for 1997/98. In 1992, the company was (partially) privatized with a fully depreciated set of production and pipeline assets. Gazprom was bequeathed a huge pipeline infrastructure combined with a production capacity that it has thus far, not needed to utilize to its fullest extent. While it is certainly true that, by 1992, much of the network was ageing and needed a great deal of remedial work, extravagant western claims regarding leakage rates, have tended towards exaggeration.[17]

Table 2: Russian Gas Production and Transmission Assets 1992–98

	1992	1997	1998
Russian Production (bcm)	640.4	569.3	591.0
Gazprom Production (bcm)	602.7	533.8	553.6
Pipelines (000km)	140.2	148.2	148.6
Compressor Stations:			
Number	224	246	
Capacity (Kw)	36.5	41.8	

Sources: Gazprom, *Annual Reports*, David Cameron Wilson, *CIS and East European Energy Databook*, Eastern Bloc Research (various years).

Much attention and investment in the post-Soviet period has been devoted to refurbishment of export pipelines because, as we shall see in the next section, foreign currency earning potential of Gazprom's Soviet inheritance was colossal.

3.2   Trade Strategy in the Soviet Era

An important Soviet institutional arrangement for dealings with foreign markets was that exports were dealt with by the Ministry of Foreign Trade (or Foreign Economic Relations). The very early contracts were negotiated by Soyuznefteexport – the oil export division of the Ministry of Foreign Trade. In the early 1970s, the Ministry established a separate gas export division, Soyuzgazexport, which handled all foreign trade contracts until the break-up of the USSR. Following the break-up (and even before the establishment of Gazprom as a joint stock company), all gas export contracts negotiated in the Soviet era were legally transferred to Gazprom – and the export division was renamed 'VEP Gazexport'.

Table 3 shows how gas trade developed during the final twenty years of the Soviet Union's existence, divided into imports and exports with a sub-division for exports to Soviet allies in Europe – members of the Council for Mutual Economic Assistance (or Comecon) – and 'west' European countries. In historical perspective, it comes as some surprise to discover that until the early 1970s, the Soviet Union was a net importer of gas; not until the latter part of that decade did the country become a substantial exporter.

3.2.1 Soviet Import Policy: Iran and Afghanistan

The development of Iran–Soviet gas trade was initially based on a joint economic co-operation project between the countries whereby the Soviet Union would build an iron and steel plant at Isfahan, in return for deliveries of natural gas. For Iran, such an arrangement had the two-fold benefit of achieving a long-held ambition to develop an indigenous steel industry, while simultaneously commercializing a portion of the gas (associated with oil production) which was being flared. For the Soviet Union, it provided not only a useful foreign policy linkage with its southern neighbour, but also gas supplies that were logistically useful for its southern republics, given that the location of domestic production was moving further north and east (Ebel 1970:155–60). The Iranian gas trunkline (IGAT) was completed on schedule in 1970 and contracted to deliver a plateau volume of 10 bcm/year to the Soviet Union until 1984. Initially the IGAT project

Table 3:   Soviet Natural Gas Trade 1970–91. Billion Cubic Metres

	1970	*1975*	*1980*	*1985*	*1991*
Exports					
Yugoslavia			2.1	3.9	4.5
Romania			1.5	2.0	5.4
Bulgaria		1.2	4.6	5.5	5.7
Hungary		0.6	3.8	4.0	5.9
Poland	1.0	2.5	5.3	6.0	7.1
Czechoslovakia	1.4	3.7	8.7	10.5	13.7
Germany (East)		3.3	6.1	6.2	n/a
Total Central/Eastern	2.4	11.3	32.1	38.1	42.3
Turkey					4.1
Finland		0.7	0.9	1.0	2.9
Austria	1.0	1.9	2.9	4.2	5.2
Switzerland					0.4
France			4.0	7.3	11.4
Italy		2.3	7.0	6.3	14.5
Germany (West)		3.1	10.7	12.5	24.4*
Total Western	1.0	8.0	25.5	31.3	62.9
Total Exports	3.4	19.3	57.6	69.4	105.2
Imports					
Iran	1.0	9.6	0.5		2.5
Afghanistan	2.6	2.9	2.5	2.4	
Total Imports	3.6	12.5	3.0	2.4	2.5
Total Net Exports	-0.2	6.8	54.6	67.0	102.7

*   unified Germany

Source: *Vneshnyaya Torgovlya SSSR* for various years. Gazprom data for 1991.

was so successful that another more ambitious project (IGAT II) was agreed in 1975. The second project was in essence a displacement agreement whereby Iran would export more than 16 bcm/year to the Soviet Union. More than 14 bcm of Soviet gas would be then delivered to four European countries (Germany, France, Austria and Czecho-slovakia) with the balance being retained by the Soviets as a transit fee and for compressor fuel (Stern 1980:79–80).

Even before the 1979 Iranian revolution and the overthrow of the Shah, the gas projects were running into commercial difficulties. In debates which have had strong echoes during the following two decades, many in Iran argued that the gas was being sold too cheaply.

In the event, gas trade collapsed almost immediately following the arrival of Ayatollah Khomeini's Islamic regime. Exports were abruptly cut off, causing serious hardship in the southern Soviet republics in the middle of a severe winter, and the IGAT II project was cancelled, with the pipeline partially built. Despite a brief resumption just prior to the break-up of the Union, the trade was never re-established on a continuous basis (Ibid.:95–6).

Trade with Afghanistan was the product of the 1957 Soviet–Afghan exploration assistance agreement which resulted in the discovery of the Khwaja Gogirdak fields in the Shibargan region of northern Afghanistan, near the Soviet border. Further assistance agreements to develop the field led to an eventual export of 2–5.3 bcm/year starting in 1967. Early payment for the gas was reflected in the Soviet construction of a gas-fired power station and a fertilizer plant (Ebel 1970:160–63; *Petroleum Press Service,* June 1970:207–9). The Soviet invasion of Afghanistan in 1979 and the subsequent deterioration of the regional security situation, meant the end of reliable gas trade and deliveries ceased entirely in the mid-1980s. It was never clear how much this was due to the volatile political situation, and how much to the exhaustion of the resource base.

3.3.2 *Soviet Export Policy in Europe*
In Cold War Europe, aside from the political and strategic distinctions, there was a clear political and commercial distinction between the Soviet Union's allies in Europe and the 'West European' countries. The former belonged to the Council for Mutual Economic Assistance known by the acronym Comecon (or the initials CMEA) and traded amongst themselves in non-convertible currencies or barter goods. The USSR, German Democratic Republic, Hungary, Poland, Romania, Czechoslovakia and Bulgaria were full Comecon members; Yugoslavia was an associate member.[18] By contrast, the Soviet Union traded with Western Europe in hard currencies, although as we shall see, as far as gas was concerned this involved a substantial barter element in the early years of the trade.

The Comecon Countries. The true beginning of Soviet gas exports to Europe can be traced back to 1946 when very small quantities were exported to Poland. But there was little increase in volumes over the next two decades until the Bratstvo (Brotherhood) pipeline, delivering gas to Czechoslovakia, was completed. It was the (marginal) extension of the Bratstvo pipeline which allowed the first deliveries to Austria in 1968, at which time only two Comecon countries – Poland and

Czechoslovakia – were together importing less than 2 bcm of Soviet gas.[19] Not until the early 1970s did a spur line from Bratstvo allow Hungary to receive Soviet gas.[20] The major increase in world oil prices in 1973–4 had a very significant impact on the development of Soviet exports to Comecon countries. While it produced a huge hard currency windfall for the Soviet economy, it also emphasized the opportunity cost of exporting large quantities of oil to the Comecon countries which were paying with non-convertible currencies and barter. For this reason, and also because problems in the Soviet oil industry were becoming apparent at that time, the Soviet Union made it clear to Comecon allies that they could not expect any increase (and indeed should expect some reduction) in oil deliveries.[21] In compensation, they would receive much greater deliveries of Soviet gas, but in return for this, they would be expected to make a significant contribution to the development of Soviet gas fields and pipelines. This was the origin of the Orenburg and Yamburg pipeline projects.

The Orenburg pipeline project was signed in June 1974, allowing for the joint construction of a 2677 km pipeline from the Orenburg field to deliver, starting in 1980, 15.5 bcm/year of gas to the six main Comecon members (1.5 bcm to Romania and 2.8 bcm/year to each of the other five) (Hannigan 1980). Although the original idea was for each country to construct its own sector of the 1420mm (56 inch) diameter line, the lack of experience in dealing with pipe of this size meant that the Soviets laid and welded almost the entire pipeline receiving financial (or other) compensation from the importing countries. The Orenburg (or 'Soyuz') pipeline project accounts for the very sharp increase in deliveries in Table 3 between 1975 and 1980.

Thereafter, deliveries increased only slowly until the Yamburg (or 'Progress') pipeline project was agreed in 1985. The new pipeline (one of six being built from the Yamburg field to the western part of the USSR), would deliver an average of 22 bcm per year to the six countries starting in 1988.[22] The volume commitments were expressed in terms of total volumes of gas to be delivered over a period of time, usually ten years. For the Yamburg pipeline, the European Comecon countries again were asked to construct sections of the pipeline and this time, more than 1300km (out of more than 4500km) were built by the GDR, Poland and Czechoslovakia, and 29 compressor stations. In total, the European Comecon countries provided construction work worth 2.6bn rubles within the Soviet Union, and 1.8bn rubles worth of their own equipment and materials. They also paid for 1.6m tons of pipe imported from Europe and 340m rubles worth of foreign currency for other imported equipment. The Orenburg and Yamburg pipelines were government-to-government agreements which guaranteed the importing countries a volume of gas paid for in soft currency or barter goods. Seen at the time by many in the West as exploiting the importing countries, these agreements proved to be extremely useful after the break-up of Comecon, when trade was moved to a hard currency basis.

The 'Hard Currency' Markets. The first contract signed with the Austrian company OMV in 1968, with deliveries starting in that same year, bore many of the hallmarks of the trade as it was to evolve during the next three decades. First, the initial deliveries of gas were paid for by reciprocal exports of large diameter (1220 and 1420mm) steel pipe, which made possible the construction of the export pipeline. Second, this export of large diameter steel pipe had only been made possible by the lifting in November 1966 of the NATO embargo on pipe exports.[23] Subsequent signing of long-term export contracts with Ruhrgas (Germany), Gaz de France, and SNAM (Italy) followed the same pattern with government credits supporting deliveries of large diameter pipe and turbines (to run the compressor stations along the route of the pipelines), which were paid for by the initial deliveries of gas.

Through the 1970s, the circle of countries receiving Soviet gas widened to West Germany (1973), Finland and Italy (1974), and France (1976).[24] Three interesting commercial details from those early contracts are worth noting: first that (unlike almost any other long-term gas contract of that era in Europe) the Soviet contracts did not specify a source for the gas. The gas was physically delivered initially from fields in the Ukraine, but switched to Siberia as volumes increased and new fields (in particular Medvezhe) moved into production. But in any event, the buyers were content that sufficient reserves existed and that the Soviets had the expertise to move the gas the necessary distances to their borders. Secondly that the prices in those early contracts were within 10 per cent of the price of Dutch gas. In the 1970s, the Soviets are believed to have used the price of Dutch gas as a 'marker' to which around 10 per cent could be added or subtracted, depending on the availability of Dutch gas in the markets into which they were selling. Third, the gas was of a lower calorific value than normal European specification gas and needed to be blended into the West European systems.

Trade expanded slowly but steadily in the 1980s until, approaching the Tenth Five Year Plan (1981–85), the Soviet planners had included the construction of six large diameter gas pipelines from Siberia to the west of the country. The choice of the field(s) from which this pipeline system was intended to be developed, was somewhat confused: some claim that the development was intended to be from the Yamburg field, but was switched to Urengoy because production at the latter was well under way and conditions were less challenging. Others refer to the project as the 'Yamal' pipeline (a title which was not to be heard again for another decade), suggesting that the gas could have come from any of the fields in north west Siberia. Some time around 1978 (again according to which sources one believes), either the Soviet negotiators mentioned to their German counterparts that one of these pipelines could be made available for exports to Western Europe; or Ruhrgas negotiators inquired whether any additional gas could be made available for export. The result became known as the Urengoy pipeline project.

From a political point of view, the Urengoy project could not have been more unfortunately timed. In late 1979 the Soviet Union invaded Afghanistan, an act which gave rise to trade sanctions by the United States. The following year Ronald Reagan was elected president of the United States with a philosophy of pursuing a much more aggressive policy against (what was perceived to be) Soviet expansionism. As negotiations continued through 1981 and the signing of contracts drew nearer, the imposition of martial law in Poland drew a furious response from the White House. Sanctions on American-supplied equipment for the pipeline were imposed immediately and these were extended extra-territorially in 1982, such that subsidiaries of American companies in Europe were prevented from fulfilling contracts (principally for the supply turbines) that they had already signed.[25] The main American arguments were that the pipeline would:

(i)   compromise the security of European energy and gas supplies
(ii) place the importing countries more firmly under Moscow's political influence
(iii) result in the transfer of technology, and the earning of hard currency revenues would enable the Soviet Union to strengthen its defence capabilities.

There ensued an upheaval in relations between the United States and West European governments which was finally resolved in a series of uneasy compromises. First, the volumes of European imports were scaled down from initial estimates (for commercial as well as political reasons). Secondly, fewer turbines were sold to the Soviets, causing the substitution of domestically produced equipment for imported units. Thirdly, OECD countries – using the forum of the International Energy Agency – agreed to 'avoid undue dependence' on a single source of imported gas (IEA 1984:72–3 Appendix A, Annex 1). This was translated by diplomats to suggest that Soviet gas should not constitute more than one-third of the consumption of major European countries (specifically Germany, France and Italy).

The Urengoy pipeline was built on time and, starting in 1986, began to deliver additional volumes to Western Europe, the effect of which can be clearly seen in the increase in volumes in Table 3 between 1985 and 1991. However, 'the pipeline episode' as it was referred to throughout the 1980s, left a set of lasting constraints on the freedom of action of major European importers. Whilst none of the importing companies (and probably none of their governments) believed that the American arguments had any serious merit, trans-Atlantic relations were too important to compromise by any further disagreements over Soviet gas imports. Aside from exports to new markets such as Turkey – supplied through an extension of the line through Romania and Bulgaria – Soviet exports to Western Europe stabilized in the late 1980s.

3.2.3 Export Policy Outside Europe

While Soviet gas exports to European markets were getting under way, much discussion took place during the 1960s and 70s about the possibility of developing liquefied natural gas (LNG) trade with both the United States and Japan. Post-Soviet developments in oil and gas development around Sakhalin Island (to which we return in Section 4) have obscured the fact that discussions on this development date back to 1966 and the first Japan–Soviet Economic Co-operation Committee. For most of this thirty-year period, the possibility of exports of Sakhalin gas to Japan has been spoken of in terms of LNG, but at the beginning of discussions, pipeline gas supplies were considered as an option.[26] Another LNG project involving the Japanese (but also the US) market, was the Yakutia project, whereby gas would be piped from the fields in Yakutia (now Sakha Republic) to be liquefied at a coastal site (Nakhodka was most frequently mentioned but other locations such as Olga and Magadan were also considered). By the late 1970s, around 1000 bcm of reserves which were required for the project had been proven.[27] Finally, a major LNG project using gas from the Urengoy field was planned to supply the US market. The Urengoy (sometimes referred to as the 'North Star') LNG project would have required gas to be piped 2500 km to Murmansk and liquefied for shipment to the USA (Kosnik 1975).

These projects failed to make progress because of a mixture of political and commercial obstacles. Yakutia and Urengoy LNG would have been relatively high cost projects even at the energy prices of the 1970s and early 1980s. However, with the coming of the Reagan administration and gas deregulation in the United States, any basis for such projects rapidly evaporated. For Japan, the lack of a Peace Treaty with the Soviet Union, continued disputes over territory, and the tendency to follow the political lead of the United States, meant that the political conditions never existed between the governments for trade on this scale, involving significant economic inter-dependence. Japanese government reluctance to enter into a closer economic and political relationship with the Soviet Union was mirrored in the lack of enthusiasm of Japanese gas buyers to import Soviet supplies. The attitude of Japanese buyers towards Soviet gas stood in sharp contrast to their much greater keenness to develop LNG trade with south east Asian countries. Thus while periodic Soviet–Japanese discussions took place, no progress was made, and the Soviet side – increasingly preoccupied with European trade – gradually lost interest. Not until well into the post-Soviet era (as we shall see below) was interest rekindled.

4.   Export Strategy in the post-Soviet Era

As we saw in Section 3, the legacy inherited by Gazprom from the Soviet era, both in domestic and international terms, was enormous. The company accounted for 95 per cent of the country's gas production and, from Siberia westward had a transmission and wholesale monopoly of all large customers, including distribution companies. The Russian gas export company, VEP Gazexport had become a wholly-owned subsidiary of Gazprom, and the sole exporter of Russian gas outside the former Soviet Union. Exports to former Soviet republics are handled by a different division of Gazprom.

During the Soviet era there were two distinct markets for Soviet gas: the Central/East European countries which were members of the Council for Mutual Economic Assistance (CMEA), and the markets of OECD Europe. In the post-Soviet era also, two distinct markets for gas exports have evolved: the former Soviet republics, and European countries; or in Russian terminology the 'near abroad' and 'far abroad'.

4.1   *The Former Republics: Managing Dependence and Interdependence*

The break-up of the Soviet Union created a set of trading relationships between newly emerging sovereign states, which (with one significant exception) had formerly treated gas trade as an internal transfer of energy without financial significance. Gas trading relationships between former Soviet republics and particularly the triangular relationship between Russia, Turkmenistan and the Ukraine, may yet have important consequences for exports to European markets in the post-Soviet era.

The statistics in Table 4 are not entirely consistent and contain a certain amount of interpretation on the part of the author. Nevertheless, they can be regarded as a reasonably accurate picture of Russian gas deliveries both before and immediately following the break-up of the Soviet Union. What these figures do not show is the pattern and extent of inter-republic trade during the Soviet period. The essentials of this trade were that Russia supplied: the Ukraine, Belarus, Moldova and Kazakhstan, while receiving gas from Turkmenistan and Kazakhstan. Turkmenistan supplied Kazakhstan and Uzbekistan; and (via Russia) Ukraine, Georgia, Armenia, and Azerbaidzhan, as well as Russia itself. In Central Asia, Turkmenistan was (and remains) the major exporter but Uzbekistan supplies Kazakhstan, Kyrgyzstan and Tadzhikistan. Kazakhstan exports small quantities of gas to Russia. The exact details of exchanges, particularly between the Central Asian republics, and between the latter and Russia are particularly complex.

For our purposes, the key issues in terms of trade are that outside Central Asia, republics receive virtually their entire gas supply either from Russia, or from Turkmenistan through the Russian system. The exception was the Ukraine which received gas from both republics to

Table 4: Russian Exports to Former Soviet Republics, 1990–98. Billion Cubic Metres

	1991	*1992*	*1993*	*1994*	*1995*	*1996*	*1997*	*1998***
Ukraine	60.7	77.3	54.9	57.0	52.9	51.0	49.2	53.4
Belarus	14.3	17.6	16.4	14.3	12.9	13.7	15.2	15.8
Moldova	2.5	3.4	3.2	3.0	3.0	3.2	3.3	3.3
Georgia				0.4			0.1	0.7
Lithuania	6.0	3.2	1.9	2.1	2.5	2.6	2.2	2.2
Latvia	3.2	1.6	1.0	1.1	1.2	1.1	1.1	1.6
Estonia	1.9	0.9	0.4	0.6	0.7	0.8	0.8	0.7
Kazakhstan		1.7	1.1	0.4			0.1	2.2
Total*	90.0	106.4	78.6	78.8	73.2	73.0	72.1	79.9

*   totals do not add for all years
**   preliminary

Source: Gazprom statistics for respective years

supplement its substantial (but dwindling) domestic production. The key issues in terms of transit are that:
- all pipelines taking Turkmen gas exports outside Central Asia pass through Russia, putting Gazprom in complete control of around three-quarters of Turkmenistan's exports.
- more than 90 per cent of Russian gas exports to Europe pass through the Ukraine; around 15 per cent pass through Moldova, and with the opening of the Yamal pipeline (see below) Belarus is increasingly becoming an important transit country.

The break-up of the USSR caused immediate and continuing problems for gas trade between all of the republics. The essence of these problems has been demands for gas and transit tariffs to be paid for at prices and in currencies, which (with the possible exception of Russia) none of the recipients can afford. Refusal and/or inability to pay resulted in the amassing of huge debts to suppliers (principally Russia and Turkmenistan) and periodic cutbacks in supply because of non-payment. The proportions of this debt for 1995–98 are shown in Table 5 and are clearly not trivial; they also amount to a high proportion of total debt owed to Russia by the former republics. When Gazprom has cut deliveries because of debt, this has caused not only hardship but, in cases where gas has been in transit to third countries, the diversion of supply intended for those countries. While the most important problems have arisen in the Ukraine, similar events have been common in trade between Central Asian and Caucasus countries.[28]

Table 5: Debts for Gas Supplies owed to Gazprom by former Soviet Republics. Million Dollars

	1995		1996		1997		1998 (9 months)	
	Value of Gas Supplied	% of 1995 Bills Paid	Value of Gas Supplied	% of 1996 Bills Paid	Value of Gas Supplied	% of 1997 Bills Paid	Value of Gas Supplied	% of 1998 Bills Paid
Ukraine	1,966.37	80.10	745.10	90.36	791.82	88.85	982.70	70.26
Belarus	854.03	73.50	212.12	71.53	97.22	91.46	217.15	64.79
Moldova	335.92	48.25	509.03	5.87	531.55	0.00	601.55	0.00
Baltic Countries	80.29	85.70	57.67	81.92	15.08	95.84	6.34	96.93
Total*	3,156.32	66.15	1,466.26	84.57	1,450.29	85.78	1,801.40	64.55

*   all CIS countries included

Source: Fadeev (1998)

In terms of relationships with Russia, the former republics can be divided into four groups:

4.1.1 *The Baltic States*

Latvia, Lithuania and Estonia were first to leave the Union and as a consequence were, by 1992, required to pay prices which (in terms of level and currency) resembled European border prices. These higher price levels combined with economic restructuring, and the availability of lower cost (principally Russian) gasoil and high sulphur fuel oil, caused Russian gas deliveries to these countries to fall sharply in the post-Soviet period. By 1997 some recovery of export volumes had occurred, but only to about 40 per cent of the 1991 level. While these countries are still regarded by Gazprom as deliveries to 'former Soviet republics', rather than 'exports to Europe', this seems to be more a political and institutional legacy, rather than a commentary on the ability and willingness of the countries to pay promptly in hard currencies at price levels which equate to those elsewhere in Europe.

There have certainly been payment problems, especially in Lithuania and Latvia, but these have improved greatly since 1996 and in any case pale into insignificance in comparison with the larger debtors (in Table 5). They are also tempered by Gazprom's equity shares in the gas industries of both countries. In addition to having a 41 per cent share in the main Estonian gas company Eestigaz, Gazprom also has a 16.25 per cent stake in Latvias Gaze (and is likely to increase this share). It is negotiating to purchase a stake in Lithuania's Lituvos Dujos and seeking to build a new pipeline across Lithuania to deliver gas to the Russian enclave of Kaliningrad (*GBI*, October 1997:VIII). Gazprom's desire to use the existing storage facilities in Latvia – particularly when the Belarus–Poland ('Yamal') pipeline comes on-stream, will become an important factor in gas trade relationships.

4.1.2 *Ukraine, Belarus and Moldova*

The story of Russia's relationships with these countries since the break-up of the Union is one of managing gas debt in the face of bills which customers in these countries are unable to pay. In terms of volume, Canadian gas trade with the United States is the only other bilateral gas trade world-wide which exceeds Russian trade with the *Ukraine*. During the 1990s, Russian deliveries to the Ukraine have been the equivalent of 50–80 per cent of its European export volumes. Another way of looking at these volumes is that during this period they have been roughly equivalent to the annual gas consumption of Italy.

In the immediate post-Soviet period, the Gazprom-Ukraine

relationship was characterized by periodic crises of non-payment involving threats of disconnection and counter-threats of diversion, some of which have been carried out. Ukrainian inability to pay for the huge volumes which it had contracted was accompanied by a desire to demonstrate control over Gazprom's deliveries to Europe. Since the break-up of the Soviet Union, much publicity has been given to unauthorized diversions of Russian gas exports in transit to European countries. Diversion of supplies by the Ukrainian gas industry, has been the product of a complex set of circumstances and negotiating positions. The principal factors are accumulated debt to Russian and Turkmen suppliers, and the degree to which non-payment can be considered a justified reason for cutting back these supplies. On numerous occasions, Gazprom has accused the Ukrainian gas industry of having taken gas from the export pipelines for its own needs. In some instances, the Ukrainian government and importers have accepted that such irregularities have taken place; at other times, they have strenuously contested such allegations.[29]

Irrespective of the validity of Gazprom's allegations, the company's freedom of action is severely constrained and financial arrangements are complex. There is an annual negotiation of export volumes and prices between Gazprom and: the Ukrainian government, Ukrgazprom, a number of different Ukrainian gas marketing companies; or a mix of all three. The elements of this negotiation are: volumes, prices, transit fees, treatment of existing and new debt. The Gazprom position has been dominated by two concerns:

• that the volumes of gas being delivered to Ukraine are so large that the revenue consequences of non-payment cannot be ignored.
• that any disruption of exports to European countries – for however short a time, even if it has no noticeable impact on European gas consumers – does damage to Russia's reputation as a secure supplier of gas to its convertible currency markets.

This latter point provides the reason why, despite the debts and periodic diversion of gas supplies, Gazprom has taken a relatively conciliatory stance towards the Ukrainian actions, and made great efforts to avoid confrontation. The Russian position has, as we shall see below, contrasted sharply with that of Turkmenistan which has cut deliveries for long periods due to non-payment and disputes over prices. The Turkmen position has periodically brought Gazprom to the position of sole supplier to the Ukraine.

Ukrainian political sensitivity towards Russian influence has been a considerable obstacle to a commercial solution in which Gazprom takes some degree of ownership in Ukrainian gas transmission and storage assets. A large part of the Ukraine's 35 bcm of storage capacity was built for the specific purpose of ensuring security of Soviet (now Russian) exports to Europe. Unlike its counterparts in Belarus and Moldova, successive Ukrainian governments and/or the Ukrainian parliament have refused to countenance significant Gazprom equity shares in Ukrainian gas enterprises.

Gas deliveries have become an issue of national importance in the political and security relationship between the two countries, having featured in the package of agreements which have included issues such as the future of the Black Sea Fleet and Ukrainian nuclear weapons. The inter-governmental agreement signed between the countries in February 1994, which set out a framework for the terms of sale and transit for a ten-year period, provided a useful reference point in this relationship but failed to provide a sound commercial basis for the trade. Nevertheless, by the late 1990s, much of the tension had disappeared from the Gazprom-Ukraine gas relationship as both sides recognized the need to make progress towards some longer-term contractual commercial framework which both sides are able to honour. The 1998 negotiation appeared to be a significant step in this direction but lacked a comprehensive solution for dealing with the debt which Gazprom claim various Ukrainian organizations – both state-owned and private – have accrued for gas deliveries since 1991.[30] The transit provisions of the Energy Charter Treaty may provide a useful international framework within which to conduct future discussions in the search for a lasting solution to these problems.[31]

Compared with the Ukraine, Gazprom's other bilateral gas trades pale into insignificance in volume terms. But deliveries of 14–17 bcm per year to *Belarus* are by no means negligible. The country currently provides transit for up to 7 bcm per year to Poland, but the importance of Belarus as a transit route for Russian exports will increase significantly in the future. Largely because of the desire to diversify away from dependence on the Ukraine, but also for logistical reasons, a second export corridor – the 'Yamal pipeline' – is being established through Belarus and Poland to Germany (see below).

Gazprom's relationship with Belarus is underpinned by a January 1994 inter-governmental agreement which sets out the sale and transit relationships between the countries over a twenty-year period. Under this agreement the assets of Beltransgaz – the gas transmission company – were intended to be transferred to Gazprom under a 99-year lease.[32] In return, Russia is said to have agreed to double its deliveries to Belarus by 2010 although it is not clear how the country would use such large quantities of gas. A more plausible outcome, at least in the short term, is that Belarus would use gas received from transit payments from the Yamal pipeline (see below) to reduce its existing gas bill from Russia.

With an annual requirement of only 3–4 bcm, it is easy to forget Russian sales to *Moldova*. However, the country is also an important transit route along which all gas deliveries to south eastern Europe (Romania, Bulgaria and Turkey) pass. As early as 1994, Gazprom began to set up joint ventures with the Moldova gas industry. In 1998 the Moldovan parliament confirmed a government proposal to set up a new company, AOOT Moldova Gas, which would be owned in equal shares by Gazprom and the Moldova government and would include the assets of the gas in the whole country including the Dnestr region (*GBI*, March 1998:IV).

4.1.3 Central Asia: Turkmenistan and Kazakhstan

During the Soviet era, Russia received significant quantities of gas from *Turkmenistan*. This was the only intra-Soviet gas trade arrangement to which real monetary values could be applied. In return for supplying volumes – which in 1990 reached nearly 80 bcm – to other Soviet republics, including Russia, Turkmenistan received a hard currency 'quota' for gas it was deemed to have exported to Europe. How this quota was calculated is not known. During the period 1990–93 for which data is available, the quota varied between 15–25 per cent of the volumes which were supplied to former republics.[33] How these volumes were translated into revenues and in what currency these revenues were paid, is not known. However, the arrangement broke down almost immediately following the break-up of the Union, and ceased by 1994.

Immediately after the break-up, Turkmenistan demanded payment for its gas from all former republics, including Russia, in hard currency at 'world prices'. There followed a catalogue of disputes over non-payment and non-delivery of gas between Turkmenistan and all of its former Soviet customers, of which the problems with the Ukraine were the most serious – since volumes of up to 25 bcm/year were involved (Miyamoto 1997:45). A variety of methods were attempted to find a new basis for regularizing Turkmen deliveries to Ukraine and other former republics. The most notable of these was the formation in November 1995 of Turkmenrosgaz – a joint venture between Gazprom, Turkmengazprom and a trading company Itera – which was given the right to handle all sales of Turkmen gas (Ibid.:49–51).[34] As payment became an increasing problem in the former republics and commerce retreated to a barter basis reminiscent of Soviet times, Gazprom has increasingly used the trading company Itera (in which it has an equity interest) to organize and monetize the barter share of its trade with the former republics. The company places considerable reliance on Itera's opinion as to whether trade is viable at a particular price and this appeared to be a major reason for the problems in the Turkmen–Ukraine relationship as Itera made it quite clear that gas was not saleable in the Ukraine at the price being demanded by the Turkmen sellers.

In mid-1997, the Turkmen government unilaterally dissolved Turkmenrosgaz due to debts which had not been paid by Itera with respect to deliveries of gas to Ukraine. During 1998 it became clear that neither Gazprom nor the Russian and Turkmen governments could agree a commercial basis for any significant resumption of Turkmen gas exports outside the Central Asian region which had ceased in March 1997 (*GBI*, December 1997:XIV and February 1998:XI). It appears that, following a meeting in August 1997 with the Russian prime minister and the Turkmen president, Gazprom's chairman made a decision that it was impossible to find an acceptable long-term basis for supplying Turkmen gas to former Soviet republics (principally the Ukraine) and that these markets would henceforth need to be supplied with Russian gas (*GBI*, September 1997:VIII). At the beginning of 1999, a new initiative by the Turkmens saw an annual contract signed for delivery of 20 bcm of gas to Ukraine. The difference from previous arrangements is that sales within Ukraine and transit through Kazakhstan, Uzbekistan, and Russia is being arranged by Itera. Gazprom has no direct commercial involvement in this transaction.

Russian gas trade with *Kazakhstan*, even during the Soviet period, never involved large volumes, although the exchanges between the countries were logistically useful. For many of the same reasons as in the Turkmen case, the break-up of the Union quickly saw the trade reduced to negligible levels, although some Kazakh gas is still sold in the Ukraine. The sudden increase in volumes in 1998 (see Table 4) was somewhat unexpected. The principal Russian interest in Kazakh gas in the post-Soviet era was the inclusion of Gazprom in a joint venture to develop the Karachaganak gas field (with significant oil and very large gas reserves) in northern Kazakhstan. In early 1995 Gazprom signed a production sharing principles agreement with partners which included British Gas and AGIP, to restore production capacity at the field to (relatively low) Soviet levels in anticipation of paving the way for a major export project through Russian pipelines (potentially) to Europe (*GBI*, March 1995:1). Barely a year later, Gazprom dropped out of the joint venture, on the grounds that the non-Russian partners were unwilling to recognize the financial contribution which Gazprom had made to opening up the field in the Soviet era, and that the company was unwilling to contribute additional finance to the venture unless that contribution was recognized (*International Gas Report*, 5 July 1996:9). By 1998, other foreign partners had joined the project, and oil production and export (via the Caspian Pipeline Consortium's system) was under way. Large-scale development of Karachaganak's gas resource development remained uncertain, following a very firm announcement by Gazprom's chairman in 1997, that neither Kazakhstan nor Turkmenistan would be allowed to export gas to European markets using the company's pipeline system (*GBI* September 1997:VIII). There were signs in early 1999 of a softening of attitudes towards Central Asian gas, at least as far as exports to CIS countries are concerned.

4.2   Europe

Table 6 shows Russian gas exports to Europe during the period 1991–97. In aggregate terms, the expansion of Russian gas exports to Europe has not taken a smooth upward path. Volumes did not exceed 1990 levels until 1995, and after two years of very rapid growth dipped again in 1997. The next section looks at the evolution of Gazprom's trade with two different groups of countries:

(i)   member-countries of the OECD in the pre-1990 period, which might be called the 'old West'.[35]

(ii)   countries which were former political and security allies of the former Soviet Union.

4.2.1   The 'old West': WIEH/Wingas and the Trading House Strategy

The reunification of Germany and the end of the post-war era in Europe, gave rise to equally historic events in the German gas industry. With the industry of the former German Democratic Republic (GDR) available for acquisition, the two major West German gas companies, Ruhrgas and BEB, purchased 35 per cent and 10 per cent respectively of the East German transmission company (which was to become known as) VNG.[36]

Around this time, Gazprom devised the strategy of trying to move 'downstream' into European gas markets, on the basis that its practice of selling gas at the border of the importing country meant that the importing company was able to capture a large amount of the profit

Table 6:   Russian Natural Gas Exports to Europe 1991–98.[1] Billion Cubic Metres

	1990	*1991*[2]	*1992*	*1993*	*1994*	*1995*	*1996*	*1997*	*1998*
Former Yugoslavia	4.5	4.5	3.0	2.7	2.3	2.0	4.0	3.9	3.7
including									
'Yugoslavia'							2.11	2.06	1.80
Croatia							0.97	1.14	1.20
Slovenia							0.49	0.50	0.50
Bosnia							0.42	0.14	0.20
Macedonia								0.001	0.002
Romania	7.3	5.4	4.4	4.6	4.5	6.1	7.15	5.09	4.70
Bulgaria	6.8	5.7	5.3	4.8	4.7	5.8	6.03	4.95	3.80
Hungary	6.4	5.9	4.8	4.8	5.2	6.3	7.71	6.52	7.30
Poland	8.4	7.1	6.7	5.8	6.2	7.2	7.14	6.75	6.90
Czech Republic	6.6	}13.7	6.8	}13.2	}13.8	}14.9	9.44	8.43	8.60
Slovakia	6.0		6.0				7.04	7.09	7.10
Total Central/Eastern	**46.0**	**42.3**	**37.0**	**35.9**	**36.7**	**42.3**	**48.5**	**42.7**	**42.2**
Greece							0.01	0.16	0.90
Turkey	3.3	4.1	4.5	5.0	4.7	5.7	5.63	6.70	6.70
Finland	2.7	2.9	3.0	3.1	3.4	3.6	3.73	3.64	4.20
Austria	5.1	5.2	5.1	5.3	5.1	6.1	6.02	5.57	5.70
Switzerland	0.3	0.4	0.4	0.4	0.4	0.4	0.39	0.40	0.40
France	10.6	11.4	12.1	11.6	12.2	12.9	12.35	10.91	10.90
Italy	14.3	14.5	14.1	13.8	13.8	14.3	13.99	14.22	17.30
Germany	26.6	24.4	22.9	25.8	29.6	32.1	32.87	32.52	32.50
Total Western	**63.0**	**62.9**	**62.1**	**65.0**	**69.2**	**75.1**	**75.0**	**74.1**	**78.5**
Total Europe	**109.0**	**105.2**	**99.1**	**100.9**	**105.8**	**117.4**	**123.5**	**116.8**	**120.7**

1   the years 1991–93 do not take the Turkmenistan quota (see text) into account
2   final year of the Soviet Union's existence

Source: Gazprom

from the sale of gas. The folklore of the European gas business has it that Victor Chernomyrdin, then Chairman of Gazprom, proposed to the Chairman of Ruhrgas that the two companies should form a joint marketing venture to sell gas in Germany, and was rebuffed in a way which gave serious offence. Whatever the truth of this story, the consequences were to prove far-reaching.

In October 1990, Wintershall (which also owned 15 per cent in VNG) announced a co-operation agreement with Gazprom at the heart of which was a joint venture company to market Russian gas in the eastern part of Germany.[37] Prior to this announcement, Wintershall had been known only as a small German gas-producing company,

owned by the giant chemical company BASF. The origins of the joint
venture with Gazprom can be found in BASF's periodic disputes with
Ruhrgas over the price of gas to its chemical and petrochemical
businesses. BASF had become frustrated with its inability to obtain
(what it saw as) a reasonable price for gas, and had proposed building
a pipeline – the MIDAL line – from Emden (a major landfall for
Norwegian gas supplies to Germany) via Kassel to Ludwigshafen (the
headquarters of BASF). The initial refusal of North Sea gas producers
to sell to anybody other than their traditional customers would
probably have meant that Wintershall's plans would have failed for
lack of gas supplies, had not Gazprom embraced it as a partner.

The alliance – earlier known as Wintershall Erdgas Handelshaus or
WIEH, later to be supplemented by another joint venture, Wingas –
was thus able to start by building two major pipelines: STEGAL
carrying Russian gas from St Katheriny on the German/Czech border,
to join the MIDAL line south of Kassel (see Map 2).[38] In addition to
these pipelines, the Wingas venture has also built:

- the Jagal pipeline: for Russian gas from the new Belarus–Poland
  line.
- the Wedal line giving it the ability to bring British Interconnector
  gas into Germany.
- the Rehden storage facility.

As far as can be ascertained, at the outset at least, Gazprom was not
required to contribute finance to the joint venture. The relationship
was therefore clear: BASF/Wintershall contributed money, Gazprom
contributed gas.

For Gazprom, the Wintershall joint venture provided an opportunity
to operate in a foreign commercial organization as an equal partner,
with its executives in senior management positions. It also provided
market intelligence as to true costs and margins involved in the German
gas market. No longer did Gazprom have to accept the view of the
importing company as to how Russian gas should be priced, it could
form a view based on first hand knowledge. But perhaps the most
important advantage of the Wingas experience was that it struck fear
into all of Gazprom's other traditional partners in European countries.
If Gazprom could find, and form an alliance with, a company prepared
to compete with Ruhrgas – a company whose position, prior to 1990,
had seemed unchallengable – it could do the same to its traditional
partners in other countries.

The success of that strategy was illustrated by Gazprom's Volta
joint venture with the Italian company Edison Gas, announced in

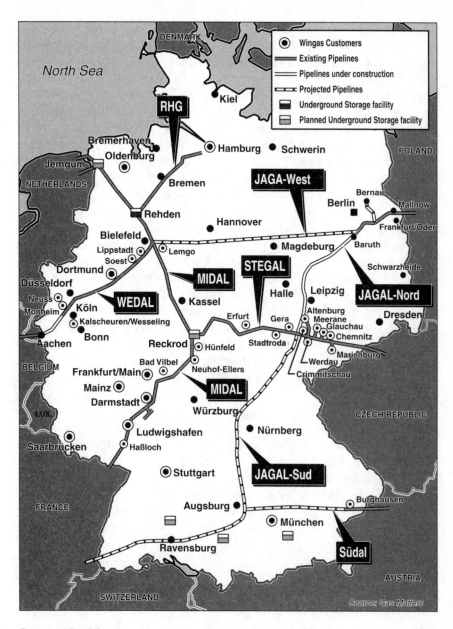

Source: Gas Matters

Map 2: New German Gas Pipelines

1995, to move an additional 10 bcm into the Italian market. This was an indication of Gazprom's ambitions in terms of expanding deliveries to one of its largest export markets. In May 1998 Edison announced that the project had been postponed, but from Gazprom's perspective, the threat of taking on a new partner had the desired effect of persuading SNAM (Gazprom's long-time Italian partner) to sign contracts for additional volumes (*International Gas Report*, 29 May 1998:4).

The principal drawback for Gazprom from the Wingas experience was the resulting pipeline-to-pipeline competition between Ruhrgas and Wingas, which drove down prices in the German market. With Wingas, competing head-to-head with Ruhrgas for customers in the German market, Gazprom found that to some extent Russian gas supplies being sold by both companies were competing against each other, resulting in reduced prices and therefore margins on sales. In the early years of competition, this was an acceptable price to pay for market entry, market intelligence and as an important demonstration to other European gas companies. But by 1998, these advantages had been established and Gazprom's German strategy changed fundamentally with the signing of a new co-operation agreement with Ruhrgas, and the latter's purchase of Gazprom equity (see below). Whether or not Gazprom had 'forgiven and forgotten' Ruhrgas's (real or imagined) offences in the past, it is clear that by the end of 1998, the company had a much more even-handed view of its two major German customers.[39]

During the 1990s, Gazprom established its model of 'trading houses' throughout Europe. In reality these are joint ventures which are focused on marketing and pipeline construction, or a mix of both activities. Table 7 shows the joint ventures established in sixteen European countries. Notable exceptions are the Czech Republic and Britain (where no Russian gas is yet sold) but where Gazprom has a 10 per cent share in the Interconnector pipeline project. Although it is difficult to generalize about the role and activity of these ventures, three categories can be identified:

(i)   Those which are (or are intended to be) involved principally in pipeline construction and operation, such as Yugorosgaz, Europol Gaz, Blue Stream and North Transgas.

(ii) Those which are already handling (or will in future handle) substantial amounts of gas under long-term contracts sold in their respective countries. Wingas/WIEH, Gasum, Panrusgas, Wirom, Progresgaz Trading and Slovrusgaz come under this heading.

(iii) Those which principally trade gas outside the framework of long-term contracts: GWH, Gaz Trading, Fragaz and Promgaz.

Table 7:   Gazprom's Principal Gas-Related Investments in Europe

Country	Title	Equity %	Principal Foreign Partner	Status[a]
Germany	Zarubezhgaz	100	n/a	JSC
	WIEH	50	Wintershall	TH
	Wingas	35	Wintershall	TH
	Zarubezhgas Erdgashandel	100	n/a	JSC
	VNG	5	Ruhrgas/BEB	JV
France	Fragaz	50	Gaz de France	JSC
Italy	Promgaz	50	SNAM	JSC
	Blue Stream[b]	50	ENI	JV
	Volta[c]	49	Edison	JV
Slovakia	Slovrusgaz	50	SPP	JV
Austria	GWH	50	OMV	TH
Britain	Interconnector	10	British Gas	JV
Finland	Gasum	25	Neste	JSC
	North TransGas	50	Neste	JSC
Poland	Europol Gaz	48	PGNiG	JSC
	Gaz Trading	35	PGNiG	TH
Hungary	Panrusgas	50	MOL	JV
Serbia	Progresgaz Trading	50	Progres	JV
Serbia/				
Montenegro	Yugorosgaz	50	Progres	JV
Macedonia	GA-MA	40	Government	JSC
Romania	Wirom	25[d]	Romgaz	JSC
Bulgaria	Overgas	50	Multigroup	JSC
	Topenergy[e]	100		JSC
Turkey	Gama Gazprom	45.3	Botas	JV
	Turusgaz	45	Botas	JSC
Greece	Prometheus Gas	50	Kopelouzos	JSC

a) JV = joint venture; JSC = joint stock company; TH = trading house.
b) Blue Stream is a joint venture aimed at the construction of an offshore pipeline across the Black Sea to Turkey.
c) in 1998 it was announced that the Volta pipeline project had been shelved. The fate of the joint venture is not known.
d) Wirom is a 50/50 Joint Venture between Romgaz and WIEH
e) in 1998 Gazprom bought out the Bulgarian investors in Topenergy.

It is difficult to obtain information regarding how much gas these marketing ventures buy, sell or market, but for example Panrusgas has a licence to import 225 bcm of Russian gas to Hungary in the period up to 2015 with annual deliveries of up to 12.5 bcm (*Gas Matters*, December 1996:10–13). Promgas has a short-term contract to provide SNAM with 0.3–0.4 bcm/year, but the company also has a 25 per cent share of an 8 bcm/year long-term contract (in which SNAM is the major importing party) concluded as part of the Yamal–Europe project. Promgas also has a long-term contract for 2 bcm/year which will start in 1999.

4.2.2 The Former Comecon Countries: From Loyal Allies to Valuable Markets

In the aftermath of independence from the Soviet Union and the break-up of the Comecon economic area, the former member-countries of that organization were placed in an extremely difficult financial situation. Starting in 1990 the Soviet Union demanded that energy deliveries should be paid for in hard currency and at 'world prices'. Of considerable assistance to the former Comecon members was that they had all participated in development co-operation projects connected with the Orenburg and Yamburg gas fields (see Section 3). These included government-to-government co-operation agreements which guaranteed deliveries of gas under soft currency and/or barter arrangements until the late 1990s, and proved immensely useful for Central and Eastern European countries for smoothing the path to full commercial relationships with Gazprom. Nevertheless, gas imports fell sharply under the combined pressure of adjusting to hard currency payments and economic reform and restructuring programmes, only briefly regaining 1990 levels in 1996 before falling again the following year (Table 6).

In the decade since the end of the Communist era, perceptions of gas trading relationships with Russia passed through a number of different stages. Immediately following independence, in the transition to hard currency payments at European price levels, it was difficult to believe that these countries would be able to afford the 'inevitably higher prices' that would need to be paid to bring non-Russian gas through new pipelines to this region. Within five years of independence, the economies of central Europe – principally the Czech Republic, Hungary and Poland – began to recover, and energy and gas demand began to rise. At that time, the perception was that Russia's economic and political hold over these countries would be sufficiently strong that Gazprom would seek to punish those intent on diversification away from Russian supplies.

But gas companies in the Czech Republic, Hungary and Poland were actively negotiating to bring non-Russian supplies to the region. The contracts signed by the Hungarian company MOL in 1995 with Ruhrgas for the delivery of 0.5 bcm annually (starting in 1996) which was expanded to 0.91 bcm/year (in 1998), and in 1996 with Gaz de France for 0.4 bcm/year, were viewed more as 'security measures' than as real diversification. The major breakthrough for diversification arrived in April 1997 with the agreement between the Czech company

Transgas and Norway's GFU. The agreement provided for the almost immediate start of deliveries and the eventual increase in deliveries to 3 bcm/year by 2000. Indicative of the prevailing market conditions, the Transgas had no fewer than five offers of gas from different suppliers, of which two were non-Russian and three were Russian gas either directly or by displacement (*Gas Matters*, April 1997:1–7). Apparently decisive in the eventual choice of the Czechs, was a political threat made by the Russian ambassador to Prague regarding the Czech application for NATO membership, and a desire for a source of gas physically separate from Russian production and delivery systems. This long struggle between Gazprom and the Czech authorities had been notable for the steadfastness with which the Czech Government had resisted the formation of a joint marketing company with Gazprom – the only major buyer of Russian gas to have taken this stand. In late 1998, the matter appeared to be settled when Gazprom and the Czech Transgas signed long-term contracts for supply and transit (*Interfax Petroleum Report*, 23–9 October 1998:17) . Gazprom established a wholly-owned company Gas-Invest in Prague, which is intended to become involved in the gas business.

In south eastern Europe, former political loyalties also began to wear thin. In 1998, Romgaz signed a contract with Ruhrgas for delivery of 0.5 bcm/year starting in the winter of 1999, with an option to increase to 2 bcm by 2005 (*GBI*, April 1998:XIV). As in the Hungarian case, this may seem to be only a symbolic diversification, but it was an important statement of future aspirations. However, it is in Bulgaria that some of Gazprom's most difficult problems have arisen. The gas sales and transit contracts signed in 1998 between the president of Gazprom and the Bulgarian deputy prime minister represented the culmination of more than a year of problems between the two sides, and did not appear to guarantee a smooth evolution of transit and trade in the future (*GBI*, May 1998:1). Political change in Bulgaria led to greatly increased sensitivity to the sovereignty issues connected with foreign – especially Russian – commercial activity in the country. This centred on two issues:

(i)   transit tariffs for Russian gas.
(ii) the role of Topenergy – originally a joint venture between Gazprom and a group of Bulgarian companies – and the extent to which that company should be allowed to market gas within Bulgaria in competition with the state-owned Bulgargaz.

In April 1998, after two years of (often bitter) negotiations, Gazprom signed sales and transit agreements for the period up to 2010 with the

Bulgarian government which involved increasing transit volumes to nearly 19 bcm (14 bcm of which are allocated to supplies for Turkey). The other part of the agreement was that Topenergy became a wholly-owned subsidiary of Gazprom, although the role that company would be allowed in transmission and sales within Bulgaria, remained unclear.[40]

In the 1990s, diversification of gas supplies in Central and Eastern European countries appeared to be as much connected with an assertion of economic independence, national sovereignty and a demonstrative break with the economic ties forged during the Communist era, as with security of gas supplies. It is uncertain whether all of the former CMEA countries – especially those in south eastern Europe – will have the same opportunities to diversify supply options. In any event, the inherited dependence of former Comecon countries on Russian gas is so great that, for the foreseeable future even for the Czech Republic and Hungary – the two countries with the greatest level of diversified imports – the objective will be less that of achieving 'independence', and more about restructuring commercial relationships in order to achieve a more politically acceptable framework of economic and energy 'interdependence'.

There is a strong case for believing that, under normal commercial circumstances, much of what is represented as real physical – as opposed to contractual – diversity of supplies may be an illusion. Increased network interconnection, combined with the ability of transmission companies to trade gas amongst themselves, means it is impossible to state with certainty that the Czech Republic is *actually* receiving gas of non-Russian origin, or that deliveries by Ruhrgas to Romania will not *in fact* be Russian gas. However, even if this should be the case, contractual diversification achieves three important goals:

(i)   an important assertion of economic (and hence political) independence.

(ii) an assurance that, should any supply problems occur with respect to Russian gas, others have a contractual commitment to deliver alternative supplies.

(iii) a negotiating lever ensuring that Russian gas remains competitive with other supplies.

For these reasons, contractual diversification is likely to continue; both MOL (Hungary) and the Polish Oil and Gas Company (PGNiG) have indicated that they wish to incorporate a significant quantity of non-Russian gas within their import portfolios.[41]

Given the strong Gazprom opposition to diversification, there must be a question as to whether better commercial deals can be struck with Gazprom by excluding other sources of supply and agreeing to sell jointly with part-Gazprom-owned marketing companies. By 1998, there were indications that both Slovakia, Poland and Bulgaria had managed to negotiate new sales contracts which included a significant degree of barter trade. In particular, the announcement of the joint Gazprom/ SPP trading house Slovrusgas, was accompanied by a government statement which appeared to suggest that all Russian gas imported into Slovakia would be paid for by a mixture of barter and transit payments involving no currency of any kind – hard or otherwise (*Gas Matters*, October 1997:6–11).

For this reason, it is uncertain whether all of Gazprom earnings from sales to Central East European countries, shown in Table 8, can be counted as 'hard currency'. Other statistical discontinuities mean that it is difficult to be completely confident about the dollar figures in the table. Nevertheless, the figures illustrate both the magnitude of Gazprom's foreign earnings, and the importance of gas in total Russian foreign currency earnings. From a corporate perspective, the comparison with oil is misleading since although hard currency earnings from oil exports are significantly greater than gas (and barter has been largely eliminated), they are diversified across a number of companies.[42] This is the reason why, although total earnings are only just over half those of oil, Gazprom as the sole gas-exporting company is Russia's largest corporate foreign currency earner.

Table 8:   Russian Hard Currency Earnings From Energy as a Percentage of Total Merchandise Exports[a]

	Oil and Oil Products		Natural Gas		Coal and Coke		Electricity		Total Energy[b]	
	$bn	%	$bn	%	$bn	%	$bn	%	$bn	%
1993	11.8	27.0	7.4	17.0					19.2	44.0
1995	14.9	22.7	9.8	14.9	negl	negl				37.6
1996	21.2	29.5	10.7	14.9	0.03	negl	0.2	0.03	32.1	44.7
1997	19.8	27.9	10.8	15.5	0.03	negl	0.2	0.02	30.7	44.2

a) These figures are for 'far abroad' exports (i.e. not including CIS countries) Because of barter trade, dollar figures (especially for natural gas exports) may be misleading.
b) 1993 figures are totals for oil and gas only

Sources: 1993 figures from *Ekonomika i Zhizn*, 16, April 1994:5; 1995–97 figures from *Vneshnyaya Torgovlya*, 1–3, 1997:65; and 1–3, 1998:65.

4.2.3 Wider Europe: The Switch from North to South – Yamal to Blue Stream
Since the break-up of the Soviet Union, Gazprom's export strategy in
Europe has been shaped by three unexpected developments:

(i)   Falling gas demand in Russia and other former Republics – a
      trend which is likely to accelerate with market-based economic
      reform and payment enforcement – has resulted in a very large
      quantity of gas available for delivery to European countries at
      relatively low marginal cost.
(ii) Difficulties in the transit relationship with Ukraine, providing
      strong incentives for diversification of export routes.
(iii) Increased competition between suppliers of gas to European
      markets has resulted in Gazprom needing to focus on short-term
      market opportunities.

From the late 1980s, it was intended that the main increase in Russian
exports to Europe in the late 1990s and the first decade of the twenty-
first century would be achieved through the building of two pipelines
from the Yamal Peninsula fields (Stern 1995:13–14). The original plan
was to build six 56 inch (1420 mm) pipelines running from the
Bovanenko/Kharasevey field complex to link with the existing northern
pipeline corridor at Ukhta (see Map 1). From Ukhta, the domestic
lines were intended to service the north west and centre of the country,
while the export lines would follow the existing Northern Lights system
through Belarus, branching at Brest into Poland and thence to
Germany (see Map 3). In 1994, Gazprom was still suggesting that
production from the Yamal fields would reach 170 bcm per year (i.e.
six pipelines). But the original plan to start production from Bovanenko
by 1997 was progressively delayed until little is now heard about either
field development or any pipelines supplying the domestic market. By
1995, Gazprom announced that six pipelines had been reduced to
three, running between the Peninsula and Torzhok, from where two
export lines will continue to Belarus and Poland, avoiding the
traditional Ukraine/Slovakia/Czech Republic route (Map 3). Since
then, attention has been fully focused on the export lines which are
said to be being built 'from the market to the fields'.

Even the first export line, which is intended to carry 29.3 bcm into
Germany, has been significantly delayed. In 1996 a pipeline connection
was established between Poland and Germany allowing small quantities
of gas to flow. But as of October 1998, sections of the line through
Belarus and Poland were still under construction with the final sections
estimated to be completed by late 2000 or early the following year; the
line may not be brought up to full compression until 2002 (Rezunenko

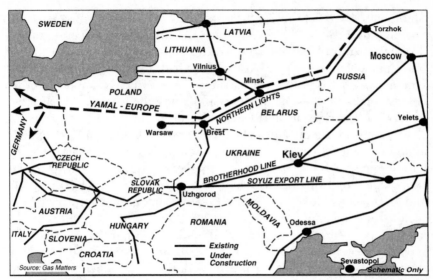

Source: Gas Matters

Map 3: Russia's Gas Export Routes

1998). There are many reasons for the long delays constructing the pipeline, of which Gazprom's shortage of capital is the most important. However, it became increasingly clear that, in the early 1990s when Gazprom were trying to sell additional gas, buyers had no requirement for long-term contract gas in such large quantities. Contracts covering much of the initial capacity of the line have been signed with Wingas (10 bcm/year), SNAM (8 bcm/year) and Gasunie (4 bcm/year but under special circumstances, see below). Nevertheless, the build-up period of these supplies is apparently very long and, anticipating the onset of gas-to-gas competition in north western Europe, may be even more protracted. The Belarussians have proved to be less than fully co-operative, with suggestions that problems similar to those experienced with Ukraine are beginning to surface even before the line is completed. For these reasons, Gazprom's urgency to complete the Belarus–Poland (Yamal) pipeline evaporated from the perspective of export expansion, but remained very real in terms of route diversification.

The other possible pipeline route diversification option for north west European countries – but at a far less advanced stage of development – is the North Transgas project – a pipeline which would run via the Nordic countries, avoiding all former republics and Central and Eastern European countries. The gas for such a project might either originate from existing Siberian fields or from the giant

Shtomanovskoye field in the Barents Sea where an international joint venture consortium has already been in existence for several years.[43] The principal problem with the North Transgas pipeline and a similar but separate project – the Nordic Gas Grid, for which the European Union has co-sponsored a feasibility study with a group of Nordic energy companies – is the distance (and hence the cost of gas delivered) to baseload markets in north western Europe.[44]

In terms of significant volumes of new exports, the company's attention switched from northern to southern Europe where Turkey had become the fastest growing gas market on the Continent. Demand is estimated to grow from less than 10 bcm in 1997 to 54 bcm by 2005 and 80 bcm by 2020.[45] With such significant growth prospects and such strong competition elsewhere on the Continent, the Turkish market has attracted a great deal of attention from aspiring gas suppliers (see Map 4). Aside from Gazprom, the Turkish company Botas has signed import contracts with Iran for pipeline gas, and Algeria and Nigeria for LNG. A number of Middle Eastern and Central

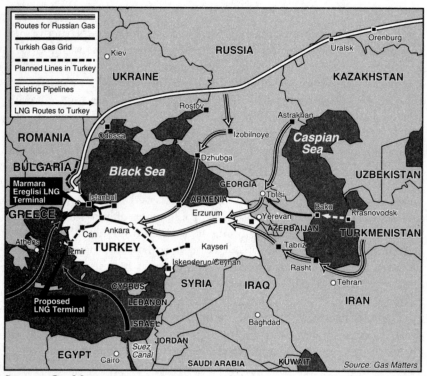

Source: Gas Matters

Map 4: Gas Pipeline Routes to Turkey

Asian gas suppliers have plans to export pipeline gas to Turkey, as do a number of LNG suppliers. Assuming that some of these new projects are credible and financeable, the Turkish market could become very competitive over the next decade. This will certainly be the case if the power generation market expands more slowly than anticipated, which is why it was very important for Gazprom to secure a large share of this market for Russian gas before other suppliers are in a position to sign contracts. The crucial step was taken in December 1997 when – in addition to the 14 bcm/year already under long-term contracts – Gazprom and Botas signed a long-term contract for 16 bcm/year commencing in 2000 through the 'Blue Stream' pipeline across the Black Sea.[46] Blue Stream will in fact comprise two lines: the first delivering 0.5 bcm in 2000 rising to 3 bcm in 2001, 6 bcm in 2002 and 8 bcm in 2003 when a second line would be commissioned.

At present, all the Russian gas delivered to Turkey passes through Romania and Bulgaria – 'the western route'. There is also a possible route to Turkey through the Caucasus countries – Georgia and Armenia (the 'eastern route'). Gazprom's increasing frustration with the demands of transit countries, and the need for a diversity of export routes, provided the principal rationale for the Blue Stream pipeline. In the autumn of 1996, Gazprom expressed a preference for the Black Sea route and since that time, problems in its relationship with Bulgaria (discussed above) have confirmed – for the company at least – the wisdom of that decision. Although the eastern route – where a capacity of up to 8 bcm/year is being created – appears *on paper* to be an alternative to Blue Stream, the distance to the major Turkish centres of demand is much greater – the border with Armenia is 900 km from Ankara. In addition, there are few market opportunities along the very mountainous route through which such a line would need to pass. Moreover, Gazprom is acutely aware of the potential for political instability in the Caucasus region.

The western route and Blue Stream will give Gazprom access to the two major centres of demand in Turkey: the western Istanbul/ Marmara region, and the central region around Ankara. The pipeline link between them will give Gazprom some flexibility of delivery and provide some security for Botas in case of problems with either route. Any gas delivered by the eastern route will presumably be consumed in that region of the country (around Erzurum and Igdir), but that is a less important and more distant prospect in Gazprom thinking. The company's strategy in relation to the Turkish market appears to be to take the baseload in both the western region and around Ankara; and eventually to take some of the eastern market. If demand in one of the regional markets does not develop as fast as anticipated, then infrastructure development can be slowed down. If it develops faster, it can be accelerated. The most important element is that with contracts having been signed, it will be very difficult for competitors to displace Russian gas as the baseload supply in the west and central regions, which are likely to be the largest, fastest growing and most lucrative markets. In early 1999, the project took a significant step forward with the announcement of a joint venture agreement between Gazprom and ENI (see below).

There is much at stake for Gazprom with respect to Blue Stream. If, like Yamal, this project falls behind schedule, then either Gazprom risks losing large parts of the Turkish market to competitors, or has to fall back on the transit relationships of the western route where (as we have seen) significant problems have been encountered in the 1990s. Given that Turkey will provide a very large proportion of the increase in Gazprom's exports over the next decade, it will be very important for the company that Blue Stream succeeds.

4.3   *Strategic Alliances and other Corporate Relationships*

4.3.1 *The Alliances: BASF, Shell, ENI, Ruhrgas and Lukoil*
Gazprom's first 'strategic alliance', although not hailed in these terms when it was formed, was the relationship with BASF which created the WIEH and Wingas joint ventures.[47] However, since 1997 Gazprom has announced a policy of creating such alliances with a limited number of companies. In October 1997, Gazprom and Shell announced that they had formed a strategic alliance aimed at developing, primarily oil reserves owned by Gazprom, but also gas projects both within and outside Russia (*Gas Matters*, November 1997:1–3). There are a number of different elements to the alliance including: oil and gas pipeline projects in southern Europe (specifically Turkey), gas swap opportunities throughout Europe, and power generation projects in Central and Eastern Europe. Shell also pledged to match a public bond offered by Gazprom which was intended to raise $1bn on international markets. (Because of unfavourable stock market conditions and the subsequent Russian financial crisis, neither the bond offering nor Shell's matching funding took place during 1998.) However, the centrepiece and initial focus of the alliance is the production of condensate in the giant Zapolyarnoye gas field in Siberia.

In February 1998, the ENI/Gazprom strategic alliance was announced. Areas for co-operation similar to those of the Shell alliance were set out, but the only specific joint development project is that the two companies will work together on developing condensate from the Astrakhan gas field in southern Russia (*Gas Matters*, March 1998:1–4).

In both cases, speculation has centred on the possible natural gas consequences of the alliances. Both have specific liquids development projects related to very large gas fields, neither of which have yet been fully developed by Gazprom. In both cases, the foreign partner has clear opportunities and incentives to finance and develop natural gas for sale in Europe. This will be particularly relevant in the ENI relationship where large-scale development of Astrakhan gas could provide a non-Siberian source of supply for the Turkish market – a move which might be welcomed by Gazprom.

The signing, in early 1999, of a memorandum of understanding to create a separate joint venture agreement for the Blue Stream pipeline with the capacity in the line divided ENI 50 per cent, 50 per cent Gazprom, will focus particular attention on possible sources of gas (*Gas Matters*, February 1999:10–12). This was a very important development, not simply because of the importance of the Blue Stream project for Gazprom (noted above), but because for the first time, Gazprom has been forced to concede capacity in an export pipeline to a joint venture partner which has apparently undertaken to arrange financing (mainly) from Italian sources guaranteed by the Italian export credit agency SACE. This throws up the interesting question as to where the joint venture partner's gas will originate. While Gazprom might prefer to simply sell additional Russian gas to ENI, the Italian company will undoubtedly wish to tie the development either to gas production from the Astrakhan field, or possibly to production from the Karachaganak field (in Kazakhstan) where its subsidiary AGIP is a joint venture partner.

Thus far the alliances have a number of elements which are indicative of Gazprom's wider strategy:

(i) The development of oil reserves. We saw in Section 2 (Table 1) that Gazprom has significant undeveloped oil reserves which could provide a major additional revenue stream for the company.

(ii) The need for technical support of projects where money has already been invested. Although Gazprom produces some crude oil, it has had considerable difficulty in developing and maximizing the value of the liquids in its gas fields. It therefore makes absolute sense for the company to bring in partners at fields where some of the general infrastructure has already been built (in support of gas production), but where specialized technology and equipment for processing of liquids is lacking.

(iii) The need to raise money. Gazprom's financial stringency is the principal factor holding back new developments. Large financially powerful international companies can provide multi-billion dollar finance, and financial and technical credibility to projects which might otherwise be unattractive to lenders.

At the end of 1998, the relationship between Gazprom and Ruhrgas appeared to be transformed into a strategic alliance by the latter's purchase of 2.5 per cent of Gazprom's equity – a figure which the German company intends to increase to 4 per cent by forming a joint venture with Gazexport (Thornhill and Corzine 1998). This constituted a major additional linkage between the two companies following their May 1998 agreement. The principal elements of this new relationship are (*Gas Matters,* June 1998:6 and September 1998:1–6; Ruhrgas Press Release, 21 December 1998):
(i)   the extension of existing contracts to 2030, but with more flexibility in delivery volumes.
(ii)   an increase in volumes (starting from 2010) of around a quarter.
(iii) Gazprom rights to transit gas through Ruhrgas network.
(iv)   an extension of technical co-operation between the companies.
(v)   further (as yet unspecified) projects

Following the announcement, it remained unclear whether the shareholding would give Ruhrgas representation on Gazprom's board, but the fact of being the largest foreign shareholder is likely to confer some degree of special treatment, particularly if the company purchases the other 2.5 per cent of government equity which will be offered for sale in 1999.

The strategic alliance announced in November 1998 between Gazprom and (the Russian oil company) Lukoil is potentially very significant and has repercussions for Gazprom's non-Russian allies (*Gas Briefing Europe,* December 1998:2). The alliance covers oil and gas, both within and outside Russia, activities spanning the entire physical chain for both fuels and beyond, including heat and power generation and equipment manufacture. Such a comprehensive agreement for companies which already have powerful foreign allies (Shell and ENI with Gazprom, Arco with Lukoil) suggests that there are strong synergies between the businesses of both companies.

The intention is that Gazprom will help Lukoil commercialize the gas which it produces; while Lukoil will give Gazprom similar help in the oil and refining sector. The specific regions and projects on which the alliance will focus are:

First, co-operation in the major Russian oil and gas production regions (Yamal-Nenets, Timan-Pechora) and the Caspian region; secondly processing and transportation of crude oil and associated gas in Timan Pechora; thirdly modernization of the Orenburg gas processing plant.

This last project is particularly interesting given that the Orenburg plant processes a limited quantity of gas from the Karachaganak field in Kazakhstan, where Lukoil took over Gazprom's 15 per cent stake in the joint venture (see above). The Lukoil connection could provide a way for Gazprom to be brought back into the project, which might also affect Gazprom's view of the gas development at Astrakhan, the centrepiece of its collaboration with ENI.

The alliance on the oil side should be complementary with what Gazprom has agreed with Shell. But it may bring Gazprom into – at least into proximity with – Lukoil's joint venture with Conoco, where additional crude oil transmission capacity is apparently needed. Nor should it be forgotten that Shell formed a consortium with Lukoil and Gazprom which exhaustively considered the purchase of, but eventually decided not to bid for, the Russian state-owned oil company Rosneft.[48]

4.3.2 Other Major Corporate Relationships

Aside from the strategic alliances, Gazprom has other corporate relationships which, while significant, are not in this category. One of the most intriguing is that signed with the Dutch company Gasunie in mid-1996. This provides for Gasunie to take deliveries from Gazprom which will start in 2001 at around 1 bcm/year and increase to 4 bcm/year thereafter (*Gas Matters*, June 1996:1–2). However, this is not intended as a simple sale and purchase agreement, but rather as a way for Gasunie to provide 'hub services' for Russian gas in the form of: transit, quality management, storage, technical support and back-up services. There is much speculation regarding the extent to which the contract protects Gasunie's Dutch market by prohibiting sales of Russian gas to other customers in the Netherlands. However, from Gazprom's perspective there are significant attractions to having the right to 'park' Russian gas in the Netherlands in the summer months, and then call upon it for delivery to customers in winter months when temperature and weather conditions make physical delivery of Russian gas more difficult and expensive.

Another much more tenuous alliance between Gazprom and its European gas supply competitors is the co-operation agreement with the Norwegian suppliers Statoil and Norsk Hydro covering exploration and technical assessment of environmental conditions in the Pechora

Sea, as well as a number of other areas in the Russian north and offshore (*International Gas Report*, 12 June 1998:15). Although little of immediate commercial significance seems likely to arise from such co-operation, it opens up a formal line of communication between the companies which is undoubtedly useful for discussing other commercial issues.

Aside from these specific alliances and corporate relationships, Gazprom has a range of other agreements and joint ventures, mainly with equipment contractors, turbine manufacturers and steel companies.[49] A co-operation agreement was signed in late 1998 with the Swedish company ABB covering a very wide range of activities in gas and gas and oil development (Almskog 1996). Most immediately, ABB will be participating in providing two compressor stations for the Polish section of the Yamal pipeline, with a view to providing similar equipment for Blue Stream. ABB is also a major global player in power generation and the development of combined-cycle gas-fired power stations. This could be a very promising area for future co-operation between the companies, both within and outside Russia.

5   Conclusions

5.1   Trade Strategy in the Soviet Era

During the Soviet era, it was difficult to discern a consistent policy or strategy relating to gas trade, partly because of the bureaucratic divide between the Ministry of the Gas Industry and the Ministry of Foreign Trade. In the 1960s and early 1970s, it appeared that the strategy was driven more by foreign policy than commercial considerations. From the late 1970s onwards, commercial considerations – principally the earning of convertible currency – became the most important priority.

Foreign policy was particularly important for the early import strategy. Both Iran and Afghanistan were considered strategically important countries where a key element of Soviet foreign policy was to curtail US influence and economic involvement to the maximum possible extent. In the case of Iran, gas imports were also intended to be serious business as considerable logistical advantages could be gained by avoiding the need to build long pipelines to take Soviet gas to the southern republics. In the 1970s, as Table 3 shows, the early development of the export trade with Europe might not have been possible without imports. However, as Iranian and Afghan governments changed and the security and reliability of both suppliers sharply deteriorated, logistical advantages were replaced by problems of security arising from regional dependence on external sources of supply. Furthermore, from a commercial standpoint, the Soviets realized that IGAT II had been a serious mistake in allowing the Iranian gas to gain a contractual foothold in the European market. In the longer term therefore, the Iranian revolution was a very welcome development for Soviet gas export strategy, as it allowed a faster development of Soviet exports, and eliminated a potentially important competitor on European gas markets.

The early motivations for exports to Comecon countries, were more political and strategic than economic. However, after the major increase in world energy prices in 1973/74, the increasing Soviet imperative to replace oil exports – which could be sold easily and highly profitably on world markets – with gas which was abundant, had a clear commercial logic. The problem was that the export potential of gas was restricted by the complexity of the necessary logistical arrangements. Nevertheless, the ensuing Orenburg (Soyuz) and Yamburg (Progress) joint co-operation projects went a long way towards establishing natural gas as a major fuel source throughout the Central and Eastern European countries. The contribution made by these countries to the development of these fields and associated pipelines, was considerable.

In the countries of 'the West', the motivation to export gas was clearly commercial, but emerged initially as a marginal extension of the pipeline network west from the Comecon countries. Those who questioned whether Soviet exports to Europe could ever be considered 'profitable', when judged by 'market economics', tended to miss the point that both the pipeline extensions, and the additional strings of pipeline necessary to create the export business, were themselves marginal when judged against the scale on which the Soviets were developing the industry. Since no country has ever (or will ever) simultaneously built six 56 inch (1420mm) pipelines in a single development, several thousand kilometres (some of which was) across permafrost terrain from a multi-trillion cubic metre field, there are few yardsticks against which to judge the commercial viability of such a project. By the time the Russians came to consider such a project again in the 1990s, it was clearly not commercially viable; but equally crucial was that demand, on that scale, no longer existed for such a huge increment of supply.

The other sense in which gas exports were marginal in the Soviet era was in comparison to the huge revenues being earned from oil exports. In aggregate terms, gas exports to hard currency Europe became significant only during the second half of the 1970s. By the beginning of the 1980s, the Urengoy pipeline signalled a major expansion of the trade, and while the Reagan administration attempted to represent this pipeline as a serious security threat, the reality was that gas trade had become serious business. This is evident from Table 9 which shows how hard currency earnings from natural gas grew from negligible proportions in the early 1970s to more than $4 billion in the 1980s. While these earnings had fallen by the time of the break-up of the Union, following the fall in oil prices after 1986, they remained substantial.

During the 1980s, as imports faded from the scene, exports to both groups of countries in Europe surged, nearly doubling during the decade. The lack of success in promoting LNG projects with both Japanese and American companies might have been of more consequence if political limitations on European deliveries had remained a serious problem. However, for as long as Cold War politics prevailed and a conservative Republican administration was in the White House, it was uncertain how much further Soviet gas could expand in, at least the NATO countries of, Europe. The political changes of 1989–91 were thus perfectly timed for the expansion of Russian gas exports.

At the break-up of the Union therefore, Gazprom inherited a physical and contractual export infrastructure delivering more than 100 bcm to thirteen European countries including:
• long-term contracts with 'west' European countries exceeding 60 bcm/year, accounting for more than 10 per cent of the Soviet Union's hard currency earnings.

Table 9:   Soviet Hard Currency Earnings From Energy as a Percentage of Total Merchandise Exports*

	Oil and Oil Products		Natural Gas		Coal and Coke		Total Energy	
	$bn	%	$bn	%	$bn	%	$bn	%
1972	0.6	19.9	negl	0.8	0.2	8.2		28.9
1975	3.2	40.5	0.2	2.7	0.4	5.0		48.2
1981	11.2	58.3	4.0	20.8	0.2	0.9		80.0
1985	10.9	53.8	4.1	20.2	0.3	1.5		75.5
1990				11.0				

* These figures are for world market exports. Because of barter trade in both the dollar figures (especially for natural gas exports) may be misleading. Dollar figures are also subject to interpretations of exchange rates during the Soviet period.

Sources: 1972–85 figures from: Jonathan P. Stern, *Soviet Oil and Gas Exports to the West,* Gower: RIIA, Energy Papers No. 21, 1987, Table 30, p. 123. 1990 figures from *Vneshnyi Ekonomicheskie Svyazi SSSR, 1990.*

- contractual relationships with former communist allies amounting to nearly 50 bcm/year.
- a highly experienced export division (Gazexport) with a substantial contractual track record.

By any standards, this was a tremendous platform from which to launch the new company.

5.2 *The post-Soviet Era*

Gazprom's export strategy became less easy to compartmentalize into country categories because of the inter-dependence characteristic of pipeline gas trade. In a situation where gas is simultaneously being sold to, and transited across, multiple countries, relationships within and between countries along the route become strongly inter-linked. It is therefore somewhat artificial to strongly differentiate between the former republics and Europe. However, this differentiation does serve to emphasize the importance of the former republics for Gazprom's export strategy, and this is the reason why it is necessary to devote considerable space to this subject. Without the maintenance of stable relationships with the former republics, neither Gazprom nor its European customers can be confident about continuity and expansion of gas trade.

5.2.1 *The Former Republics*
In the post-Soviet era, there have been two basic sets of problems:
(i) non-payment by buyers in the Ukraine, Belarus and Moldova; all of which are important for the transit of gas to European customers which cannot therefore be summarily cut back or cut off when they do not pay their bills.
(ii) aspirations of Central Asian sellers, principally Turkmenistan (but also Kazakhstan), to sell gas to European customers using transit through Gazprom's pipeline network, while refusing to supply gas to former Soviet customers who do not pay their bills.

Underlying the problems of gas trade with the former republics have been the general foreign policy and security relationships between Russia and these new sovereign states. This has meant that gas negotiations are invariably conducted at presidential or prime ministerial level and include many factors other than gas. As far as sales and transit to Ukraine, Belarus and Moldova are concerned, the commercial problems of non-payment and late payment remain unresolved, but a framework is being developed within which they can be contained. For Belarus and Moldova this framework includes substantial Gazprom equity stakes in the gas industries of those countries. Such ownership does not resolve the non-payment problem, but it allows Gazprom greater oversight and control of gas flows. For Ukraine, where Gazprom's principal transit vulnerability lies, the company has been denied ownership in the gas industry, but appears to have won acceptance of two principles: that escalating gas debt cannot be tolerated and that diversion of supplies in transit to Europe is unacceptable. In all these countries, the payment problems are very similar to what Gazprom faces in its domestic market and await resolution at a political level; specifically substantial progress towards the enforcement of prompt payment of cost-based prices. Until the payment situation is regularized, the problem of managing inter-dependence with these countries will remain especially difficult, However, Gazprom has become more adept at this task as the post-Soviet era has progressed. While periodic debt crises are to be expected in the future, transit crises should be avoided unless they are a symptom of wider political problems.

In Central Asia, Gazprom's strategy in the immediate post-Soviet (as in the Soviet) period had been to use Turkmen (and possibly also Kazakh and Uzbek) gas to satisfy Ukrainian (and other former Soviet) demand in order to alleviate the burden of non-payment, and reduce the costs which would have been involved in accelerating the development of Siberian supply. In return for using its gas in this way, Gazprom rewarded Turkmenistan by giving it a hard currency quota for a 'notional' export of gas to Europe. The *quid pro quo* was very clear to Gazprom: in order to obtain access to hard currency, Turkmenistan was required to deliver agreed volumes of gas to Ukraine and endure the same payment problems associated with those deliveries which Gazprom was suffering.

When Turkmenistan refused to share the burden of supplying non-paying former republics, Gazprom first cancelled the hard currency payment arrangements and then attempted to move the relationship to an entirely different basis using a trading company to barter goods in exchange for gas. But in the post-Soviet era, developments both within Russia and in European gas markets significantly reduced the value of Central Asian gas to Gazprom. The fall in gas demand, both within Russia and the former republics, meant that Gazprom had excess supply and began to 'shut in' production capacity in Siberia.[50] Central Asian gas was therefore no longer essential, or even a substantially less expensive option, for supplying the needs of the Ukraine and others.

Externally, growing competition in Europe meant that Gazprom was increasingly concerned to protect the markets for Russian gas, and eliminate any suggestion that Central Asian gas should be transported through its system to compete in European markets. In this respect Gazprom's post-Soviet attitude to Central Asian gas has parallels with the (aborted) Soviet displacement contracts for Iranian gas in the 1970s: initially attractive because of logistical advantages, displacement agreements which allow competitors to gain a foothold in European markets using Russian pipelines, make little commercial sense. For most of 1997 and the whole of 1998, no Turkmen gas was supplied through Russian pipelines to other CIS countries. In early 1999, deliveries recommenced on a different basis with the trading company Itera handling both sales and transit contracts, eliminating any direct commercial involvement by Gazprom. It is too early to say whether this new approach will be successful.

5.2.2 Europe

Diversification of routes and security of supply: The credibility of Gazprom as a secure supplier is heavily dependent on a combination of the successful management of the Ukrainian relationship, and the creation of alternative export pipeline corridors to European markets. Gazprom's response has been to plan a diversification of routes avoiding the Ukraine:

(i)   north – through Belarus and Poland – the Yamal pipeline.
(ii) further north still – Finland, Sweden and the Baltic Sea – the North Transgas and/or Nordic Gas Grid pipelines.
(iii) south – across the Black Sea to Turkey. The routes to Turkey have also been complicated by transit problems with Bulgaria – where Gazprom has been facing a combination of political instability and greatly increased political sensitivity to Russian ownership of transmission pipelines. This has confirmed the company's determination to pursue the 'Blue Stream' pipeline across the Black Sea.

Aside from diversification of routes, Gazprom has both investments and contractual relationships which enhance security of supply and give its customers additional confidence that, in the event of a disruption, it could draw upon alternative supplies:

• at least 4 bcm/year will be available from 2001 by virtue of its contractual relationship with Gasunie.
• the Wingas joint venture has not only its own storage at Rehden in Germany but has contracted to use additional storage in Slovakia.

- Wingas has purchased gas from British producers to be delivered through the Interconnector pipeline; these supplies could be increased using the capacity which Gazprom owns by virtue of its equity in the Interconnector.

Competition and Financial Stringency: As the 1990s progressed, chronic non-payment problems and a preponderance of barter trade in the Russian and former Soviet markets, focused Gazprom even more strongly on European customers in order to raise revenues. However, this coincided with the beginning of gas-to-gas competition in European markets. In northern Europe, Gazprom felt this most keenly with the announcement of the Netra pipeline bringing Norwegian gas to the eastern part of Germany in competition with Russian gas. Former political allies of the Soviet Union in central and eastern Europe – taken for granted as a captive market in communist times – began to look to other suppliers as a combination of increased purchasing power and a desire for supply diversification, met increased keenness to sell on the part of (principally) North Sea producers. The 1997 Norwegian contract with Czech TransGas was a landmark in this process. Following that contract, there have been strong indications that other countries – notably Slovakia and Poland, but also Bulgaria – were using the threat of supply diversification to extract more favourable terms from Gazprom, with a (partial) return to the barter trade deals of the Communist era.

For Gazprom this is part of the emerging reality of an increasingly competitive European gas market, a development already accepted as inevitable by the top management of Gazprom (see Chairman Rem Vyakhirev's speech to 1997 World Gas Conference in *Gas Matters*, June 1997:1–5.) This may account for the increasing emphasis on supply to south European markets, particularly Turkey, and the beginnings of interest in developing pipeline connections with markets in East Asia. In both of those regions, competition is (arguably) not well-advanced and – even allowing for the 1997–98 Asian financial crisis – demand growth is projected to be rapid, providing a strong contrast to Gazprom's traditional European markets.

However, with Gazprom's established supply and transmission capacity the company should be in an excellent position to take advantage of market opportunities. In Europe, Gazprom's established marketing companies and trading houses throughout Europe should give the company an excellent platform to take a much more pro-active and aggressive role in maintaining and expanding the market share for Russian gas throughout the Continent. In this respect, Gazprom is well ahead of its supply competitors in European gas markets.

The principal problem which the company faced in 1998 was unprecedented financial stringency caused, in large part, by economic crisis and political instability within Russia. The company projected that it would make a loss of $2–3 billion in 1998 (*International Gas Report*, 11 December 1998:9). The combination of these problems has meant that during the post-Soviet era it has become increasingly difficult for the company to raise the finance it needs by traditional means.[51] This has severely affected export development as Gazprom's Norwegian and British competitors built pipelines which have taken market share ahead of the Yamal pipeline, which should have been completed around 1996–97, but has been delayed until 2000–01. To avoid similar market pre-emption in Turkey, it will be essential that the Blue Stream line stays on (or close to) its planned schedule.

Strategic Priorities and Strategic Allies: During 1998, the combination of Russian economic crisis and a 15–20 per cent fall in European gas export prices gave rise to a rethink in Gazprom's strategic priorities. With limited funds available, and little scope to raise money on international markets, Chairman Vyakhirev announced a cut of two-thirds of the company's investment programme which would be refocused on five important priorities (see Vyakhirev 1998):

- exploration and production in new fields
- modernization of equipment at existing fields
- refurbishment of the transmission system
- completing the construction of the Yamal–Europe pipeline
- construction of the Blue Stream pipeline to Turkey

It is difficult to see that financial stringency will soon disappear, and for that reason there must be doubts about the company's ability to complete even these priority tasks satisfactorily. They are likely to be regularly re-examined to discover ways of achieving them at least cost. The immediate consequences for export policy will be to defer and delay any substantial new investment which is not immediately required, and which will not yield short-term returns. In concrete terms this means that foreign projects other than Yamal–Europe and Blue Stream can continue to be discussed, but there is not likely to be any funding available for them until the company's (and probably the country's) financial situation improves. This puts into context the likely time frame of Gazprom's other export projects such as North Transgas and Barents Sea (Shtokmanovskoye), as well as recently expressed ambitions for exports to east Asia (China, Korea and Japan). For the next several years, it will be virtually impossible for the company to embark on any significant export project – existing or new – without near-total funding from external sources. To the extent that such projects may require several billion dollars of new greenfield investment, as in east Asia, they may be particularly difficult to develop.

It may be that gas development in Asia will crystallize the distinction between Gazprom's strategy, and the strategy and capabilities of other possible Russian gas suppliers. With no Gazprom involvement thus far in the established export projects, Sakhalin, Irkutsk (Kovykhta) and Sakha, this is an opportunity for other Russian energy companies to establish themselves with foreign partners. It remains to be seen whether they will be able to take this opportunity, or whether as these projects move towards reality, Gazprom will 'inevitably' become involved.

Because of financial stringency and difficulties in borrowing additional funds, the role of foreign investors and strategic alliances with foreign partners has taken centre stage during 1997 and 1998, because these companies can contribute finance to Gazprom's projects directly. The Shell and ENI alliances are principally aimed at development of liquids rather than gas; although the latter is certainly not excluded within the framework of the agreements. In early 1999, the signing of a memorandum of understanding for the Blue Stream joint venture indicated that ENI will make a major contribution to the organization and financing of the pipeline in return for 50 per cent of its capacity. In the early 1990s, Gazprom faced a choice between allowing foreign ownership, and hence a degree of control, of the Yamal (Belarus–Poland) export pipeline, and delaying construction. It chose the latter and may have missed market opportunities as a result. This has been an important learning experience and if Gazprom finally allows a foreign company to purchase equity in an export pipeline, this will be a major step forward in the company's alliance strategy.

How Gazprom's current alliances will play out in the future is uncertain. To some extent this uncertainty is a general comment on the nature of alliances and joint ventures between companies which cannot see how their business interests may or may not coincide in the future. But in this case there is also a fundamental dilemma for Gazprom as to whether these company are allies, or competitors. At one level, there are obvious projects for collaboration; at another, companies such as Shell and ENI clearly have interests in a range of European companies and are sponsors of projects which may be in direct competition with Gazprom's export sales. Ruhrgas is in a different category and, as by far the largest foreign shareholder in Gazprom, it will be interesting to see how the companies co-operate within, and beyond, Germany.

The extent to which these major foreign alliances – and major corporate relationships which have been announced with other foreign companies – prosper or wither, will depend on whether the benefits to both sides are sufficiently substantial that the differences can be resolved. Major differences are likely to arise for two reasons. Firstly, foreign partners will probably be reluctant to contribute multi-billion dollar finance in a climate of low prices and great uncertainty. Secondly, there will be reluctance on the part of Gazprom to allow foreign partners into its core business, both in terms of owning production capacity and capacity in pipelines. To the extent that the existing alliances fail to make the progress anticipated by the partners, Gazprom can be expected to continue to seek relationships with foreign companies – particularly those with multi-billion dollar finance to contribute to projects. To the extent that the company's foreign relationships do not make satisfactory progress, then alliances with Russian companies, such as Lukoil, may have a greater immediate impact on Gazprom's business.

5.3   Gazprom in the Twenty-first Century: Monopoly, Liberalization or Demerger?[52]

Gazprom's organizational future is strongly bound up with the presidents and governments which are likely to rule Russia over the next decade and their policies towards economic reform and industrial organization. Clearly a president and government strongly committed to market-based economic reform and liberalization would be a greater threat to Gazprom's current organizational structure than a political elite happy to preside over more centralized management of the economy. Yet no simplistic parallels should be drawn between economic philosophy and the ability and willingness of a government to change industrial organizations, particularly when foreign and private shareholdings are involved. Personal connections between the president, government ministers and Gazprom will continue to be important, although the bond between the company and its former president Victor Chernomyrdin, when he assumed the post of prime minister, is unlikely to be repeated.

Both the IMF and the World Bank have been influential thus far in the restructuring and liberalization of Russian industry (including the gas sector). The strong preference and recommendation of both agencies is for the break-up or 'demerger' of vertically integrated utilities into multiple companies competing through a regulated pipeline network or networks. During 1998, as the Russian government became increasingly beholden financially to the IMF, (real or imagined) calls for the break-up of Gazprom were heard again, and rejected by the government (Thornhill 1998). Given the degree of economic sovereignty which would be involved in any such decision and the degree of resistance which it would meet – both politically and within the company itself – it is unlikely that a future Russian government would agree to any external demand to break up Gazprom, unless it had already decided upon this course of action. In early 1999, in what may be a reaction to IMF pressure, a Bill was being debated in the Duma which would maintain the high pressure transmission system as an indivisible network, and ensure that the state would retain a share of at least 25 per cent plus one share in that network (*Interfax Petroleum Report*, 15–21 January 1999:7–9).

However, even if demerger is unlikely to be a short-term development, this does not mean that the company's structure, functions and relationships with government will remain static. Government financial pressures on the company will remain considerable. The financial crisis of 1998 has shown how important Gazprom is to government finances and the country's financial stability. At a time of uncertainty and instability, it would seem impossible to change the structure of a company which is providing 25 per cent of all taxes collected (as opposed to all taxes owed), and 15 per cent of foreign exchange earnings. In such a situation, it is very difficult to oppose the continued existence of a centralized, vertically integrated Gazprom.

By contrast, looking forward to a time of economic reform and prosperity in Russia and the other countries of the former Soviet Union, where the majority of gas customers pay their bills in full and promptly (and do not continue to receive gas if they do not), Gazprom's position could be entirely different. Gazprom's earnings would be truly gigantic and the company's current image of economic saviour might, in the eyes of politicians, be transformed into that of an unmanageable political and financial entity. In such circumstances, the political attraction of retaining the company as a single vertically integrated unit would diminish. Thus in a Russia where economic reform had taken place, or was at least seriously under way, government pressure for Gazprom to be demerged into smaller entities would probably intensify. This would be due less to any likely government conversion to a philosophy of competition and liberalization, and more to the increasing threat which successive Russian politicians will perceive arising from the financial and political power of Gazprom.

5.3.1 Production and Transmission

The reform programme laid out in Section 2 was always overly ambitious, but by 1999 progress had been made towards the creation of corporatized production and transmission units trading by means of transfer prices. Transmission companies appeared to have transferred their sales functions to the newly-created marketing division Mezhregiongaz (MRG). Transmission tariffs, if only as internal financial transfers, must therefore have been devised and implemented, a development which constitutes a major step towards restructuring and liberalization.

However, if taken to the extreme of demerger, the political, financial and institutional complexities of further restructuring should not be minimized. Production is highly concentrated, both geographically and corporately (in the hands of three production associations) in Siberia. A structure of demerged production companies selling their gas through an open access transmission system (controlled either by a single company or multiple companies) would place significant power and wealth in the hands of three new companies in the Yamal–Nenets region of Siberia. This transfer of economic power to the regions may not be attractive to Moscow politicians.

Moreover the prospect of structural change only adds to the climate of uncertainty for further privatization of the company, and in particular the sale of shares to foreign investors. Sufficient uncertainty already exists in Russia, without adding the prospect of the company being broken up and thereby losing both the advantages of vertical integration, and de facto monopoly of production and transmission. Investors may baulk at handing over billions of dollars to government or to the company itself, without assurances about the future structure of the company.

Privatization aside, until the problem of non-payment and non-cash payment by Russian customers is resolved, or at least reduced to manageable proportions, the effect of demerger could be to plunge many of the newly-created production and/or transmission companies into immediate bankruptcy. When non-payment and barter problems have been resolved – or at least substantially reduced – demerger would become a viable option. Competition and liberalization will be accelerated due to the reduction in gas demand within Russia, arising from bankruptcy and the start of conservation and efficiency measures which will greatly inflate the existing 'bubble' of excess supply. This would provide ideal conditions for competition between producers, and potentially between transmission companies with unused capacity, competing for business. On the other hand, given the geographical concentration noted above, the potential for collusion between existing producers may be equal to, or greater than, the potential for competition.

If Russian politicians should decide against a step as drastic as demerger, they would still have the option to ease the path of gas producers and resource-holders other than Gazprom, to sell their gas in competition with the dominant player. Oil producers with associated gas already account for some 35 bcm/year; not a large quantity of gas compared with Gazprom's production, but far from negligible. Moreover, as noted in Section 2, Gazprom owns the rights to only 70 per cent of Russian reserves, leaving substantial gas resources in other hands. Some of the most interesting commercial prospects may be in smaller fields located closer to centres of demand. Nevertheless, there will be a problem of persuading investors to open up new fields at a time of surplus supply and low prices, when their only opportunity to commercialize their resource will be via the transmission system owned by the dominant player. It is this prospect which could lead back to considerations of demerger.

5.3.2 *Exports: Structures and Strategies*
The demerger of Gazprom's production and transmission units would hugely complicate existing export contracts with European companies. All of the current long-term contracts are held by Gazprom (with Gazexport being the negotiating partner), and stretch out over the next two decades. In terms of revenue earnings, these are the crown jewels of Gazprom's current assets currently earning around $8 billion per year, a figure the company expects to increase to $15.5bn by 2005 (*Interfax Petroleum Report*, 5–11 June 1998). The demerger of Gazprom would cause immense difficulties in terms of which entity would continue to hold the contracts. If a residual Gazprom company still existed after the production and transmission assets had been demerged into different companies, there would be no guarantee that the entity would have the financial means to purchase sufficient gas from production companies for the management of 150–200 bcm/year of long-term contract gas. If there was no residual Gazprom company, the existing long-term contracts would presumably be allocated between the successor production companies. Such an allocation might amount to a complete renegotiation of contracts for around one-third of European gas demand – a highly destabilizing prospect for European markets.

Given opportunities and incentives, Russian and foreign companies might be prepared to open up smaller gas fields, and perhaps revisit older fields (where recovery could be increased with more advanced technology). Development of fields west of the Urals which would involve relatively low transmission costs to markets, would have obvious commercial advantages. By this means, competition between suppliers, for consumers in Russia and beyond, could develop. This would also give a major opportunity to Central Asian gas producers – freed from the embrace of a vertically integrated Gazprom – to negotiate directly with a range of customers, Russian and non-Russian, with their gas being delivered by a transmission-only successor company (or companies).

If Gazprom were to be demerged into production and transmission units, a proliferation of exporters will certainly develop consisting of: former Gazprom production companies (and also transmission companies if this were to be allowed by the government and regulators), oil companies and a variety of other industrial conglomerates, including foreign energy companies. Even if there is no demerger and Gazprom remains in roughly its present form, it would be unrealistic to expect that other gas producers will not attempt to export gas using the company's pipelines. The 1999 contract between Turkmenistan and Ukraine with transportation being arranged by Itera might be seen as the beginning of such developments. In the future it is likely that Gazprom will face increased competition at home, as well as abroad.

Anticipating future strategy in a situation of multiple Russian gas exporters is an overly ambitious task at the present time. But it does underline the increasing need to differentiate between Gazprom's export strategy and the strategy of others which may enter this business. This leads back to re-emphasizing the perverse profitability of Russian gas deliveries to different markets, a situation which has remained constant since the Soviet era. Instead of customers nearest to the centres of production being the most profitable, the opposite is the case: Russian customers yield the smallest returns and European customers, several thousand kilometres further away, the greatest. In the late 1990s, with European gas prices falling and likely to remain at historically low levels for an extended period, the attraction of these markets will be reduced for Gazprom and other potential Russian exporters.[53] By contrast, any improvement in the payment situation in Russia and the CIS countries could dramatically improve the commercial attractiveness of these customers.

Entering the twenty-first century, as long as any market-type economic reform within Russia (and CIS countries) is anticipated, these markets will become more valuable and export markets less valuable. In such a situation, the commercial assumptions which have underlain export strategy during the 1968–98 period, and have led to ever greater expansion of exports to foreign countries may no longer be applicable. In the late 1990s, and arguably for at least the first five years of the next century, Russian gas deliverability will remain surplus to the needs of markets, both domestic and foreign. But as that situation changes and significant new upstream investments are required, economic viability calculations may appear completely different to a new generation of Russian gas executives, and the commercial logic of increasing exports to European gas markets may become increasingly questionable.

Notes

1.. For an authoritative account of Gazprom's creation see Kryukov and Moe 1996: Parts II and III.
2. Decrees 538, 539 and 1333, Ibid
3. Ownership at 31 December 1997, *Interfax Petroleum Report*, 31 July–6 August 1998:11.
4. At that time, the two positions were combined in the person of Boris Nemtsov. During the tenure of the Kiriyenko government (until August 1998) he retained his position of Deputy Prime Minister with overall responsibility for the energy sector, with Sergei Generalov as Energy Minister.
5. *RAO Gazprom, IAS Consolidated Financial Statement*, 31 December 1996.
6. Ibid., 1997. Current figures can be found on the Gazprom website: www.gazprom.ru.
7. Reuters, 2 July 1998 reported Deputy Prime Minister Boris Nemtsov as saying that the government owed Gazprom R13bn while Gazprom owed the government R12bn. In October 1998 with the appointment of a new tax chief by the Primakov government, it was announced that Gazprom had overpaid 1.5bn rubles to the government. *Interfax Petroleum Report*, 16–22 October 1998:13.
8. The tax will be 5% of customs value but not less than 2 Euros/tonne, *Interfax Petroleum Report*, 29 January–4 February 1999:3–4.
9. All volume figures in this chapter are expressed in Russian billion cubic metres (bcm) measured at 20 degrees centigrade. To be converted to standard cubic metres, figures must be reduced by 7%.
10. For more details on the Gazprom reorganization see Moe and Kryukov (1997).
11. In old rubles, Russian sales amounted to 51,112bn while European sales earned 47,359bn. *Gazprom IAS Consolidated Financial Statement*, 1997.
12. One of the classic Soviet texts is Orudzhev 1976.
13. Bovanenkovskoye, Kharasoveiskoye, and Kruzenshternovskoye. These are

the fields which are eventually intended to form the supply source for the Yamal pipeline.

14. For the early history of Soviet pipeline development, see: Orudzhev (1976:43–68). For later history see Seligman (1999).

15. See Wilson, *Soviet and East European Energy Databook*, op.cit.

16. The huge expansion of gas-fired generation was not in fact originally intended by the planners. It was forced upon them because of the imperative to free up oil for export, and the relative failure of the coal and nuclear industries to develop as fast as had been expected.

17. Gazprom's official leakage rate is in the range of 1–2 % of throughput (not dissimilar to other countries with similar aged networks). However, this only includes the high pressure network and does not include gas which may be vented at the wellhead, or associated gas flared during the course of oil production. The low pressure networks, which are not under Gazprom's control, probably have much higher leakage rates, but lack of metering means that accurate data are unavailable.

18. These were the members in Europe and hence the countries of interest here. There were also non-European members such as Mongolia and Cuba.

19. For details of the Bratstvo pipeline see Stern 1980:58–61, Chabrelie 1993:.7.

20. A chronology of imports from Comecon countries can be found in Peebles 1980:169–72; Ebel 1970:138, Table 48 shows exports to Poland during the period 1950–68.

21. The energy relationships – including payment relationships – between the Soviet Union and Comecon were immensely complex and have been roughly generalized here; see Park 1979:Ch. 6.

22. More commercial details of the Progress pipeline can be found in *Eastern Bloc Energy*, August 1988:4; physical details can be found in Chabrelie 1993:16–18.

23. The details of the Austrian contract can be found in Ebel 1970:135–7; for a detailed explanation of the 1962 pipe embargo see Jentleson 1986:113–18.

24. The early energy, gas and equipment trading relationships between the major European countries and the Soviet Union can be found in Stent 1982.

25. For a contemporary account see Stern 1982. The best account of the equipment embargo and its repercussions is in Jentleson 1986:Ch.6.

26. Ebel 1970:151 has a map of three pipeline proposals for Sakhalin exports to Japan dating from the late 1960s, which mirrors the options being considered in the mid to late 1990s.

27. For the background to the East Asian gas projects, see Keun-Wook Paik 1995:Ch.7. A useful update on specific projects can be found in Keun-Wook Paik and Jae-Yong Choi 1998.

28. For example in the trades between Turkmenistan, Kazakhstan and Uzbekistan; and between Turkmenistan, Azerbaidzhan, Georgia and Armenia.

29. Ukrainian interruptions are worthy of separate study in themselves, but an analysis of the problems in the first few showed that: first, these episodes have not involved a *complete* interruption of deliveries to Europe, but rather a *reduction* of deliveries which (in one case) have reached 50% of one importer's supplies. Second, these reductions can be measured in terms of days; only one episode appears to have exceeded a week. Third, there has always been ample warning of these reductions, allowing importers to make other arrangements. Stern 1995:60–61.

30. Under the 1998 agreement, the Ukraine received 52 bcm of gas priced at $50 per thousand cubic metres ($/mcm); a considerable price reduction from the 1997 price of $80/mcm. This was achieved by means of a similar reduction in the transit tariffs charged by Ukrgazprom from $1.75/mcm per 100 km to $1.01–1.09/mcm/100km. In practice this means that around 30 bcm out of the 52 bcm of total deliveries was received in respect of transit (the actual figure will depend on the volume of gas actually transited to Europe), and the remaining 22 bcm would be priced at $50/mcm. Gazprom and Ukraine finally agreed to trade 52 bcm this year. *Gas Matters*, January 1998:12–13; *GBI*, March 98:IV; June 1998:IV. The agreement held during 1998 and although debts increased to $1 billion by the end of the year, this did not prevent the signing of a 1999 supply and transit agreement. *Gas Briefing Europe*, December 1998:13.

31. *Energy Transit: the multilateral challenge*, Energy Charter Secretariat: Brussels, 1998.

32. This was agreed in 1993 and confirmed when Beltransgaz was converted into a joint stock company in 1996. However, as far as can be ascertained the measure has still not been approved by the Belarussian parliament. *Interfax Petroleum Report*, 30 March 1998.

33. The quota reached a high of 15.6 bcm in 1991 (although the high point of deliveries to former republics was reached the previous year at 78.7 bcm). Miyamoto 1997:46–7.

34. Turkmenrosgaz was also intended to carry out exploration and pipeline construction although no details of any projects were ever made public. This was one of the reasons given by the Turkmen Government for the winding up of the company

35. It is important to be clear about dates because in 1996, Poland, Hungary and the Czech Republic became OECD members.

36. For more details on the development of the German gas industry after reunification, see Stern 1998:139–55.

37. It is worth pointing out that, although this has been included in the post-Soviet era, in fact the relationship was forged more than a year before the break-up of the Union. Whether the joint venture would have prospered to the same extent if the Union had remained intact, can only be guessed.

38. WIEH was the original seller of gas to VNG in the eastern part of Germany, but otherwise came to act as a marketing company outside of the country. Wingas is the joint venture which both owns and builds pipelines, and which markets gas, in the western part of Germany.

39. In late 1998, at the official rapprochement between the companies, Chairman Vyakhirev summarized the whole Wingas/Ruhrgas episode as follows: 'The establishment of Wingas is attributable to the fact that our plans for participating in shaping the German market did not initially have any positive results. There are probably deeper roots to the matter. Somebody did not want Ruhrgas and Gazprom to stay together. I do not want to burrow in this dirty linen. After all that happened before I became head of Gazprom.'
     This suggests that the continuing rift between the companies was strongly associated with Viktor Chernomyrdin and it may not have been a coincidence that the healing of the rift was achieved when he had been replaced as prime minister. *Gas Matters*, September 1998:1–6.
40. The unresolved issue remains whether Topenergy is free to sell to customers within Bulgaria, or whether it must sell to Bulgargas. *GBI*, May 1998:1.
41. The Polish Oil and Gas Company is said to have been in negotiation with both Gasunie and Statoil (GFU) for a total of 6 bcm per year. *GBI*, March 1997:4; *International Gas Report*, 2 October 1998:20.
42. In 1997, thirteen Russian companies exported crude oil plus a large number of joint ventures. Wilson 1998:34, Table 136.
43. The foreign partners are: Conoco, Neste, Norsk Hydro and Total. *Gas Matters*, October 1995:XV.
44. North Transgas Oy is a joint venture between Gazprom and Neste. Three routes to northern Germany are under consideration: Finland and Sweden, Finland and then offshore, from St Petersburg offshore all the way. *European Gas Markets*, 14 September 1998:6–7; *Nordic Gas Grid: an overall feasibility study of the possibilities to integrate and develop the natural gas markets in the Nordic and Baltic countries*, TEN Program of the European Community, October 1998.
45. Demand estimates from the Turkish company Botas, *Gas Matters*, May 1998:1–8.
46. Ibid, The Blue Stream pipeline system will be 1213km in length running from Izobilnoye, north of Stavropol in Russia's North Caucasus region across the Black Sea to Ankara. It will be supplied with Siberian gas and will use the storage facility at Stavropol for back-up supplies.
47. Aside from the gas marketing joint ventures discussed above, there are other projects such as: the ethylene and polyethylene plant to be located near the gas fields at Novyy Urengoy in Siberia; gas flow control equipment; computer hardware and software. BASF has also arranged finance for the Yamal pipeline. Ibid, July 1993:12–14; *GBI*, February 1996:8.
48. The Rosneft privatization could come back on the agenda, at which point the possibility of purchasing the company's assets in the Sakhalin 1 joint venture could be of serious interest to all three companies. *GBI*, April 1998:7.
49. As of October 1994, the list included a number of companies from six countries. *International Gas Report*, October 1994:13–17. This does not include specific joint ventures such as the 'Northgas' JV with the American company Farco.

50. These issues are dealt with at much greater length in the author's previous work (Stern 1995).
51. Details of Gazprom's share issues and international borrowings can be found in the company's 1997 Annual Report, parts of which are available on the company website: www.gazprom.ru
52. Some of the ideas in the remainder of this section were first expressed in Stern 1998:161–4.
53. Reasons for expecting European price levels to remain low are contained in the author's work, Stern 1998.

References

Almskog, K. (1998), speech at the Royal Institute of International Conference, *Natural Gas: Trade and Investment Opportunities in Russia and the CIS*, Moscow, 6–7 October.

Campbell, R.W. (1967), *The Economics of Soviet Oil and Gas*, Resources for the Future/Johns Hopkins.

Chabrelie, M.F. (1993), *European Natural Gas Trade by Pipelines*, Paris: Cedigaz.

Eastern Bloc Research, various issues.

Ebel, R.E., (1970), *Communist Trade in Oil and Gas*, Praeger Publishers.

Energy Transit: The Multilateral Challenge, Brussels: Energy Charter Secretariat.

European Gas Markets, various issues.

Fadeev, B.T. (1998), 'Deliveries of Gas to CIS Countries and the Baltic States', paper given to RIIA Conference, Moscow, 6–7 October.

Gas Briefing Europe, various issues.

Gas Briefing International (GBI), various issues.

Gas Matters, various issues.

Gazprom (1997, 1996), *IAS Consolidated Financial Statement*.

Hannigan, J.B. (1980), *The Orenburg Natural Gas Project and Fuels-Energy Balances in Eastern Europe*, Ottawa: Carleton University, East-West Commercial Relations, Research Report No. 13.

Interfax Petroleum Report, various issues.

International Energy Agency (1984), *Energy Policies and Programmes of the IEA Countries, 1983 Review*, Paris: OECD.

International Gas Report (various issues).

Jentleson, B. (1986), *Pipeline Politics*, Cornell University Press..

Kosnik, J.T. (1975), *Natural Gas Imports from the Soviet Union: Financing the North Star Joint Venture Project*, Praeger.

Kryukov, V. (1997), 'Gazprom – Financial Flows and Management: The Need for Internal Transparency', in proceedings of the Conference, *Reform in the Russian Gas Industry: Regulation, Taxation, Foreign Investment and New Export Prospects*, London: RIIA.

Kryukov, V. and A.. Moe (1996), *Gazprom: Internal Structure, Management Principles and Financial Flows*, London: RIIA.

Miyamoto, A. (1997), *Natural Gas in Central Asia: Industries, Markets and Export Options of Kazakhstan, Turkmenistan and Uzbekistan*, London: RIIA.

Moe, A. (1997), 'The Reorganisation of Gazprom: Scope and Impact' in proceedings of the Conference, *Reform in the Russian Gas Industry: Regulation, Taxation, Foreign Investment and New Export Prospects*, London: RIIA.

Nordic Gas Grid: an overall feasibility study of the possibilities to integrate and develop the natural gas markets in the Nordic and Baltic countries (October 1998), TEN Program of the European Community.

Orudzhev, S.A. (1976), *Gazovaya Promyshlennost' po Puti Progressa*, Moscow.

Paik, Keun-Wook (1995), *Gas and Oil in North East Asia: policies, projects and prospects*, London: RIIA.

Paik, Keun-Wook and Jae-Yong Choi (1998), *Pipeline Gas in Northeast Asia: Recent Developments and Regional Perspective*, London: RIIA, Energy and Environmental Programme Briefing Paper No. 39.

Park, D. (1979), *Oil and Gas in Comecon Countries*, Kogan Page.

Peebles, M.W.H. (1980), *Evolution of the Gas Industry*, Basingstoke: Macmillan.

Petroleum Press Service, various issues.

Rezunenko, V.I. (1998), 'The Yamal-Europe Project', a paper to the Royal Institute of International Affairs Conference, *Natural Gas: Trade and Investment Opportunities in Russia and the CIS*, Moscow, 6–7 October.

Seligman, B. (1999), 'Key factors influencing the reliability of trunk gas pipelines in the West Siberian North', Unpublished PhD Thesis, Scott Polar Research Institute, Cambridge.

Stent, A.E. (1982), *Soviet Energy and Western Europe*, Praeger: the Washington Papers, No 90.

Stern, J. (1998), *Competition and Liberalisation in European Gas Markets: A Diversity of Models*, London: RIIA.

— (1995), *The Russian Gas Bubble: Consequences for European Gas Markets*, London: RIIA.

— (1987), *Soviet Oil and Gas Exports to the West*, Gower: RIIA.

— (1982), 'Specters and Pipe Dreams', *Foreign Policy*, Fall: 21–36.

— (1980), *Soviet Natural Gas Development to 1990*, Lexington Books.

Thornhill, J. (1998), 'Nemtsov rejects Gazprom break-up', *Financial Times*, 27–28 June.

Thornhill, J. and R. Corzine, (1998), 'Ruhrgas boldly goes where other groups fear to tread', *Financial Times*, 23 December.

Vyakhirev, R. (1998), 'Gazprom's Strategic Priorities in the Context of the Development of the Russian and Global Economy', a paper presented at the Royal Institute of International Affairs Conference, *Natural Gas Trade and Investment Opportunities in Russia and the CIS*, Moscow, 6–7 October.

— (1996), address to the Conference, *Natural Gas Trade and Investment Opportunities in Russia and the CIS*, London: RIIA.

Wilson, D.C. *Soviet and East European Energy Databook*, various years.

CHAPTER 5

NORWEGIAN GAS: THE STRUGGLE BETWEEN GOVERNMENT CONTROL AND MARKET DEVELOPMENTS

Ulrich Bartsch

1.   Introduction

In 1962, a representative of Phillips Petroleum walked into the Ministry of Industry in Oslo and expressed interest in an exploration licence for the Norwegian North Sea. At this time, Norway did not have the legal framework for issuing such a licence. Nor was there much belief in the potential of the North Sea. A pessimistic Norwegian geologist at the time promised to drink all the oil which would ever be produced from the Norwegian continental shelf (NCS). History proved him thoroughly wrong, and Norway is now the second largest oil exporter in the world.

This chapter covers the history of hydrocarbon extraction in Norway, and the strategic position the country has taken up to prepare for the future in a changing European gas market. The central thesis is that Norway will defend the current institutional framework with centralized, government-controlled gas marketing against attacks from free-trade advocates and competition authorities, and the liberalizing market environment in Europe. The rationale is that a strong centralized structure is needed as a tool for resource management. The benefits derived from integrated resource management are seen to outweigh any possible costs in terms of a lack of market orientation and flexibility, as long as existing contracts continue to be honoured. In fact, the institutional structure might well be able to cope with an onslaught of a large number of small-volume buyers. Recent signs of increasing flexibility in contractual terms for Norwegian gas are cited in support of this argument. Losses which might arise from a fractionation of the gas market and a break-down of take-or-pay contracts are nevertheless seen as potentially very damaging, and Norway therefore resists regulatory change in Europe.

The chapter is divided into five parts: first a general overview of discoveries and reserves. It is shown that oil will be more important than gas in terms of revenues for Norway well into the next century, although the reserve base is shifting in favour of gas. Second, the history of sales negotiations, the development of the institutional framework, and the pipeline infrastructure to the UK and the European mainland. We shall show how gas sales went from depletion contracts to volume contracts when the giant Troll field was discovered, which guarantees sales while smaller fields are brought on stream.

The institutional framework grew gradually into the current centralized system, where all gas sales are negotiated by the Gas Sales Committee (Gassforhandlingsvutvalget, GFU), which consists of representatives of the three Norwegian companies Statoil, Norsk Hydro, and Saga. Likewise, a flexible, massive pipeline system was built over the last twenty years, the biggest off-shore system in the world. Gas is delivered through one pipeline to the UK, two lines to Emden in Germany, one to Zeebrugge in Belgium, and the most recent, a pipeline opened in October 1998 to France. Sections 2 and 3 of this chapter give the reader a complete overview of the status quo of the Norwegian hydrocarbon industry and gas exports.

The next three sections provide more of an intuitive understanding of motivations which led to the developments described before. Section 4 includes a discussion of Norwegian attitudes to the petroleum industry, and the cultural and socio-economic background necessary to understand the formation of petroleum policies. It is argued that central control over petroleum activities is of the highest importance for the Norwegian public, in order to achieve the best possible resource depletion results as seen for society as a whole. In Section 5, an account of the history of the national oil company, Statoil, is given. It is shown that the company has become increasingly independent over the years, leaving the shackles of the role of revenue collector for the state, and becoming more like any other international petroleum company. Critics see a danger in this independence because of a perceived lack of effective control and discipline imposed on other companies through the stock exchange. The last section discusses the changing marketing strategies of the past, and looks into the medium-term future.

2.   Discoveries and Reserves

2.1   *The Discovery of a New Oil and Gas Province*

Some months after the first request for an exploration licence on the Norwegian Continental Shelf, work started to put the legal framework in place so as to enable the issuing of such a licence. A Royal Resolution in May 1963 claimed sovereign rights for Norway over exploration and development of natural deposits to feasible depths, although not beyond the median line in relation to other nations. This followed international maritime agreements from 1958, according to which the 'continental shelf' refers to the seabed and subsoil of the submarine areas adjacent to the coast but outside the areas of the territorial sea. Norway then concluded agreements on the delimitation of the continental shelf south of Lat. 62° North with Britain and Denmark in 1965, and with Sweden in 1968. All of these agreements were based on the median line principle.

Ironically, an investigation of the sea bed between Norway and the UK might easily have led to a different solution, which would have given virtually all the wealth of the North Sea hydrocarbon reserves to the UK. Not far off the Norwegian coast the sea bed subsides to depths between 300 and more than 700 metres in the Norwegian Trench, which could have been regarded as the end of the NCS, especially since technology at the time did not permit development of resources beyond a depth of about 200 metres. Subsequently, all the Norwegian hydrocarbon discoveries were made to the west of the Norwegian Trench, a lot of them straddling the median line, and hence would have been in UK waters.

Phillips as the first company interested in Norway, applied in 1962 for exclusive rights to all of the NCS, in line with the concession agreements in other oil regions at the time – a request which was rejected by the Norwegians. Instead, the first licensing round was held in 1965, in which all the Norwegian off-shore areas south of 62° North were announced. After receiving eleven applications, the government awarded 22 production licences comprising 78 blocks. This was the most comprehensive licensing round in Norway (Ministry of Petroleum and Energy 1998:45). The foreign companies then starting work in Norway included Amoco, Elf, Esso, Phillips, Shell and Total. On the Norwegian side, only Norsk Hydro was in a position to take part. The two other Norwegian companies, Statoil and Saga founded in 1972, were not in existence at the time of the first licensing round but later acquired an interest in the Ekofisk licence.

The first well was drilled in 1965, the same year in which the licensing round was held. Initial results were disappointing, and some American companies had started pulling out of the NCS when Phillips announced the discovery of the Ekofisk field in 1969. With recoverable reserves then estimated at 140 million tons of oil and 130 billion cubic metres of gas, Norway suddenly was in the spotlight of the international petroleum industry, and the country had to come to terms with the implications of being a petroleum producer. Ekofisk original recoverable reserves are now estimated at more than 500 million tons oil equivalent, of which about 40 per cent remain.

The second licensing round was held in 1969, which was only aimed at providing supplementary blocks to production licences already awarded. The first major discovery of unassociated gas in the Frigg field followed from the second round in 1971. The field straddles the median line between Norway and the UK with about 110 billion cubic metres of recoverable gas on the Norwegian side. In the third round, 32 blocks were awarded, in which the state participated for the first time with a 50 per cent interest.

Three years after the discovery of the Frigg field, Statfjord was found. It is one of the largest oil fields of the North Sea, and has a geology which allowed rapid exploitation, and yields a high recovery factor of more than 60 per cent. In the autumn of 1979, Shell's exploration well in block 31/2 found gas, the first indication of the giant Troll field, which is now estimated to contain around 1300 billion cubic metres of gas. Already at the beginning of October 1979, Arve Johnsen, the Managing Director of Statoil, pointed out that the find 'could be Norway's Groningen' (Johnsen 1990:88).[1] We will see later how this judgement proved to be true in more than one sense.

2.2   *The Oil Bonanza, But Even More Gas*

Total discovered and undiscovered resources in Norwegian waters are currently estimated at between 10 and 17 billion cubic metres of oil equivalent (bcm oe). At the end of 1997, total remaining reserves, i.e. recoverable hydrocarbons in existing developed fields, are put at 1.7 bcm oil, and around 1000 bcm of gas, which adds up to a total of 3 bcm of oil equivalent. Remaining discovered resources, i.e. reserves plus resources in discovered but undeveloped fields are estimated at 2.5 bcm oe of oil, and 3000 bcm of gas (see Table 1) (Ministry of Petroleum and Energy 1998:23). This shows that Norway's resource base is strongly shifting from oil to gas. Oil production has reached 3.1 million barrels per day estimated for 1998, or 230 million cubic metres,

Table 1:   Remaining Discovered Resources and Reserves

	Oil mill. m³	Gas bill. m³	NGLs mill. ton	Oil Equiv. mill. m³
The North Sea				
Remaining Discovered	1963	2337	113	4447
Of Which Reserves	1289	969	70	2350
The Norwegian Sea				
Remaining Discovered	545	615	99	1289
Of Which Reserves	445	204	24	680
The Barents Sea				
Remaining Discovered	18	168	6	194
Of Which Reserves	0	0	0	0
Total				
Remaining Discovered	2526	3120	219	5930
Of Which Reserves	1735	1173	94	3031

Source: Norwegian Petroleum Directorate

whereas gas production stood at 25 bcm throughout most of the 1980s and early 1990s, but is increasing fast to a plateau of 100 bcm in 2005, with exports slated to account for 75 bcm. In that year, gas production will constitute 30 per cent of total hydrocarbon production, increased from the current 19 per cent. Current commitments in gas sales contracts require this plateau to be held until at least 2015 (Ibid.:27).

Oil production is forecast to peak early next century and then decline, but oil equivalent gas production will not overtake oil before about 2013. On a net revenue basis, Norway will therefore remain an oil nation rather than a gas nation for a considerable time to come. It should be noted that on a net revenue basis, the dominance of oil is likely to remain for a longer time than on an energy content basis, because of the high investment and production costs for gas as compared with oil. This reinforces the assessment that Norway is an oil nation, and will therefore for the foreseeable future prioritize oil over gas production.

As shown in Tables 2 and 3, Oseberg is the highest producer among the fields on the NCS, with about 400 thousand barrels per day, followed by Gulfaks, and Ekofisk, which after twenty years still produces more than 300 thousand barrels of oil per day. Table 3 shows the dominance of Troll in the gas reserves figures, with more than 500 bcm certified reserves. Troll produced almost half of all gas produced in 1997, and Ekofisk is the second largest producer. Note that among

Table 2:   Major Oil Fields

| | Remaining reserves at end 1997 | | | Production 1998 |
| | Oil | Gas | NGLs | Oil |
	mill. m^3	bill. m^3	mill. ton	bl/d
Ekofisk	171	47	6	323,000
Troll II	162	65	-	257,000
Heidrun	128	13	-	236,000
Snorre	116	3	2	190,000
Oseberg	103	16	6	403,000
Gullfaks	90	9	1	344,000
Statfjord	88	18	5	293,000
Draugen	81	-	-	190,000
Norne	72	-	-	132,000
Valhall	66	17	2	93,000
Eldfisk	49	27	2	N/A
Others	233	743	43	691,000
Total	1,359	957	67	3,152,000

Source: Norwegian Petroleum Directorate

Table 3:   Major Gas Fields

| | Remaining reserves at end 1997 | | | Production 1998 |
| | Oil | Gas | NGLs | Gas |
	mill. m^3	bill. m^3	mill. ton	bill. m^3
Troll I	15	563	-	20.6*
Sleipner West	-	128	27	1
Troll II*	162	65	-	-
Ekofisk*	171	47	6	8
Eldfisk*	49	27	2	N/A
Statfjord*	88	18	5	2
Sleipner East	-	13	11	7
Others	874	97	16	28
Total	1,359	957	67	46

* Predominantly oil fields

Source: Norwegian Petroleum Directorate

the seven major gas fields shown in Table 3, five are associated gas fields, among them Troll II.[2]

In the 1998 National Budget total wealth in the petroleum sector is estimated as the net present value of future cash flow, using a discount rate of 7 per cent. It is estimated at 2100 billion Norwegian kroner (NOK) and the state's share of this is billed at NOK 1900 billion, or roughly 90 per cent of the total (Ministry of Petroleum and Energy 1998:17). This is probably why the Norwegian fiscal regime is regarded by international oil companies as one of the toughest in the world. The high figure for the state's share reflects the tough fiscal regime operating in Norway, as well as the high direct participation of the state and participation through the national oil company Statoil.

3.   Becoming a Major Gas Supplier

Until the middle of the 1980s, petroleum activities in Norway were concerned with oil fields, with gas seen more as a by-product, valuable but not exciting as compared with oil. Still today, oil has priority over gas because of the higher profitability. 'Sell more gas, find more oil' was a phrase coined by then Minister of Petroleum and Energy Arne Øien in the 1980s, expressing the Norwegian attitude towards the two hydrocarbons. At that time the gas reserves were seen as ample, whereas the precious oil was seen as running out in the near future. Of course, the importance of gas exports has increased dramatically over the years, and the perception of this importance likewise.

Recently, a certain shift in emphasis has begun to emerge, captured by Bengt Lie Hansen, Director of Norsk Hydro, as 'find more gas'. Apart from selling available non-associated gas, in the 1980s Norway was concerned with creating outlets for associated gas in order to be able to produce oil. The flexibility to produce associated gas was achieved with the Troll/Sleipner Gas Agreements, which included the right-of-way for associated gas from other fields. In contrast to that, it now seems that existing sales contracts stretch gas production capacity to the limit, because more and more gas is needed for injection in oil fields for Enhanced Oil Recovery projects (*Norsk Olje Revy* no.3 1998:8). In fact, the build-up of gas production from Troll and Oseberg lately has been reduced in order to safeguard liquids production from these fields. Gas has gained a much more prominent role as a means to produce more oil, as well as in its own right.

This section presents an overview of the history of Norwegian gas marketing and gas negotiations, and the development of the institutional framework regulating gas sales. Firstly, it is shown that the history of gas sales negotiations distinguishes earlier field depletion contracts from the volume contracts since the Troll negotiations in 1986. The section shows the tremendous importance of Troll in bringing about a major shift in marketing strategy, because of the size of reserves and the possibility of using Troll as a swing producer to bring smaller, more risky fields and associated gas from oil fields into production. Secondly, the development of the institutional framework for gas sales in Norway is presented. The current system is seen as essential by the Norwegian authorities in order to integrate oil and gas depletion policies from a resource management standpoint.

3.1   The History of Gas Sales

3.1.1 Caught between a Cartel on the Continent and Protectionist Britain

Until 1985 with the negotiations for gas from Troll and other fields, Norway sold gas on the basis of field depletion contracts, as opposed to contracts specifying a certain volume per year over a number of years. Depletion contracts merely stipulate that all the gas produced from a specified field over its production lifetime will be delivered to a buyer. The buyer therefore carries part of the geological risk coming from the uncertainty of actual production volumes and depletion time. With volume contracts as opposed to field depletion contracts, this risk is entirely carried by the seller, who guarantees certain yearly deliveries, usually over contract periods of 10 to 25 years. It is the seller's responsibility to find the necessary reserves to supply the contracted volume. This responsibility is usually only taken on when a succession of fields are available for development with large reserves relative to contracted production, or as in the case of the Netherlands and later Norway, when one giant field can act as swing producer to back up volumes from smaller fields.

The first major discovery in Norway, the Ekofisk field, is an oil field with associated gas. Sales negotiations were held between Phillips representing the sellers, and the British Gas Corporation on one side, and a consortium of continental European buyers on the other side. The continental consortium brought together the most important continental gas companies: Ruhrgas, BEB, and Thyssengas from Germany, Gasunie from the Netherlands, Gaz de France, and Distrigaz from Belgium. The negotiations were held under the leadership of Ruhrgas, and export contracts were later signed on a bilateral basis between all the sellers and buyers.

In the Ekofisk negotiations, the continental buyers offered better conditions for Norwegian gas, and the first gas pipeline was built to Emden in 1977, while the oil was initially loaded on tankers from the platform in the field, and later piped to the British Teesside terminal. Geographical diversification might have played a part in the decision to send gas to the continent. British Gas at the time tried to ensure the availability of Norwegian gas for their own market, but half way through the negotiations realized that the Frigg field offered substantial reserves and could probably be obtained at a better price. Ekofisk therefore lost in attractiveness. Also, the company was not accustomed to buy gas at a price linked to competing energy, and was not prepared to concede to Norwegian demands.

When the Frigg field was discovered, the next major look at gas marketing from Norway became necessary. Complications arose from the fact that Frigg lies on the median line between the UK and Norwegian parts of the North Sea, and a consulting firm was charged with working out a division of the resources, which took about two years.[3] The resulting division gave Norway about 60 per cent of the resources. Complex negotiations about landing pipelines then followed. In the end, two parallel gas pipelines were built, one to transport British gas, one for Norwegian gas. Similar to the Ekofisk oil pipeline, and all subsequent Norwegian pipelines, it was agreed without much delay that Norway should have jurisdiction over the line for Norwegian gas right up to the metering point in St. Fergus, an issue which became the major stumbling block two decades later when negotiations started for an extension of the original Frigg treaty.

The next step in Norwegian marketing of gas was the sales of Statfjord gas. Statfjord is one of the biggest oil fields in the North Sea, although Oseberg, Gullfaks, and the Ekofisk area are currently producing at higher rates. Oil production was to start in 1979, and associated gas could initially be reinjected. From the mid-1980s however, gas had to be produced as it would have otherwise compromised oil production. Sales agreements had to be signed during 1980/81. The transport of the gas became the crucial question.

Already in 1976 the Norwegian Storting (Parliament) had started thinking about a Norwegian gas gathering system and transporting Statfjord gas first to the Norwegian mainland, and then to the continent. The landing of oil and gas in Norway had been an objective laid down in the Royal Resolution of 1963, which started the exploitation of petroleum resources. But it proved technically infeasible until the end of the 1970s, when pipeline technology had advanced sufficiently to make a crossing of the Norwegian Trench possible. A project group consisting of members from the Ministry of Petroleum and Energy, the Petroleum Directorate, and oil companies was created in 1977. The group concluded that unless further gas was found on the NCS, the system would not be profitable. But in May 1980, after rejecting proposals by Phillips to build a transport line, or to include

Statfjord gas in the British gas gathering system, the idea came up that Heimdal gas could be included, which would make a landing of gas in Norway and transport to the continent via Ekofisk and Emden profitable.

The Heimdal field development had been postponed indefinitely in 1976 when reserves had been adjusted downward to the point where development was not seen as profitable. A little earlier, sales negotiations had been nearly concluded with British Gas Corporation for the reserves in the field. Inclusion in a transport solution for Statfjord changed the outlook for Heimdal significantly. In addition, in late 1980 appraisal work on the Gullfaks field had progressed sufficiently, and it became clear that also the associated gas from Gullfaks could be included in the Statfjord pipeline system. Another small field, Ula, was included when it was realized that the buyers, BP and the German Gelsenberg, could not circumvent the continental buyers consortium, of which more will be said in section 6. The idea of combining centrally the transportation of gas from several fields, which would not have been profitable on their own, was put into practice.

From January 1980 sales negotiations were conducted both with British Gas Corporation and the continental buyers consortium, which had bought Ekofisk gas before. Statfjord straddles the median line, like Frigg. The relations between Statoil's leadership and British Gas were not at their best at the time, as Arve Johnsen's account of the negotiations clearly shows. For example, he reports that after the first meeting with BG in January 1980, he set a date and time for BGC to hand in a bid for the Statfjord gas. Donald F. Cooper of BGC felt this was not an appropriate treatment of the biggest gas company in Europe, and had the British ambassador intervene with the Ministry of Oil in Oslo (Johnsen 1990:131). A year later, BGC was given another opportunity to buy Heimdal gas before a final decision was made to include it in the Statfjord pipeline. James Allcock, then chief negotiator for BGC, went to Stavanger on 17 January 1981 and submitted his offer. Arve Johnsen recounts that it was not competitive, and Allcock was so informed by the Statoil leadership, and was given a 'one hour break to call London for possible new instructions. He did not receive these, and that was that' (Ibid.:142).

These two anecdotes show a certain lack of goodwill between Statoil (i.e. Arve Johnsen) and BGC. The British price most probably was competitive with the continental offer. But not surprisingly the British were not willing to pay an additional premium in order to compete against the strategic opportunities seen by Statoil in the integrated transport solution to the continent. The gas was sold to the consortium, and Statoil boasted that it received the highest price ever for gas imports to Europe. However, before any gas was sold the oil price collapse in 1986 allowed the buyers to declare *force majeure* and trigger the price renegotiation procedure. Critics allege that nobody ever believed the Statfjord contract would be implemented, but that it was merely a way to convince investors and the government of the viability of the Statfjord pipeline.

The marketing of Sleipner gas, starting in the same year in which Statfjord was signed, did nothing to improve Norwegian relations with the UK. Sleipner came on the selling block in the winter of 1982/83. There are actually two fields, which are geologically separate, Sleipner West and East. Sleipner West is polluted by large quantities of CO_2, and therefore has to be blended with other gas to achieve a useable mix. The UK was thought to be the obvious market for the gas. Negotiations with BGC were concluded in January 1984, but the contract never received approval from the British authorities.

After the contract was presented to the Department of Energy in London, contacts were made between the two Ministers of Energy, Peter Walker and Kåre Kristiansen. In April, it was indicated that the volumes should be reduced by 20 per cent, to give greater room for an expected expansion of UK gas production. Britain also wanted assurances that British suppliers would be awarded a certain part of construction contracts, and that gas liquids would be landed through a pipeline on the British Orkney Isles. In principle, the UK government had no say in the matter, and the Norwegians pointed out that any changes in the already negotiated contract would have to be agreed between BGC and Statoil based on commercial principles, and could not be determined politically. The two companies sat down over the summer, but soon it became clear that a commercial basis for the liquids transport could not be found. Kåre Kristiansen was given the last word, and after another meeting with Peter Walker it was announced in February 1985 that the British government 'said thanks, but no thanks, to imports of Sleipner gas' (Johnsen 1990:228).

It emerged later that two British oil companies, BP and Shell, had lobbied the government to phase out imports from Norway, in order to boost indigenous British production (Ibid.:226). Allegedly, when the Norwegian authorities were looking for the culprits, Shell escaped the wrath of the Norwegians, whereas BP did not: BP had better contacts in the British Department of Energy, and tried to convince them that imports from Norway were not in the best interest of the UK. Shell on the other hand went to the Treasury to achieve its goal. BP did not consider, however, that the Department of Energy keeps good contacts with the Norwegian Ministry of Oil and Energy, which was subsequently informed. The British Treasury in contrast has little contact with the Norwegians. In the next licensing round therefore BP was punished with a meagre award of areas, whereas Shell was left unaffected.[4]

In the spring of 1991 the Norwegians signed a contract over 2 bcm per year of gas to be delivered to National Power in the UK. Another contract was signed with Scottish Power, and Statoil and Norsk Hydro also planned to participate in the construction of a gas-fired power station in Scotland, which would have used the gas. Further, deliveries of 5–7 bcm per year were under negotiation with British Gas, to be delivered from Sleipner West, Visund, or the Midgard field in the Haltenbanken area (*Euroil*, March/April 1991:13). However, the Scottish Power contract was never finalized, and it was cancelled in 1994, after negotiations had stalled a year earlier, and the National Power contract was simply rolled over every year, a consequence of the British insistence on renegotiation of the Frigg treaty. This happened despite the strategic alliance between Statoil and BP set up in 1990, which should have taken care of at least part of the lobbying problem discussed above. So if Sleipner West was indeed the field to have supplied the Scottish Power volumes, the UK authorities actually rejected it twice.[5]

The rejections of the Sleipner and Scottish Power contracts were instances where a European government intervened to the detriment of the Norwegian commercial position (more are presented in Section 6). The two cases above involving the UK are all the more significant because the intervening government showed a strong commitment to free market principles, at least domestically, and is one of the driving forces of European gas liberalization. The Norwegian negotiators might be forgiven some cynicism regarding liberalization considering Norway's experience even as late as the 1990s.

Incidentally, the Norwegians could of course have taken the British government to court for not allowing commercial imports. But quite obviously they did not want to open a Pandora's box by initiating an investigation by the European competition directorate (DG IV) into gas selling practices, which might have led to unwanted interest in the Norwegian system as well. This investigation nevertheless came later, when Marathon filed a complaint against the GFU.

3.1.2 *The Frigg Treaty*

Some years later towards the end of the 1980s imports from Norway were on the agenda again. But Peter Morrison, Minister of Oil at the time, was still negative, and surprisingly frank about the protectionist motives of a government otherwise strongly committed to free market principles: 'We would have to look at it in terms of the development of the North Sea. If there was possible damage to the further development of the North Sea, because the companies felt we weren't going to buy their gas, we would have to look at it very closely' (*Noroil*, August 1989:30) The vehicle to be used to 'look at it' was the treaty covering the Frigg pipeline, as Colin Moynihan stated two years later: 'We will consider a new treaty related to a possible new sales contract on the basis of the concrete contents of the treaty... No British government can ignore the resource situation on the UK shelf when such a treaty is to be considered' (*Norsk Olje Revy*, March 1991).

The UK insisted on a renegotiation of the Frigg treaty, which in their view covered only deliveries of Frigg gas. The Norwegians did not see the need for a renegotiation. The treaty was drawn up in connection with the depletion contract covering the Frigg field, but two other fields were allowed to use the line, Lille Frigg in 1993, and Froy in 1995. It was therefore thought that the original treaty already covered fields outside the area and remained valid until declared void by the governments.

The major sticking point in the negotiations which followed was the legal status of the Norwegian line: the Norwegians, as an old shipping nation, insisted on following the flagstate principle, according to which the regulation and general jurisdiction over a ship is held by the country where it is registered. Norway therefore claimed jurisdiction over the complete Frigg line until it reaches the terminal in St. Fergus in Scotland, whereas the British negotiators argued that they should have jurisdiction over fixed installations on their part of the continental shelf beginning at the median line between the UK and Norway.

The UK side defended the hard stance on the grounds that the UK needed control over the line once it came to the point of abandonment, but in addition wanted to make sure that they had a say over the use of the line for UK gas. The Norwegians accused Britain of using the jurisdiction issue merely as a way of obstructing Norwegian imports with a protectionist motivation. Negotiations petered out during 1993, because both sides kept close to their original positions – the Norwegians did not see the use of offering a compromise, given their belief that the renegotiation was merely the vehicle to keep their gas out of the UK, and any compromise therefore would be followed by new obstacles.

Lately, negotiations have been taken up again, and a breakthrough was achieved towards the end of 1997, in which the UK obtained major concessions from the Norwegians: they explicitly concede jurisdiction over the Norwegian pipeline in the twelve miles of UK territorial waters, but taxes and tariffs remain in the hands of the relevant government at the pipe inlet. More significantly, the new treaty opens the way for regulated third-party access. In Article 16 of the new treaty, the two governments pledge to assist companies wishing to use spare capacity in the pipeline for their gas. It is agreed that any applicant for capacity use who fails to obtain a fair offer from the pipeline company can approach the relevant government to 'request access' and the principles are spelled out that are to be applied during consultations between the two governments regarding the application.

The provision which could well be regarded as a bombshell in the history of Norwegian gas exports follows in paragraph 7: if after consultations the relevant government is convinced that an applicant has not received a fair offer for pipeline capacity, it can impose access at 'terms and conditions as it may specify'. Moreover, the two governments also agree to adhere to international arbitration in case they cannot find an agreement in the consultation period.

This means the UK government can impose access to the Norwegian line, if a company wishes to transport gas from the UK continental shelf and excess transport capacity exists. It would be an arduous process of consultations and arbitration, but in the end Norway would have to give in. It is hard to imagine exactly what would cause Norway to try to refuse access to anybody willing to fulfil the basic conditions for the use of the line. But it is a fundamental departure from the Norwegian understanding of control over their assets. The Norwegians have retained jurisdiction over the line on the UK side of the median line, but the UK has obtained a say over the transport of UK gas through the line. It is a Norwegian victory in principle, and a British in economically relevant terms.

As such, the new Frigg treaty obviously has no impact on the other Norwegian pipelines, but it sets a precedent which will not be missed by EU regulators. The arrival of regulated third-party access to the Norwegian off-shore pipelines could alter Norwegian gas selling practices beyond recognition.

Ironically, at the end of 1998 the UK government imposed a moratorium on the construction of new gas-fired power stations, which again would put a hold on the planned Anglo-Norwegian power station which was to be the customer of Norwegian gas imports. 'It is the Frigg treaty problems in a different disguise all over again', exclaimed one Statoil official mockingly, although it is of course understood that the British gas moratorium has more to do with the domestic coal mining lobby than with Norwegian gas.

The renegotiation of the Frigg treaty was responsible for a delay of almost a decade for Norwegian imports into the UK. It brought UK operators breathing space to develop the UKCS, while it cost the Norwegians millions in revenues. It might be true that the UK would not have allowed new imports anyway disregarding any concessions offered, as suspected in Norway, and the breakthrough only became possible when the Interconnector pipeline between the UK and Belgium was in place. On the whole, the UK might be accused that they have not handled well their relations with the nearest, stable source of vital gas supplies in the twenty-first century.

3.1.3 The Troll Field and Resource Management

The Troll discovery was a major turning point for Norwegian gas marketing. It became apparent almost immediately that the size and geological properties of the field were very similar to the Groningen field, and that it therefore could easily play the same role in Norway as Groningen in the Dutch production system. Essentially, as it was put by a Statoil official, Troll could be seen as a huge gas tank with a valve on top. This makes it possible to open the valve and produce gas literally at any quantity needed, or close the valve and let other fields fulfil contract commitments. In other words, Troll could act as swing producer to guarantee gas deliveries, while smaller fields with higher geological risks could be depleted.

Later this simple picture became somewhat more complicated when production technology progressed to the point where the thin oil layer in the reservoir could be produced. This layer, at places only six metres thick, could be produced with horizontally drilled wells, and Troll ceased to be a pure gas field. This means that gas production again is subjected to oil production, substantially limiting the swing role of Troll. According to latest plans, Troll will not build up to its full 36.5 bcm export capacity until 2006, to maintain pressure and also because significant volumes of gas are needed for reinjection in the Oseberg field through the Troll Oseberg Gas injection (TOGI) scheme (*European Gas Markets*, 12 June 1998:1).

Troll is situated at a water depth of 350 metres, which meant frontier technology had to be employed and investment cost estimates were huge. For years, Statoil officials toured conferences with estimates of minimum gas prices of $5 per million Btu needed to make the investment in Troll profitable. The rejection of deliveries from the Sleipner field to the UK then inadvertently came to the aid of the Troll project: tying in Sleipner, which could be developed much more quickly, meant that the infrastructure for gas production from Troll could be built in stages, with initial deliveries and revenue flows from Sleipner. With hindsight, Statoil officials regard the repeated rejection of Norwegian gas by the UK as the best that could have happened to Norway, although the rejection of Sleipner was seen as a major calamity at the time.

Until the early 1980s, Norway saw herself in a sellers' market for gas. Demand for Norwegian gas from European gas companies eager to diversify away from Russian gas was always higher than the availability of fields for development. This ended abruptly with the huge jump in reserves brought about by the Troll find, and other factors: ample supply of gas was available in Europe, the contracts with the UK about further gas deliveries were cancelled, oil prices collapsed in 1986. The Norwegian attitude to gas sales changed dramatically: while earlier on Norway would sit back and wait for buyers willing to pay attractive prices for Norwegian gas, the emergence of a buyers' market meant that a more active role was needed to increase Norwegian volumes.

Negotiations for Troll gas started in early 1985, when Statoil became aware of problems with the UK over the sales of Sleipner gas. It was felt that a rejection of Sleipner gas by the UK would unduly weaken the Norwegian negotiating position, and some progress should have been made before this happened. From the very beginning, the Ministry of Oil and Energy in Oslo made it clear that the Troll contracts would be volume contracts, which would leave the Norwegians to decide freely which fields to develop to deliver the gas. In the event, the buyers were less happy with what was for Norway a new concept, and insisted on a specified share of 75 per cent of the total volume to be delivered from Troll.

In the middle of the negotiations, a rare strike on the Norwegian platforms incapacitated the NCS for two weeks in early 1986, which one official described as the most expensive strike in the history of Norway, and which has not been repeated since.[6] For the first time, buyers were put in doubt over the security of supplies from Norwegian fields, one of the major selling points for the gas for years. Statoil reacted swiftly by offering the creation of a gas storage facility in Emden, the landing point of the gas on the continent, capable of ensuring deliveries over a period of two weeks. The Etzel storage facility is now owned 75 per cent by Ruhrgas.

The first Troll contracts were ready for signature on 30 May 1986, but the buyers insisted that the signing should only follow a renegotiation of the pricing of the Statfjord/Gullfaks/Heimdal contracts. The Statfjord contracts were built on a very high base price, but with a generous hardship clause which made it relatively easy for the buyers to demand re-opening of price negotiations. In fact, as mentioned before, observers accused the Statoil negotiator of scoring a public relations victory with the announcement of the high gas prices achieved when the Statfjord contracts were signed, while knowing that these would never stand the test of time.

With the huge Troll contracts ready for signature and all buyers and sellers assembled in Stavanger, the sudden demands for re-opening of the Statfjord contracts put huge pressure on Norwegian negotiators. Arve Johnsen representing Norway was holed up with Ruhrgas Director Klaus Liesen for two hours and finally agreed to a significantly lowered base price, Troll was signed and the two emerged to the popping of Champagne corks (Johnsen 1990:265). This renegotiation by Statoil was undertaken without prior authorization from the licence committee for the Statfjord, Heimdal, and Gullfaks fields, and Arve Johnsen actually made it clear during the talks that he could offer the new price only for Statoil's share of the gas, whereas the others would have to agree separately. Only Marathon Oil and Conoco did not agree to the new terms. Marathon was dissatisfied with Johnsen's handling of the affair to the extent that they took Statoil to court, alleging that the negotiator had reneged on his duty to defend the licence holders' interests. Marathon lost the case at the Stavanger court in 1997.

Renegotiations of the gas price affected only the licence holders, whereas transport tariffs in the Statpipe system remained unchanged. It should be noted that Statoil has a share of 50 per cent in the Statfjord licence, but a much smaller share in the other fields delivering gas into the Statpipe system. On the other hand, it owns 58.25 per cent of the Statpipe system, with no direct state involvement. Observers see this episode as an example of the principal-agent problems between Statoil and the Norwegian state: Statoil maximizes its own interests, and the Statfjord renegotiations are seen as a redistribution of revenues from the licence holders, especially the state, to the pipeline with a much higher Statoil share. Marathon Oil has also filed a complaint with the European Surveillance Agency, the competition watchdog of EFTA, where it alleges that the Norwegian government gives hidden subsidies to Statoil by allowing the company to overcharge the users of the Statpipe system, and another complaint with the EU competition directorate about price fixing by the European buyers.[7]

The Troll contracts were signed in May 1986. In the biggest commercial contract ever seen in Norway, with an estimated total value of more than $60 billion in 1986, Ruhrgas, Thyssengas and BEB together pledged to take 8 bcm per year (with a distribution between the three of 55 per cent, 30 per cent, and 15 per cent, respectively), Gaz de France 6 bcm, Gasunie 2 bcm, and Distrigaz 2 bcm per year.

Table 4:   The Troll Contracts in 1986

	bcm/year
Germany	8.3
France	6
Netherlands	2
Belgium	2
Austria	1

Source: *Petroleum Economist*, January 1987:12.

Later, additional contracts were signed with Austria's OMV, Enagas in Spain, and SNAM in Italy. In selling directly to the Austrian market, Norway tried for the first time to challenge the position of Ruhrgas as major gas company in north-western Europe. Ruhrgas rejected the idea of becoming a mere gas transporter on behalf of another owner, and Norway finally had to give in, which meant Ruhrgas bought the gas from the GFU on the northern German border, and resold it to the Norwegians on the Austrian border. With the sales agreements with Enagas in Spain and SNAM in Italy, Norway encroached for the first time on the southern European market, until then the eminent domain of Algeria. The total extent of Norwegian contracts is hard to gauge, as this information is considered a commercial secret in Norway. Nevertheless, we have collected an indication of existing commitments (shown in Table 5).

3.2   Building a Powerful Sales Organization

The stated aim of Norwegian gas selling policy is to achieve the best possible overall result. This is presented conclusively in a report by the Ministry of Oil and Energy to the Storting in 1986: gas should be sold at acceptable prices, producing the highest possible revenues, and gas should be transported at the lowest cost to the overall economy; a high gas sales volume is not an aim on its own; the level of co-ordination needed to achieve this goal calls for the centralization of Norwegian gas export efforts; centralized marketing of Norwegian gas is also needed because of the high concentration and co-ordination of buyers'

Table 5: Norwegian Gas Export Contracts

Company	Volume (bcm/yr)	Duration
Distrigaz 1	1.8	2028
Distrigaz 2	1.5	2028
Distrigaz 3	2.6	2022
GdF 1	3	2028
GdF 2	3.5	2028
GdF 3	8	2022
Elf	1	n/a
Ruhrgas 1	0.2	2028
Ruhrgas 2	8.3	2028
Ruhrgas 3	14.4	2022
VNG	4	2016
Deutsche Shell	1.7	2028
OMV	1.3	2022
Gasunie	3.5	2022
SEP	2	2022
ENAGAS	2.1	2022
SNAM	6	2025
Transgas	3	n/a
National Power	4	n/a
Other	3	n/a
Total	74.9	

Note: Indicative only, data collected from trade journals.

interests in the European market (Olje- og Energidepartementet 1986–7:58f).

The institutional setting of gas marketing in Norway developed in several phases. In the early period for fields discovered under licences awarded before 1973, no formal provisions for gas discoveries were made in the licensing agreements and the field operator undertook to sell the gas on a field depletion basis. Both the Ekofisk and Frigg gas contracts were concluded under this arrangement, with Phillips Petroleum negotiating for Ekofisk, and Elf Aquitaine for Frigg.

A majority share period for licences awarded between 1973 and 1978 followed. In this period, Statoil automatically received at least 50 per cent of production interest in each licence, and then by default took leadership in gas negotiations as the most important owner, without there being any formal provision in the licence agreement. The high and more or less constant share for Statoil meant that it would be neutral as to which field to develop, in contrast to other partners who might have a high share or operatorship in one field, and low shares in others.

From the fourth licensing round in 1979, Statoil's leadership role in gas negotiations was entered formally into the licence agreements. Gas negotiations have to be held in close co-operation with the steering committee of the licence area concerned. Further, from then on all partners have the right to sign contracts for their part of production, or can take their equity gas elsewhere if offered better conditions, or for use in their own downstream interests. This is still the case in licences awarded today. This is an important provision in light of the impending liberalization of European gas markets, but it is somewhat surprising that this possibility has almost never been taken up by any party during the last twenty years.[8] Two reasons for this come to mind: firstly, it is probably difficult for any company to obtain transportation for its gas through the export pipelines, which are mainly controlled by Statoil, which in turn has no interest in allowing independent gas sales. Secondly, companies fear reprisals by the Norwegian government in future licensing rounds, if they decide to break ranks with the GFU.

From the ninth round in 1985, gas negotiations were put into the hands of a negotiating committee, consisting of the three Norwegian oil companies Statoil, Norsk Hydro, and Saga, under the leadership of Statoil, as long as at least two of the companies are present among the licence partners. This followed the re-organization of the state participation in petroleum activities, and was a natural result of the attempt to reduce the dominance of Statoil (see Section 5). The negotiating committee was first conceptualized to continue selling gas reserves on a field depletion basis. Soon after the new institutional setting was put in place, however, it became clear that depletion contracts were outdated.

With the discovery of the giant Troll field, Norway suddenly found itself awash in gas. Reserves are so huge that a high level of production can be sustained over a long period. In addition, Troll can be used as swing producer, guaranteeing security of supply while small marginal finds are produced, and associated gas is fed in. This is a major departure from the earlier years during which fields were sold and developed as soon as technically possible, and no conflicts of interest arose between the licence partners and the authorities (Olje- og Energidepartementet 1986–7:61).

In addition to the new resource management capabilities of the Troll field, the high gas volumes available meant that the market situation in Europe was a constraining factor for the development of newly discovered gas producing fields. The field approach by the negotiating committee was no longer adequate, and fields could no longer be developed as they were discovered. All development projects entered a queue, and the timing of fields since then is evaluated from a socio-economic perspective, and fields with the best overall results are given priority.

In 1986, the creation of a centralized negotiation and production planning committee was proposed in Parliamentary Report 46, 1986–7, the Gassforhandlingsutvalget (GFU), consisting of the same three Norwegian companies as the field negotiation committees before. Ironically, the first Troll contracts concluded in May 1986 were negotiated under the old system of Statoil leadership, because the Troll and Sleipner licences were awarded between 1969 and 1979. But the government made sure that the contracts fulfilled major conditions: the authorities wanted the Troll contracts to give security of supply to the buyers, but at the same time give flexibility to Norway to enable sales of gas from other fields, i.e. recognize the potential of using Troll as swing producer (Ibid.:62).

Foreign companies were excluded from the GFU mainly for two reasons: firstly because of the strong desire for Norwegian control over resource development, and secondly because of the important downstream interests of most of the foreign partners, for example Shell's interests in Ruhrgas, which meant gas sellers could be gas buyers at the same time. Availability of unallocated fields also means that partners have an increasing incentive to sell their own gas. Similarly, a problem was seen in the downstream interests of the upstream partners, conflict of interest and gas-to-gas competition could arise, and lead to downward pressure on Norwegian gas prices. Since then, Statoil and Norsk Hydro have created their own downstream interests, Statoil with Alliance Gas in the UK and, together with Norsk Hydro, a participation in the NETRA pipeline in Germany. In order to prevent conflicts of interest, the GFU therefore sold gas to Alliance Gas without Statoil participation under leadership of Norsk Hydro.

Norwegian gas sales follow a standard pattern: the Ministry appoints the GFU to negotiate volumes and prices, and in co-operation with the upstream partners decides on field allocations. The GFU can take on contract commitments without allocating specific fields to contracts because of the strength of the Troll field and the integration of other fields. Until fields are allocated to contracts, the GFU partners carry the commercial contract risk. Volume negotiations are therefore decoupled from specific field developments, and these can be optimized from a resource management perspective.

In 1993 another change was made to the institutional setting in reaction to complaints by foreign partners, who felt they were too

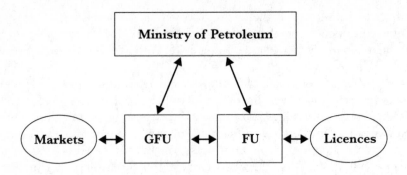

Figure 1: Institutional Framework for Norwegian Gas Sales

often bypassed by the Norwegian companies. Since then, the upstream partners are organized in the Forsyningsutvalget or Supply Committee (FU). Field development plans are submitted and ranked according to the net present value of projected volumes, where a discount rate of 7 per cent is used to determine the net present value. The Ministry of Oil and Energy decides on the allocation of contracts to fields, making sure that the most profitable fields are allocated first. Field allocations and development plans are integrated with oil development to make sure that oil output and ultimate resource recovery is optimized.

This institutional setting is in Norway widely regarded as ensuring rational resource development and maximizing the net present value of national revenues. On this basis the institutional setting is strongly defended against the European competition authorities. In this defence, no effort is made to disguise the fact that gas selling from Norway is organized in a monopoly. But, the argument goes, European competition rules do not apply to a national institution for resource management.

3.3   Gas Export Infrastructure

Norwegian gas is used for reinjection purposes on oil fields or exported to the UK and continental Europe. Almost no gas is used domestically, although this might change in the coming years if long discussed plans for gas-fired power stations are carried out. Norsk Hydro has revealed plans to build a power station using new technology to remove carbon from the gas before firing, although these were put on hold when oil prices dropped in 1998. It is hoped that carbon removal will satisfy the environmental lobby who is strongly opposed to the use of hydrocarbon fuels for power generation in a country where until now only hydropower is used.

Norway currently uses five export pipelines, one to the UK, and four to continental Europe (see Map 1). The first pipeline to be completed, Norpipe, has carried gas from the Ekofisk area to Emden in Germany since 1977. The 440 km line with a diameter of 30 inches has a design capacity of 19 bcm per year. Statoil owns 50 per cent of

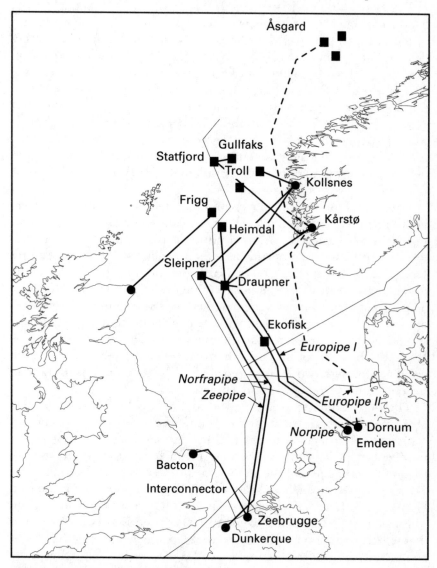

Map 1: Norwegian Gas Export Pipelines

the line, followed by Phillips with 16 per cent. Only six months after the Norpipe commissioning, the Frigg line commenced deliveries of Frigg gas to St. Fergus in Scotland. Two parallel lines transport gas from Frigg, the second is owned by the UK Frigg group. The Norwegian line has a design capacity of 12 bcm/year, but is currently limited to only about half of that. Both the British and the Norwegian lines are operated by Total Oil Marine UK.

Following the decision to sell Statfjord and Heimdal gas to continental buyers, the Statpipe system was built. The system consists of four parts: a pipeline to transport wet gas from Statfjord and other fields in the northern part of the Norwegian North Sea to a treatment terminal in Kårstø on the Norwegian west coast, where natural gas liquids are separated and exported by ship. Dry gas is then piped to the Draupner-S riser platform, where the third part of the Statpipe system delivers gas from the Heimdal field, which is relatively dry. From Draupner-S, a pipeline connects to Norpipe downstream of the Ekofisk centre, and the gas is transported to Emden. The project was initiated in 1981, and started operation in 1985. Statoil owns more than 58 per cent of the system.

With the Troll and Sleipner contracts, several new pipelines were built. The first part of the development connects Sleipner with a new pipeline to Zeebrugge in Belgium, with a capacity of 12 bcm per year, the Zeepipe IA development, and another line to the riser platform Draupner-S, Zeepipe IB. On the landing point in Zeebrugge a landing terminal was built with a 49 per cent interest of the Belgian Distrigaz. The second phase connects the new gas treatment terminal in Kollsnes on the mid-Norwegian coast with one pipeline to Sleipner, and a second line to the riser platform Draupner-E. The two lines, Zeepipe IIA and IIB were put into operation in 1996 and 1997. Finally, Troll gas flows through two 26 inch pipelines to Kollsnes and from there to Sleipner and Zeebrugge, or to Draupner-E.

The third landing pipeline on the continent is Europipe connecting Draupner-E with Dornum, and on-shore to Emden. The pipeline has a capacity of 13 bcm per year and has the same ownership structure as Zeepipe. A second Europipe is planned connecting the Kårstø treatment terminal with the storage facility in Etzel, with a capacity of 18 bcm per year, which will bring to three the number of pipelines to Germany, with a total capacity of 50 bcm per year. The construction of Europipe II is planned to begin in 1999. The Ministry of Petroleum and Energy approved in 1995 the Norfra pipeline, which was completed in 1998. It runs over 840 km from Draupner-E to Dunkerque with a capacity to transport 15 bcm of gas per year. Statoil and the Norwegian state have an interest of 60 per cent in Norfra. Another long-distance pipeline is planned to connect the Haltenbanken area in the Norwegian sea with the treatment terminal in Kårstø, covering a distance of 750 km for a volume of 20 bcm per year.

The Norwegian export pipeline system has been designed gradually, and later investments have taken careful consideration of system flexibility, by using riser platforms as hubs, such as the Draupner-S platform, which links the gas from Troll and other fields in the northern North Sea via Kollsnes to both Emden and Zeebrugge. Draupner-S also connects Statfjord and Heimdal gas directly to Emden through Statpipe, or via the Ekofisk centre through the Norpipe to Germany. Therefore, Draupner-S ties together the Statfjord/Heimdal, and the Sleipner/Troll developments. The other hub is Draupner-E, which allows Troll and other gas to flow to Zeebrugge via Zeepipe IA, to Emden via Europipe I, or after completion of the Norfra line also to France.

The system achieves a high degree of flexibility through inter-connection at the different hubs. This flexibility allows the substitution of different fields, and increases the security of supply by giving the possibility of switching between different landing pipelines, such that at least a certain volume of gas can always flow in the event of one pipeline being closed. The system as a whole will have excess capacity at least some parts of the year, as was demanded during the Troll negotiations: the buyers insisted on volume flexibility between 90 and 110 per cent in the take-or-pay contracts, with actual capacity use in the first years of operation just above 90 per cent.

Norwegian oil fields use about 30 bcm of gas per year for re-injection in order to maintain reservoir pressure during oil depletion. The biggest injection project is the Troll-Oseberg gas injection (TOGI) project, which started operations in 1991. It produces 22–25 bcm of gas per year from a sub-sea module on the Troll field for injection in Oseberg. Most of the injected gas will eventually be produced.

4.   A Tiger by the Tail: Norwegian Attitudes to Petroleum Activities[9]

When oil was discovered on the Norwegian Continental Shelf in 1969, the public largely missed the implications because it was involved in a hard, divisive political struggle over membership in the European Economic Community, which ended with a 'No' in a referendum in 1972. By the early 1970s it became clear that hydrocarbons would have a very strong role in the Norwegian economy, and a discussion over oil depletion policy started in earnest. Major decisions about the principles of petroleum policy, and state participation through a state-owned oil company, had been taken by then without much participation by the public.

The most important principle was established very early on with the Royal Resolution claiming sovereignty over the subsea resources in 1963. Since then it has been a principle of Norwegian policy that resources are the property of the state and that the state needs strong and effective control over resource use. This idea of central control is the strongest motivating force behind Norwegian petroleum policy even today.

This section tries to give an overview of the attitudes of the Norwegian public and the cultural determinants of petroleum policy in the country. It points out that the idealization of a modest lifestyle and equity, together with popular support for a strong role of the government in achieving the ideals of the society, are the determinants of petroleum policy.

4.1   *The Proud Successors of the Vikings Find Oil*

It should be properly appreciated that Norway is quite different from other petroleum countries. It is the only developed country in the world with a highly petroleum-dependent economy. Other petroleum-producing countries are either developing countries, especially the countries in the Middle East, or have more diversified economies like the USA and the UK. When oil was discovered, and became the dominant sector in the economy some years later, Norway had a highly developed legal system, and democratically legitimized public institutions.

The arrival of the major international oil companies was something of a shock to Norwegians, and was primarily perceived as a threat to the Norwegian way of life. The attitudes of the international petroleum industry in the early years might not have been very helpful. Oil companies mainly had experience in developing countries, and were used to a level of control over activities and manpower which went fundamentally against Norwegian ideas of national sovereignty and individual self determination.

Arve Johnsen, President and CEO of Statoil until 1988, encapsulates the problem beautifully in his account of the discussions between Statoil and Mobil over the operatorship of the Statfjord field, which was meant to be transferred from Mobil to Statoil around 1981. Rather than agree to the transfer, Alex Massad, then in the Mobil headquarters in New York, instead suggested the formation of a joint operating company. 'Alex Massad argued well for his cause, and he could point to several countries in Africa and the Far East who found the solution useful. *I thanked him for the lecture*, it was a good repetition of [...] arguments about the granting of concessions in 1973' (Johnsen 1990:123, emphasis added). Another example of the extent of the culture clash is the anecdote that one American oil company employed a distant relative of the Norwegian king in the vain hope of gaining influence in political circles.

Norwegian political economy is determined by a highly moral society, with an overwhelming support for equity policies. The equity ideal in Norwegian society is expressed in a comprehensive cradle-to-grave social welfare net. But it has wider implications than simply providing for the unfortunate. What Norwegians call 'janteloven' determines social behaviour to a surprising extent: nobody should try to distinguish himself from common norms of behaviour, be it through wealth, consumption patterns, or to some extent even in ways of thinking. Conspicuous consumption until recently had taboo status, and tales abound about the modest lifestyles of important personalities. Compare this to the 'gung-ho' attitudes of the American-led international petroleum industry and the problems are obvious.

For the realization of their social ideals Norwegians strongly believe in the role of the government to redistribute wealth and steer economic activities. A paternalistic interpretation of the role of the state commands a strong level of support in the electorate. Direct government participation in industry and banking is seen as a necessity, although the worldwide trend towards liberalization and privatization has not completely passed by Norway.

The concerns for directing social change result in a strong regional policy, which is based on strategic consideration and popular history and folklore. The latter consists of tales of small isolated farming and fishing communities fighting for survival, and deriving their pride from the centuries-old success of the struggle. Even today, Norwegians can often tell the exact origins of people by their accents, with each valley with two or three villages using a distinctive pronunciation. The country affords the luxury of maintaining two official languages, which are strikingly similar and cannot easily be distinguished by the foreigner.

The regional policy tries to safeguard historical settlement patterns, especially in the north of the country. Preservation of the traditional industries established in those areas, most importantly fishing and to some extent agriculture, is seen as the vehicle. This means safeguarding the environment, and controlling social change in a macroeconomic context. Norway has only about 4.5 million inhabitants, of which around one million live in the greater Oslo area. Other major cities, among them Kristiansand, Stavanger, Bergen, Trondheim, make up another million. The rest of the population lives in small cities and villages, or relatively isolated farms. Especially in the north of the country, entire coastal areas comprise small villages which are entirely dependent on fishing and shipping related industries, which are remote and were at least in the advent of the oil era cut off from much of the main land by snow over seven or eight months of the year and only reached by boat. Enabling high standards of living in these undoubtedly picturesque if somewhat unpractical places is one of the main pillars of Norwegian political economy.

Of course, the more pragmatic reasons for keeping the north of the country inhabited are strategic: the area is NATO's northern flank, with the shortest distance between the USA and Russia. It would be of greatest interest for the Russians who lack ice-free access to the Atlantic. In addition, as is becoming more and more obvious, the Norwegian Sea contains considerable reserves of oil and gas, while at the same time there is no agreement over the division of the off-shore between Norway and Russia, and the waters around Spitsbergen. It is therefore vital to keep the North inhabited, both for military logistics, and as support for the Norwegian sovereignty over land and sea.[10]

In a macroeconomic context, regional policy is associated with the monitoring of wage levels, which rose sharply with the increase in labour demand from both off-shore and on-shore petroleum industries. The rising attraction of outside work opportunities is a real threat to the northern villages. Regional policy is therefore inextricably linked to general economic policy, and leads to the attempts to slow down petroleum activities, in order to limit their impact. Observers describe Norwegian petroleum policy therefore as being determined by macroeconomists, with the help of some geologists, who point out the benefits of an integrated oil and gas depletion policy.

4.2   Foundations of Petroleum Policy

As mentioned in the introduction, a public debate over petroleum activities only started in the early 1970s. A fundamental Parliamentary Report in 1974 spells out the principles on which oil depletion policy should be based for years to come, updated by two other Reports in 1984 and 1986. The 1974 Report starts with an assessment of production possibilities for hydrocarbons over the following ten years and concludes that the forecast 'level of production would probably cause greater problems of adaptation for Norwegian society than are justifiable' (Ministry of Finance 1974:6*). Shifts in employment away from traditional industries are explicitly mentioned. A 'moderate rate' of extraction specified as targeted production of 90 million tons oil equivalent per year is therefore proposed (Ibid.). The government asserts that the oil revenues should be used to develop a 'qualitatively better society', according to the ideals of the Norwegian population (Ibid.). Elected representatives of the people must acquire genuine control over developments in all areas of the petroleum industry in order to achieve this goal.

Given the scepticism towards the international oil companies, it was clear that control would be impossible without strong competence in the petroleum industry. Therefore a national oil company, Statoil, was founded in 1972, of which more is said in Section 5. The government points to the Royal Resolution of 1963, which claims Norwegian sovereignty over the subsea resources. Oil and gas are owned by the Norwegian state, and private and international oil companies are merely allowed to help in the exploitation in return for a level of profit deemed adequate to keep them interested. 'But in future they should obtain the right to exploit these natural resources in exceptional cases only. The organizational pattern for Norwegian petroleum operations must provide Norwegian authorities with full control of all stages in the operation' (Ibid.:9*). With the creation of increasing expertise in the state oil company the role of the international companies was bound to decline over time.

Norwegian control over the activity level in the petroleum industry is mainly effected through licensing rounds. The government recognizes that once a discovery has been declared commercial, development cannot be withheld for long because companies involved have to recover investment outlays. High development costs and fast physical degradation of installations make production control after development difficult. Once a field has been developed, production should therefore follow an optimal depletion pattern and not be influenced by overall activity considerations (Ibid.).

In practice, the 90 million ton production ceiling was never a constraint, and was dropped in 1980. Oil development followed commercial considerations to a large extent, and even in the licensing rounds, acreage of interest to the companies was never withheld for long. Field developments were postponed only twice, once in the 1980s under Minister Øien, and then in 1998, although on both occasions the effect in terms of deferment of oil production was small. Twice the government decided production cuts in support of world oil prices, in 1998 it joined international efforts by a cut of 100,000 barrels per day.

4.3   *Petroleum Policy and Political Parties*

There has been very little disagreement over the broader lines of Norwegian petroleum policy over the years. Controversies have focused on details, such as the exact staging of developments. Political parties in Norway can be distinguished along two dimensions: one is the common left-right axis associated with socialistic or capitalistic attitudes the world over. The other axis is 'green vs. technology', i.e. a division between environmental and rural interests with moralistic and nationalistic attitudes on one side, and pro-technology and growth, and more pragmatic and internationalist attitudes on the other.

Along the left-right axis, Norway has a small Marxist and a medium sized socialist party (SV), and then the moderate Labour Party (AP). The centrist parties are the Christian People's Party (KrF), the Centre Party (SP), and the small Liberal Party (Venstre). To the right are the Conservative Party (Hoyre) and lastly the xenophobic Progress Party (FP). With a simple left-right division, the current government, and many governments before, would have been a Conservative-led, centre-right coalition. But the second dimension of Norwegian politics puts the socialist and centrist parties furthest in the 'green' camp, Conservatives and Labour more in the middle, and FP on the other side.

The Christian People's Party and Venstre have historically tended to compromise with the right, whereas the Centre Party played off Labour against Conservatives trying to ensure that whichever was in power would depend on its main constituency, the farmers. When Norway entered the second round of discussions over EU membership in the 1990s, support for SP increased to such an extent that a centrist coalition was seen as a feasible alternative to Labour and Conservatives, although it only came to power as a minority government in 1997.

Concerning petroleum policy, two broad issues can be distinguished: the general issue of speed of petroleum development and depletion policy, and the question of the organization of the state participation and Statoil's role. The depletion policy debate follows the 'green vs. technology' fault lines, with Labour and Conservatives usually taking a more positive, pragmatic attitude, and the centrist parties urging restraint. On the other hand, Conservatives oppose Labour and support a more commercial organization of Statoil and reduction of direct state intervention. The centrist parties have held principles similar to Labour, but in periods have been willing to support the Conservatives (in return for other favours, no doubt).

The current Norwegian government is formed by a centrist minority coalition which took over from a long-standing Labour government in 1997. Oddly, the coalition has seven seats less in parliament than the Labour Party, but is backed by ad-hoc collusion with other parties, which usually seem to be united against Labour. Originally, the minority government came into existence when Thorbjørn Jagland, Labour prime minister after Gro Harlem Brundtland, resigned after a heavy loss of seats in the general elections.

The parties making up the new government supported production cutbacks in their election manifestos and postponed investment approvals in early 1998, following their green, rural agendas. The government readily agreed to oil production cutbacks following an initiative of Mexico, Saudi Arabia, and Venezuela in March of the same year, a decision which was heavily contested by the Labour Party. It should be remembered that the majority in Parliament is still pro-technology and growth, and the government's initiatives were greatly watered down. In fact, the production cutback might not have been implemented at all had the government not committed quickly internationally, without awaiting approval by Parliament.

Whereas in the last years the state oil company has been given increasing commercial freedom, the new government is more concerned with the international expansion the company has achieved. The company has come under intense scrutiny by the public with its upstream projects in countries like Nigeria and China. It is not acceptable for Norwegians that the state oil company should be associated with human rights violation or low environmental standards, as could be the result of the foreign expansion.

5.   The Making of an International Oil Company

Following a unanimous decision by the Norwegian Storting (parliament), Den Norske Stats Oljeselskap AS, commonly abbreviated to Statoil, was founded in 1972 to take part in all activities in the petroleum industry in Norway. The state participated in exploration licences since the second licensing round in 1969 and from 1972, all state participation was channelled through Statoil. The rationale behind the creation of Statoil was the need for adequate technical and commercial expertise in the petroleum industry, in order to keep control over resource production in Norway. Significantly, Statoil was founded as a joint stock company, all the shares of which are held by the state, and the Minister for Petroleum is the general assembly. Nevertheless, the company is covered by the laws governing joint stock companies, which ensures that much more weight is placed on the company's commercial functions, than is common among other national oil companies.

Until the early 1980s, Statoil automatically received at least 50 per cent of interest in a licence area, but did not have to share exploration expenditure. In addition to the high initial share for Statoil, the licensing terms also specified a sliding scale, which meant the state could increase its participation after commerciality of a find had been declared. This brings state participation up to 80 per cent in some cases.

Norsk Hydro is one of the other two main Norwegian companies to compete in the Norwegian off-shore, and 51 per cent of shares in the company are owned by the government. Hydro has a long tradition in the energy business with worldwide interests in fertilizer production. The company is exactly between private and public, although most commentators seem to treat it as private. Nevertheless, Norsk Hydro can point to its majority owner in international dealings with state entities, and on the other hand can portray itself as thoroughly independent if need be.

In general, Hydro seems to be regarded as a private company, and is therefore much less in the limelight than Statoil. As repeatedly pointed out by Statoil leaders, Hydro is therefore in a much better commercial position. Allegedly, one of the main differences is Hydro's comparatively easy access to capital: the general assembly can decide on capital increases, and the government has to go along or lose its majority share position. Statoil on the other hand has to go to the Minister cap in hand, and parliament is likely to object to giving more money to what is perceived as an oil giant.

The third major company is Saga, and it was also founded in 1972 through the merger of several off-shore companies with only private ownership. Saga is rather small, accounting for less than 5 per cent of oil and gas production. The company gave out three different types of shares – two types of voting shares, one restricted for sale in Norway, and non-voting shares. The sales restrictions on voting shares enabled the government to prevent a foreign takeover of the company. The sales restrictions have recently been dropped, but observers do not see this as indicating a fundamental shift in attitude by the government. It is still expected that the government would prevent a foreign takeover.

In addition, Statoil acquired 20 per cent of Saga shares, and some more shares are held by the public pension fund. The big Statoil share will probably suffice to scare off any potential foreign bidder.

Statoil was rapidly built up to fulfil its double role of revenue collector for the state and commercial player on the NCS. In the words of the company's first President, Arve Johnsen, it was 'leap-frogging' ahead (1990:44), which meant that only three years after its inception, in 1975, Statoil received operatorship in the exploration phase of a new licence area for the first time. Gas exports started in September 1977 from the Ekofisk area through Norpipe, in which Statoil has a 20 per cent interest, and in August 1978 from Frigg through Frigg Transport, in which Statoil participates with 29 per cent.

In 1978, the Gullfaks oil and gas field was discovered under Statoil operatorship. The field is the second largest oil producer in Norwegian waters with a production of 344,000 barrels of oil per day on average in 1997. Statoil has a 12 per cent share in the field, Norsk Hydro has 9 per cent and Saga 6 per cent, with the rest held by the Norwegian state directly. After the heavy investment programme of the early years, Statoil reached profitability in 1980 for the first time.

5.1   From Revenue Collector to Commercial Actor

The strongly political nature of Statoil operations was always clear: as state oil company it could not escape scrutiny by political actors. These were foremost interested in the implementation of the company's role as revenue collector for the state. A sometimes difficult balancing act was required between the revenue collector role and its commercial role. Statoil was founded and built up under Labour governments, and its first President and CEO from 1972 to 1988 was a strong Labour supporter. A shift to conservative governments therefore always brought a more critical attitude towards Statoil.

Such a shift followed the 1981 election when a new government under Kåre Willoch took over. The Ministry of Petroleum and Energy embarked upon an evaluation of the state's participation in the petroleum industry. The immediate consequence was a postponement of the transfer of operatorship in the Statfjord licence. Under the licence agreement, the Ministry could reallocate operatorship between licensees after commerciality of a find had been declared. The new government postponed what was to become the first major Statoil operatorship from 1982 to 1987.

The government expressed the opinion that the power of the Statoil leadership should be reduced. Channelling all of the state's participation through one commercially oriented company was seen as inadequate. The large cash flows going through Statoil accounts meant that the power of that company was perceived to be too great both *vis-à-vis* elected organs of the state and other Norwegian industries. It was thought that a reduction of Statoil's role and parallel upgrading of the other two Norwegian companies would enhance control over Norwegian petroleum activities, although the other Norwegian companies were at least partially in private ownership. More equitable distribution of participation between all Norwegian companies was seen to enhance the pool of competence available to Norway.

In the autumn of 1984 the decision was announced to take a part of Statoil's production interests into the State Direct Financial Interest (SDFI), although Statoil retains the administration of the state's participation. Statoil was reduced to a share of around 12 per cent in most licences, even where it is the operator, on a more equal level with other companies. The influence Statoil could wield on decision making in licences was accordingly reduced. The split means that Statoil cannot force decisions on the other licence holders in the management committees, because the SDFI is taken out of the steering groups, although Statoil formally retains a high percentage by administering the SDFI on the basis of a bilateral Statoil-government arrangement. In this sense the company retains a dominant position in Norway.

On the other hand, the split means Statoil can now more freely concentrate on its commercial role, since the role of revenue collector for the state is separated out and taken care of by the SDFI. In addition, the SDFI constitutes a silent partner in all projects, contributing the majority of financing for new investments. Statoil therefore is in a much better commercial position than before the split, and concentrates on commercial tasks, with diversification both domestically and internationally. The issue of the administration of the SDFI is of course unresolved, if Statoil is becoming more independent.

In the 1990s Statoil is gradually becoming an international petroleum company like other private companies. The strategy is international diversification in upstream activities, and vertical integration into retailing of petroleum products, and gas transportation. The transition is helped by institutional changes instigated by the government. For example, starting in 1993 Norway adheres to EU rules for procurement of off-shore supplies. Also, starting with the fifteenth licensing round Statoil is for the first time competing with other companies on an equal level, i.e. the company is not automatically awarded a share in every licence. Two licences were awarded without participation by Statoil, albeit both in the high-risk Barents Sea. The company is free to decide which areas to apply for, according to commercial portfolio decisions. During the last years, officials in Norway, both from Statoil and the Ministry, have increasingly stressed that the company should concentrate on its commercial role, and a partial privatization is at least being discussed by politicians, although it seems unlikely that a majority for privatization will emerge in the near future.

5.2 Strategy for the 1990s and Beyond

In 1990, Statoil announced the formation of a strategic alliance with BP Exploration. Co-operation between the two companies was planned within three main areas: a) using existing infrastructure to transport gas to the UK and continental Europe and joint marketing of gas, b) joint research for exploration technology, and c) joint international oil and gas exploration focusing on West Africa, China, Vietnam, and the former Soviet Union (*Euroil*, September 1990:12). Statoil hoped to gain access to the UK gas market, whereas BP would benefit from better access to gas reserves in Norwegian waters.

Confident about the improved position in the UK, Norway signed a supply contract over 2.2 bcm per year of gas with UK electricity producer National Power in 1991, and a depletion contract for the Froy field close to the Frigg field with Scottish Power with a plateau volume of 1.7 bcm per year. To further strengthen their position in the UK market, BP and Statoil together with Norsk Hydro formed Alliance Gas to trade gas in the UK. This was planned to supply gas from smaller fields in the UK sector of the North Sea to customers in Britain, and had an agreement with regional power company MANWEB to sell gas to their customers (*Euroil*, May 1992:9).

In a repetition of the 1985 rejection of Sleipner gas imports, and much to the surprise of the Norwegians who thought they had taken care of at least one source of lobbying against them, the UK government thwarted these plans, with far-reaching consequences for the Norwegian presence in the UK. The British authorities under Energy Minister Tim Eggar still demanded renegotiation of the Frigg treaty, and Eggar openly admitted the breakdown of negotiations when he announced in April 1994 that 'there is no question of the line being available for Froy gas once Frigg has finished'. He asserted that there were no further meetings between British and Norwegian negotiators planned (*Euroil*, May 1994:5).

The lack of progress in the UK ultimately led to the break-up of the co-operation between BP and Statoil in the marketing of British and Norwegian gas. The break came with the liberalization of the British gas market, which left gas customers stranded with long-term contracts with high prices. The gas sold by Alliance was then exclusively BP gas from the UKCS, and BP was not interested as seller to renegotiate a deal with Alliance as buyer, where part of the losses accrued to Statoil. BP and also Norsk Hydro left Alliance Gas, which is now a 100 per cent subsidiary of Statoil. BP meanwhile has created a strategic alliance with Sonatrach in Algeria, and it is a declared aim to compete against Norwegian gas in Germany. As in the earlier parts of the drama concerning the Frigg treaty, in the early 1970s and again following the Sleipner contracts with British Gas, the Norwegians were following other options and stayed firm over the principles governing the treaty.

The alliance with BP did not break up in the international co-operation in upstream activities, and joint projects are underway in Africa and Asia. Statoil plans to spend about one-third of the total exploration budget abroad over the coming years, in order to achieve about the same share of revenue from non-Norwegian production in the next century, to prepare for declining production levels of oil in Norway. Already, Statoil is well established on the British continental shelf. As a result of the upstream diversification strategy Statoil will remain an oil company at least in revenue terms, although the reserve base in Norway is shifting strongly in favour of gas.

5.2.1 *Vertical Integration*

In the beginning of the 1990s, Norway had discovered Eastern Europe as the new strategic direction for Norwegian gas, and while the British DTI was haggling about sovereignty over the Frigg line, Statoil and Norsk Hydro were in negotiations for the NETRA joint venture with Ruhrgas. 'In the value chain for gas, especially in a low price scenario, a large part of the value is taken out in those parts of the chain where we are not present', as Harald Norvik, President and CEO of Statoil, had remarked in the autumn of 1993, to suggest a strategy of downstream integration for Statoil (*Euroil*, November 1993:17). In this light it fits well that Statoil at about the same time formed a joint venture with the Norwegian electricity company Statkraft to build a gas-fired power station in Norway, and had plans to take part in a new power station in Scotland.

In addition, the company bought capacity in the Interconnector, a return to the initial position, where Statoil and also Norsk Hydro were sponsors of the project in its early phase. The Norwegians left the

Interconnector project when Norwegian imports were rejected by the British, but lately Statoil has again shown interest in positioning itself on the short-term European gas market.

Vital experience in gas trading is also made with Eastern Gas, which Statoil acquired in the liberalized US market. In addition to providing a testing ground for trading skills in a truly liberalized market, the US presence is seen as providing a strategic opportunity to bring Norwegian liquefied natural gas (LNG) into the US market. The company sells 10–12 bcm of gas annually, 1.2 bcm of which are equity gas. It is a large trader of gas and electricity, and owns about 150 megawatts of generation capacity, mainly in the form of cogeneration projects. The construction of a liquefaction terminal is seen as the option for exploiting the gas resource discoveries in northern Norwegian waters, especially the Snøvit field. Statoil officials are optimistic that LNG could be delivered at competitive prices to the US East Coast, thereby opening a completely new export outlet for Norwegian gas.

5.2.2 *Criticism Against Statoil*

The greater commercial freedom and the decisions which have come out of that are unsurprisingly under intense scrutiny by the Norwegian public and politicians. Even before the SDFI was taken out of the Statoil holdings, the company was always suspect because of the obvious temptation to pursue company interests rather than maximize benefits for the society as a whole. This is a well-known principal-agent problem, where the principal – in this case the Norwegian public as represented by the government – employs an agent – here the national oil company – to take care of the principal's business. The incentive structure for the agent is not necessarily identical with what the principal wants him to do.

One of the main lines of criticism is based on the fact that although the company is legally a joint stock company, the state is the only shareholder, and the shares are not traded. This means there is no market price of Statoil shares, and therefore no evaluation of company performance on the stock market. Critics see this as a lack of control over the company. Both company and government have reacted to this by appointing investment banks to evaluate the value creation in the company on an annual basis, and compare it with the record of other international oil companies. The exercise is a proxy for true market discipline, but seeing the company ranked is not equivalent to seeing actual share prices fluctuate, especially since in most companies managers hold shares themselves. This repeatedly leads to calls for at least a partial privatization of the company, but politicians are afraid of foreign ownership. The market value of Statoil is likely to exceed the total market valuation of the Oslo stock exchange, and selling shares abroad would therefore be the only option in a large-scale privatization.

6.   From Sellers' Market to Rearguard Battle

Norwegian gas marketing has changed tremendously over the years, following developments in the markets, but also reserve developments at home. This section shows how it started in the blissful years of a sellers' market, in which buyers came knocking at Norwegian doors. The negotiators were successfully playing off different buyers against each other in order to achieve the best prices and conditions for Norwegian gas. At the beginning of the 1990s the strategy shifted. Since then Norway has tried to support the European monopolies – especially Norway's biggest customer Ruhrgas – by not selling to their competitors. Volume expansions for Norwegian gas are instead achieved by selling to new niche markets. Marketing has changed into a rearguard battle, where Norway joined forces with the incumbent continental monopolies, against the liberalization of the European market.

The section presents some of the steps on the way:
(i)   Norway's attempts to undermine the buyers' consortium by selling separately to individual companies, which were twice derailed by intervention from European governments.
(ii)   The strategic alliance between Statoil, Norsk Hydro and Ruhrgas for the NETRA pipeline, to deliver gas to the new growth markets in the east.
(iii)   The repeated rejection of attempts by Wingas, the biggest threat to the old order in Germany, to buy Norwegian gas.
(iv)   The dawn raids by European competition authorities on Statoil offices, starting a process which could jeopardize the institutional framework for Norwegian gas sales.

The outlook for the next two decades concluding this chapter shows that the resource base is shifting, and more gas will become available in the next 10–15 years, from new finds in the north of the country, and from gas which has been injected into oil reservoirs that are running down. A renewed aggressive marketing effort could be expected. But it has to be remembered that Norway remains an oil country, and integrated resource management is the most important driving force for Norwegian policy regarding the petroleum activities. The chapter concludes with a prediction of a tug-of-war between the politicians and bureaucrats on one side, and the commercial actors including Statoil on the other side.

6.1   Bringing Gas to Changing Markets

6.1.1   Riding the Tigers: Playing Off Buyers Against Each Other

Gas marketing in most of the history of the Norwegian off-shore could rely on strong demand for Norwegian supplies because of perceived security of supply and the wish for diversification by continental buyers. Demand was always greater than supply, and Norway could obtain relatively high prices. The Statfjord contracts were the last of this blissful era.

In order to achieve the best possible prices, Norway tried to play off buyers against each other. This was true for the Ekofisk negotiations, held in parallel with British Gas in the UK and the continental buyers' consortium, as well as for Frigg. Ekofisk gas was sold to the consortium, and Frigg gas to British Gas Corporation. The next step was selling the gas from the Statfjord field, as mentioned in Section 3. At about the same time, BP as operator approached Statoil to sell the contents of the Ula field, which was awarded in 1965 without participation of the Norwegian state, to a joint venture between BP and the German Gelsenberg. Later, additional volumes from Statfjord were included in the negotiations.

In May 1980, the negotiations were in an advanced state with all major points agreed, when Klaus Liesen, Director of Ruhrgas, visited Statoil. He was interested in buying a large share of Statfjord reserves, and at the same time enquired about the BP/Gelsenberg negotiations. Within a week, Ruhrgas then put pressure on BP and Gelsenberg to join the buyers' consortium, and also wielded its political power: it became clear that Gelsenberg would not receive approval by the German authorities if it circumvented the consortium, and Ruhrgas made it clear that it would not transport the gas (Johnsen 1990:132). This was the first time that the coherence of the buyers' consortium was propped up by intervention from European authorities.

A similar event followed during the Troll negotiations, when Statoil held separate talks with Elf for supplies to France, in order to undermine the continental buyers' cartel. Elf was the only major gas company outside the cartel, and contacts with Norway were well established, since Elf was the operator of the Frigg field, and had already bought Statfjord gas separately. At the time, all Norwegian gas supplies to the continent were landed in Emden, and therefore dependent on Ruhrgas, the leader of the buyers' consortium. The attraction of Elf was that it could be instrumental in building a new pipeline landing gas to the south-east of Emden.

In February 1986 the Belgian Distrigaz was approached by Statoil about the possibility of a new pipeline to Zeebrugge, a proposal which was supported enthusiastically. Initially, negotiations were taken up with Elf over the sales of gas from Sleipner East, the easier part of the Sleipner area which was available after the final rejection by the UK. The idea was that Sleipner could be developed relatively quickly, and Zeepipe could be built between the field and Zeebrugge, and later connected further north to Troll. In the beginning of May negotiations with Elf were well advanced and a contract was going to be signed in a matter of days.

At this point, 'it was becoming clear to Gaz de France that something was going on between Elf and Statoil' (Johnsen 1990:262). In response, GdF offered to increase offtake to include the volumes Elf was interested in buying. In the second half of May, a meeting was held between Elf, GdF, and the French authorities, and the latter insisted that GdF would be the only price negotiator for gas imports to France. The French meanwhile agreed to the new pipeline to Zeebrugge to deliver the contracted volumes. Norway secured a new export pipeline, and sold the same volume of gas as originally planned with Elf.

So the history of Norwegian gas marketing contains at least two instances of European authorities intervening anti-competitively to protect their gas companies, and in addition two instances of rejection of Norwegian gas by UK authorities, first the Sleipner gas contracts, and then Statoil's contracts with Scottish Power in Scotland. The Norwegian wish to maintain control by the authorities, and to maintain a sellers' monopoly for gas, might look more plausible in this light.

6.1.2 Finding New Markets for the1990s: The East and NETRA

Beginning in 1990, Eastern Europe was recognized as the new strategic market for Norwegian gas. All three Norwegian companies applied for a stake in the former East German Verbundnetzgas (VNG), Statoil acquired 5 per cent, and sales negotiations were initialled with Czechoslovakia, Hungary, and Poland. The next strategic move was the participation in the NETRA pipeline from Emden to Salzwedel on the border with the former East Germany, where it links up with the VNG pipeline network.

The participation agreement was negotiated between Statoil and Norsk Hydro on one side, Ruhrgas and BEB on the other, in complete secrecy for three to four years starting early in 1991. When the project was unveiled in the autumn of 1994, a stunned public was struck by the logic of the agreement. Ruhrgas and BEB were in it for two reasons: firstly, it was a welcome injection of about DM 1 billion of capital; secondly, the established German transmission companies were under increasing pressure from the European Commission and German lawmakers were threatening initiatives for regulated third-party access. The joint venture with the Norwegians could be paraded to show that the old monopolists could transform themselves, and had granted access to at least one major supplier to compete directly in an important market.

The NETRA pipeline is of obvious strategic importance for Norway, although it poses some problems for the institutional framework: the downstream integration of the two main members of the GFU causes raised eyebrows at best. It does not augur well for the integrity of the Norwegian sales monopoly when its members go their own way. In principle, if downstream interests are involved, the GFU member concerned cannot take part in the negotiations. But it is unthinkable that important negotiations take place with only Saga on the sellers' side. This might not be much of a problem in the case of NETRA, because it could be regarded as just another transport line for Norwegian gas, similar to the Norwegian off-shore lines. Sales negotiations at least with VNG were held between the GFU and an outsider. Nevertheless, the announcement of the NETRA joint venture agreement suddenly made it clear why Statoil at least, and to some extent Norsk Hydro, had been so unremittingly cool towards repeated bids by the German Wingas to buy Norwegian gas, of which more will be said in the next section. A Norwegian sales contract with Wingas, the main competitor to Ruhrgas, would inevitably have jeopardized the NETRA agreement, therefore overriding strategic Norwegian interests.

The uneasiness about the incompatibility of downstream integration with the institutional framework of Norwegian gas sales might be one reason why Statoil officials do not like to talk much about NETRA. They try to play down the importance of the project, as much as they like to play down the importance of Alliance in the UK, the other major downstream integration of Statoil. Likewise, Norsk Hydro's application for a trading licence for gas in the UK was filed and received without much fanfare. Officially, the GFU members are holding the line, while quietly preparing for changes in the European market.

Statoil and Norsk Hydro initially hold 25 per cent of the NETRA shares and therefore also capacity (with Hydro's participation one-quarter of that), which could be increased to 33 per cent for the transport of Norwegian gas. The agreement however allows the Norwegians to sell spare capacity to others. Initial capacity of the line is 16 bcm per year, which can be upgraded to 18 bcm. It will be used to transport the 4 bcm the GFU contracted with VNG, and if capacity and at the same time the Norwegian share is increased, another 2 bcm can be sold.

Three years after the NETRA agreement was unveiled, in March 1997, a sales agreement over 4 bcm per year was concluded with Transgas in the Czech Republic, which will use the NETRA pipeline. Talks are also underway with other East European countries, and a contract over the delivery of 2.5 bcm of gas has recently been signed with Poland. The latter is of some key importance for the future, as a major sales agreement with Poland could finally open the way for a Scandinavian pipeline, delivering gas from mid- to northern Norway via Sweden, possibly Finland, and Poland to the Baltic. This is in direct competition with a similar project by Russia's Gazprom, which would cover Finland and Sweden, and transport more gas to northern Germany. In addition, it clashes with Gazprom's understanding of Eastern Europe as its 'home turf'.

Statoil officials stress that they only target additional gas demand, and will not attempt to win market share aggressively from Gazprom. Again, Norway could ride on the wish for supply diversification, a return to the blissful sellers' market of the early 1980s. It has been reported that the Czechs were willing to pay a significant premium for Norwegian gas, with Gazprom offering supplies at $2.35 per mBtu, Norway lowering an initial offer of $2.69 to $2.50 per mBtu (*European Gas Markets*, March 1997:2). The future might see an extension of the NETRA pipeline further east, such that the Norwegians could deliver their gas directly to Berlin, the Czech Republic, and possibly Poland.

Another strategically important contract was signed in January 1997 with the Italian SNAM to deliver 6 bcm of Norwegian gas per year. The deliveries will be landed through the Norfra and Zeepipe lines to France and Belgium, and then through a new pipeline crossing France North to South, which will be linked to an existing pipeline through Switzerland into Northern Italy. In Italy, Norway is competing directly with Algeria, as in Spain. With parallel plans by the Sonatrach/BP alliance to bring Algerian gas to northern Europe, the European market is moving strongly towards full integration, and also towards stronger competition between the sellers.

6.1.3 Supporting the Monopolies: No Room for Wingas
Towards the beginning of the 1990s, the Norwegian attitude towards the continental buyers changed in the face of approaching liberalization of European gas markets. It is not in Norway's best interest to support this liberalization. Norwegian gas is relatively expensive to produce and deliver to the European markets, with very high investment costs. Stable, long-term contracts are perceived as the *sine qua non* of bringing Norwegian gas to market. The impression is that liberalization might lead to the disappearance of large-volume, long-term commitments, if the hitherto mono- or oligopolistic European buyers lose market share in a major way. The picture of a liberalized market with a high number of sellers and buyers and fast action on a small-volume basis runs fundamentally against the Norwegian idea of control and optimization.

Norwegian gas sales therefore no longer try to play off buyers against each other. This became clear when the German Wintershall wanted to break away from its dependence on Ruhrgas. Wintershall is a subsidiary of the chemical conglomerate BASF. The parent company, one of the largest industrial gas customers in Germany, was increasingly annoyed over the prices it had to pay the monopolist Ruhrgas for its supply and sent Wintershall looking elsewhere. The GFU declined a request on the basis of the strategic relations between Norwegian gas sellers and Ruhrgas. Selling to a major customer inside the Ruhrgas core area would have opened the door to competition between two different providers of Norwegian gas, and would have jeopardized the strategic relationship between Norway and Ruhrgas.

Wintershall did not pack up and go back to Ruhrgas, but instead entered into a partnership with Russia's Gazprom, out of which came Wingas, of which Wintershall owns 65 per cent, and Gazprom the rest. The rejection of Wintershall was a very risky strategic game by the Norwegians. Wingas went ahead with Russian gas, finally building its own pipeline network alongside the Ruhrgas lines, because the incumbent monopolist would not transport the competitor's gas.

But the issue of security of supply brought Wingas back to Norway repeatedly. Wingas saw that customers were cautious in buying their requirements, because Wingas could offer only Russian gas, whereas Ruhrgas was seen as more reliable with supplies from different sources. Wingas therefore wanted to buy Norwegian gas, and if possible also get access to storage capacity. Approaches were made in 1990 without success. The Norwegians declined to negotiate.

In the spring of 1992 a new attempt was made to acquire Norwegian gas for the MIDAL pipeline project by Wingas, which will consist of a pipeline running from the German North Sea coast south to meet the STEGAL pipeline near Frankfurt. The project is a joint venture between Wingas and Elf, the Austrian OMV, as well as Polish, Czech, Slovakian, and Hungarian companies. The group hoped to buy 10 bcm per year. Again, the GFU declined the approach by the consortium, although it left the door open for negotiations on a bilateral basis (*Euroil*, May 1992:9).

An even more elaborate effort was made in 1993 to buy Norwegian gas. In a series of meetings in the spring, Wintershall agreed on co-operation with Saga. In June the same year, a strategic alliance was outlined. This followed Saga's unease about the strategic alliance between Statoil and BP, announced in September 1990. The alliance with Wintershall would have opened for Saga to take a 14 per cent participation in Wingas. The ultimate aim of course was that Wingas would obtain a foothold in the Norwegian gas scene, and therefore obtain gas from the elusive supplier, although this was not part of the alliance agreement. Wingas simultaneously approached the GFU again for 4 bcm per year of gas supply.

Ruhrgas then increased its Troll gas volumes by 2 bcm as a pre-emptive strike, while the GFU was also negotiating the delivery of 4 bcm per year to VNG in the former East Germany. The Norwegians could then easily say that the German market could not absorb additional volumes demanded by Wingas, and turned them down again (*Euroil*, November 1993:20). Of course, half a year later the participation of Statoil and Norsk Hydro in the NETRA pipeline was announced, and what was maybe the real reason for repeated rejections of Wintershall/Wingas became clear. Saga was sacrificed in favour of a strategic stake in transport infrastructure to the new market niche for Norwegian gas.

But neither Saga, nor Wingas were ready to give up just yet. At the end of 1994, Saga created a subsidiary in Germany, Saga Deutschland. The subsidiary then agreed to sell Norwegian gas to Wingas, and approached the GFU for supplies. The plan was to buy 1 bcm per year of secure gas, and 0.5 bcm on the basis of an interruptible contract. Saga would then rent transport capacity in the MIDAL pipeline, and storage capacity in Wingas' Rehden storage facility. The interruptible gas would flow in the summer into the storage, and could be sold on with a profit in winter through the Wingas system. The 'little brother' in the Norwegian petroleum scene thought all the necessary ingredients were in place, and even if the GFU did not want to sell to the new German axis, Saga could have taken their own share of gas, as specified in the licensing agreements (*Norsk Olje Revy* no.2, 1995:6f).

The plans never came to fruition, because Saga got 'cold feet' after Harald Norvik, executive director of Statoil, spoke out vehemently against them. He said that if Saga took out their own gas, this would render the GFU into 'an empty shell'. It was not immediately clear whether this was meant to be a prognosis of a fact, or a threat by Statoil to react by circumventing the GFU system in turn, therefore leaving the small Saga out in the cold in the future (Ibid. no.8, 1995:15f). In any case, Saga dropped the attempts to take gas to Germany and take part in Wingas.

In 1998 then, Saga looked increasingly attractive as a takeover candidate. However, a foreign takeover would almost certainly lead to an abandonment of the three-headed institutional setting for gas sales with Statoil, Norsk Hydro, and Saga. The GFU system, defended on the grounds of national resource management, would not make sense anymore, if one of the members was taken over by a foreign oil company. It is therefore highly unlikely that the government would stand idle on the sidelines, if a hostile takeover attempt was becoming obvious. However, the government has no formal say over who owns the publicly listed shares. But Statoil holds 20 per cent of Saga shares and any takeover bid would be opposed by them. Saga might then be a very hard pill to swallow.

6.1.4 *Holding Off European Competition Regulators*

In 1992, Norway agreed to adhere to a European Directive concerning the tendering of supply contracts to the off-shore industry. Since then, discrimination in favour of Norwegian suppliers in off-shore construction and maintenance – once a prerequisite for companies wishing to obtain licences in Norwegian waters – has stopped. On the other hand, Norway tried for years to ensure that any European Gas Directive would not cover the Norwegian off-shore landing pipelines, especially clauses concerning third-party access (TPA). Official Norway sees TPA as a threat to the established ways of conducting the gas business.

The latest rejection of Wingas as a customer for Norwegian gas led to a more concrete conflict between Europe and Norway: it was followed by an investigation of the gas selling practices at the hands of the European competition authorities. The European Commission's competition directorate, DG-IV, which could not intervene directly since Norway is not a member of the EU, asked the EFTA Surveillance Authority (ESA), to investigate on its behalf a possible violation of Article 59 of the European Economic Area agreement. ESA officials raided offices in Norway one morning in the early summer of 1996, after calling late the preceding afternoon, giving only a token warning. The day of the raids, on purpose or not, was the very day when most of Norway's petroleum officials were to be out to attend the official opening of Troll gas deliveries.

The investigators took documents mostly from Statoil, and later in a letter in October 1996 asked for further clarifications. The Ministry of Petroleum and Energy replied with a lengthy statement entitled 'Memorandum on the Establishment and Functioning of the GFU' (20 January 1997). This document amounts to an outright rejection of the applicability of competition clauses in the EEA agreement on the GFU. It says

> a Party to the EEA agreement has sovereignty and sovereign rights over the petroleum resources on its continental shelf, and the exclusive right to resource management remains with the national state. The same applies to the right of the contracting parties to take necessary measures and apply appropriate means for resource management purposes. Measures taken or means adopted by a Party to the agreement in its exercise of such rights fall outside the scope of the EEA agreement. As a resource management instrument, the GFU has been established by the government as an integral part of the Norwegian resource management system (p.27).

The Ministry appoints the GFU members, and puts them on the job of negotiating new gas sales. In this sense, the GFU is a government instrument. The problem is however, that the state lacks direct control over the members of the GFU. Saga and Norsk Hydro are more or less private companies, but even Statoil as a 100 per cent state-owned company is incorporated as a joint stock company and therefore subject to the commercial laws regulating these companies. Intervention by the state into Statoil's commercial policies can only be effected through the general assembly, which is not a practical steering instrument, and intervention into the GFU can be effected by withdrawing the negotiation mandate, also not a very practical instrument. And government officials have pointed out on numerous occasions that Statoil should and does follow its own commercial objectives. In the words of an astute observer, 'this turns the GFU into a private majority monopoly protected by the state, but as seen from the critics' perspective to the benefit of private commercial interests (*Norsk Olje Revy*, no.8, 1995:16)'. This would be fundamentally opposed to EU/ EEA principles.

Since the clarification request and the subsequent despatch of the Memorandum by the Ministry in January 1997, nothing further has been heard about the ESA investigation. Norwegian officials are quietly optimistic that the matter is indeed closed, but of course are not going to ask ESA about the status of the investigation. ESA does not have the duty to inform Norway about the proceedings, and therefore will not report their closure. 'No news is good news' for the Norwegians.

What could be regarded as a 'close shave' for the centralized gas marketing system in Norway had at least one potentially far-reaching consequence. At the end of 1994, the Ministry had already proposed to all the companies active in Norwegian waters to review the gas transport systems. Originally, at the time, 500 different agreements regulated the transport of gas to the UK and continental Europe. After conflicts broke out over the route of the Zeepipe IIB pipeline, the Ministry urged the companies to negotiate the combination of all the different pipelines in a central transport organization.

The mammoth task of negotiating between more than a dozen international and Norwegian companies with ownership interests in the different pipelines was achieved in the summer of 1995, much to the surprise of almost everybody involved. By this time, contracts were ready to be signed which would have combined all the export pipelines except for the oldest – the Norpipe from Ekofisk – in a single transport company. Statoil was to take operatorship of the company, and administration was planned to be effected through Statoil's own administration, without the creation of a new organization which then would have been suspected of following its own agenda. The state had long before laid out the principle that transport tariffs should merely provide the owners with a 7 per cent return on their pipeline investments, in other words transport should not be seen as a profit centre (*Norsk Olje Revy*, no.8, 1995:20f).

Since then the agreement has been on the shelf in the Ministry of Petroleum and Energy. With the investigation by ESA and the European Commission, it was seen as risky to change the structure of gas transport, into a quite obvious monopoly. The Europeans had kept a watchful eye on gas transport ever since the complaints by Marathon Oil after the renegotiations of the Statfjord contracts, and the allegations that Statoil was using its dominant position to charge monopolistic prices in the Statpipe system.

In addition to ESA and the EU DG-IV investigators, Norway also feared that a unified transport system could much more easily be regarded as part of a European pipeline network which was coming under the regulation of the EU Gas Directive. The Directive covers all pipelines downstream from gas treatment facilities. Whereas UK gas is mainly treated on shore, Norwegian gas is treated on platforms or on shore in Norway, which means the bigger part of the Norwegian offshore pipelines would have come under the Directive, with some form of third-party access looming on the horizon.

Looking at Norway's relation with the EU, history should not be forgotten. As has been pointed out, European governments repeatedly intervened to shore up support for the buyers' consortium, and quite openly rejected Norwegian imports on protectionist grounds. And much of the European gas industry is still openly monopolistic. In this situation, it is not surprising that the European calls to decentralize Norwegian gas marketing are not very appealing to those in charge. Quite in contrast, when talking to Norwegian officials one detects a strong resolve to hold on to the current institutional setting, and to wait and see what happens about liberalization of the European gas market. 'We want to see it first, before we think about changing anything.'

6.2   Outlook For the Future: More Gas and a Tug of War

The contracts with the Czech Republic, Italy, Spain, and eventually Poland, show a new direction for Norwegian gas marketing: extending the limits of the traditional market for their gas. Rather than taking up competitive positions in the European heartland, gas sales are driven to the fringes, where Norway is not yet an established supplier, and where buyers are keen to diversify away from their traditional suppliers. Officials in Norway stress that the idea is not to compete aggressively for market share, but to take part in the growth of markets.

This is an obvious attempt to signal to the other suppliers to the European markets: Norway is willing to avoid harmful aggressive competition between the three major supply countries. The Norwegians want to show that they will not encroach on established Russian markets, and hope the Russians will show similar restraint. The result could be a Cournot-style stand-off, in which each supplier accepts the others' positions, because moving against them would mean all-out war with crumbling prices. Interestingly, Russia has more or less simultaneously refocused exports from the Yamal project, which would have brought substantial new volumes to northern and central Europe, to the Blue Stream project aimed at Turkey and southern Europe. An implicit cartelization of gas supplies to Europe, against which competition authorities would be quite powerless.

To support this, Norway is building an alternative marketing route for gas: a planned Liquefied Natural Gas (LNG) plant in the north of the country, to exploit significant gas finds in the Barents Sea. At the time of writing, appraisal wells were being drilled in order to determine the reserve base more fully, especially the existence of liquids in the reservoirs, which would have to be produced first. Plans for the LNG plant are well advanced and start-up was scheduled for 2004, although this will probably slip given the fall in oil prices in 1998. Otherwise, with the lead times common in these large-scale projects, buyers would have to be found soon.

Other new outlets for gas might have to be found: only recently, the Ormen Lange field was discovered under the leadership of Norsk Hydro, which made the first discovery, and BP in an adjacent licence area, south of the Haltenbanken basin. The new field might contain as much as 400 bcm of gas, or up to one-third of the reserves of the giant Troll. In the medium-term future, with the construction of the Åsgard pipeline over 730 km from the Haltenbanken area to the gas treatment plant in Kårstø, Norway is opening the new area with large reserves. But the capacity in the Åsgard line is already filled with existing contracts, and exploiting Ormen Lange would need new markets, and would necessitate the building of additional pipelines.

The current official position is that Norway does not have much more gas to sell. Norwegian officials stress that instead of new sales they will focus on 'asset management', by which they mean the maintenance of existing contracts and relations with existing buyers. In particular, they will focus on adjusting prices competitively in the periodic price reviews, and building and maintaining strategic relationships with the traditional customers, such as Ruhrgas. Nevertheless, a look at the developments in the reserve base shows that major new sales offensives can be expected, with significant amounts of extra gas available in, say, ten years from now. This would mean that Norwegian gas exports would continue the rise which started with the Troll contracts, and the current committed volume plateau of 75 bcm is not a ceiling. Reaching 90 bcm towards the end of the next decade is a distinct possibility.

In a possible future with liberalization and fractionation of the European gas market, the institutional structure for Norwegian gas sales seems out of place as it was built to counter concentration on the buyers' side. In a new market, the GFU would be overrun by large numbers of small-volume requests. Aggressive marketing of new gas volumes would need a flexible, commercially oriented seller. But it should be remembered that the benefits of the integrated resource management possibility afforded through the current institutional framework are regarded as far greater than any gains to be had from a more commercially oriented gas marketing strategy, as long as Norway can rely on existing long-term contracts.

From a revenue perspective, Norway remains an oil country. It is surprising how strongly this point of view is supported by sources in the Ministry of Petroleum and Energy in Oslo. The belief is that widespread trading on the basis of a European spot market for gas will only be seen in the distant future, and a firm belief in a continuing presence of the major buyers of Norwegian gas is shown. And even if fractionation is about to happen, the Ministry/GFU/FU triumvirate of Norwegian gas sales is not seen as cumbersome and too inflexible for a fast-moving liberalized European market. In the Norwegian view it is precisely the centralization of decision making and the integration of production and a variety of transport pipelines which gives Norway a competitive edge.

The Ministry officials believe that the structure is able to cope, and see Norway well placed to prevail in a faster moving market. Officials point out that the transport infrastructure has spare capacity during most of the year, because it is designed to supply peak demand of about 120 per cent of base volumes. Having an integrated pipeline system, with excess capacity, and the huge Troll field as swing producer, means Norway can accommodate a very wide load variation to take account of seasonal demand patterns. Nevertheless, GFU officials when asked directly insist that their goal is to sign old fashioned take-or-pay contracts with as little flexibility as possible, which as an initial bargaining position is to be expected.

It should be remembered that the current system is designed to give the Ministry control over gas marketing in order to allow the integration of gas and oil production with the final goal of revenue maximization. The Ministry appoints the GFU and FU members, and gives them the task of negotiating on Norway's behalf. The Ministry insists on the control principle, and the GFU/FU system is only one possible way of implementing this principle. Other ways could be found, if the current system for one reason or another had to be changed, without changing the basic principle.

Officially, Statoil closely follows the argumentation of its owner. The most important basis for gas marketing is seen in the Report to the Storting No. 46 from 1986, i.e. in a government document as opposed to a strategic marketing one would expect from a commercial company. But at least the door is left ajar, in that representatives admit the possibility of fast liberalization of European gas markets. Statoil officials are more sanguine about the ability of the current setting to secure markets for Norwegian gas in the future. The leadership acknowledges that as a hedging strategy, Statoil should be prepared for this possibility, be it remote or imminent. Downstream integration policies are therefore followed cautiously, as for example with the acquisition of Alliance Gas in the UK, and the participation in NETRA. This is consistent with the 'asset management' approach, which tries to maintain existing customer relations.

As shown during the Troll negotiations, Norway is capable of marketing aggressively when large new reserves are to be developed. During those negotiations, Statoil agreed to a significant reduction in the prices for Statfjord and Heimdal gas in order to secure large new contracts. But Norway has shown in the past that selling gas is not an aim in itself, and that volumes can be held back from the market when the conditions are not right. With the very comfortable fiscal position, and excellent macro-economic parameters now apparent in the country, this attitude might prevail.

An interesting struggle will then ensue between the Ministry and Parliament on one side, and the commercial actors including Statoil on the other side, with the latter calling for more aggressive marketing efforts, the former urging conservation of resource wealth for future generations. The last twenty years of Norwegian gas marketing presented in this chapter tilt the odds towards the Ministry as the likely winner of the tug-of-war, even if the GFU breaks up and Saga becomes a foreign oil company. Norwegians have much more faith in the central government taking care of their interests than letting foreigners decide about depletion policy. No change in the central control over gas marketing is to be expected in the medium-term future.

Finally, Norway is holding on to what they think is the right way to use their resources. In the long run however, Norway is not isolated from the rest of the world. One can therefore safely assume that when the rest of the world moves firmly towards a liberal, privatized petroleum industry, the Norwegians may be the last to follow, but in the end they will.

Notes

1. This and all other translations used in this chapter are the author's.
2. The Troll reservoir consists of two linked regions, one contains relatively dry gas and is operated by Statoil, and one contains much more oil than gas, where Norsk Hydro is operator.
3. The key consultant working on the division died in an accident, which delayed the process considerably.
4. This story was told by Hans Henrik Ramm, personal communication.

5. Of course, sales negotiations were undertaken without field assignment.
6. It should be noted though that the threat of strike action was perceived to be high ever since, somewhat contradicting the Norwegian effort to appear as a very secure supplier in comparison to the non-European suppliers.
7. The Marathon complaint against the Norwegian government has recently been withdrawn.
8. Both Mobil and Elf sold limited volumes to their respective affiliates.
9. The same metaphor was used for an article about the subject by Jorgen Hanisch and Martin Bould, in *Norsk Olje Revy*, no. 2, 1994:27–38.
10. This section and section 4.3 benefited from comments by Hans Henrik Ramm, personal communication.

References

Angell, V. (1975), 'Basic Facts: Norwegian Oil Policy,' Nupi-Notat, Nupi/N - 111, November, Oslo: Norsk Utenrikspolitisk Institutt.
Ausland, J. (1979), *Norway, Oil, Foreign Policy*, vol. 1, Boulder, Colorado: Westview Press.
Austvik, O.G. (1989), *Norwegian Oil and Foreign Policy*, vol. 1, Sandvika: Norwegian Institute of International Affairs.
Bergesen, H.O. and K. Sydnes, eds (1990), *Naive Newcomer or Shrewd Salesman? Norway – a Major Oil and Gas Exporter*, vol. 1, Oslo: The Fridtjof Nansen Institute.
Brundtland, G.H. (1987), 'The Politics of Oil: A View from Norway,' A. J. Meyer Memorial Lecture, Energy and Environmental Policy Center, John F. Kennedy School of Government, Harvard University.
Cornot, S. (1989), *Norwegian Gas: Reaching New Markets*, Paris: CEDIGAZ.
—(1987), *Troll: The Project, Contracts, the Outlook*, Paris: CEDIGAZ.
Det Kongelige Olje- og Energidepartement (1997–98), Olje- og Gassvirksomheten., Oslo.
Energi- og Industrikomiteen (1984), Stortingsmelding Nr. 73: Om Organiseringen av Statens Deltagelse i Petroleumsvirksomheten., Oslo.
Estrada, J., H.O. Bergesen, A.Moe, and A.K. Sydnes (1988), *Natural Gas in Europe*, vol. 1, London: Pinter Publishers.
European Gas Markets (several years), monthly trade press, London: PH Energy Analysis.
Euroil, formerly Noroil (several years), monthly trade press, London: Hart Europe Ltd.
Golombek, R., E. Gjelsvik, and K.E. Rosendahl (1996) 'Increased Competition on the Supply Side of the Western European Natural Gas Market,' Memorandum of the Department of Economics, Universitet i Oslo.
— (1994) 'Effects of Liberalizing the Natural Gas Markets in Western Europe,' Memorandum of the Department of Economics, Universitet i Oslo.
Hanisch, J. and G. Nerheim (1993), Norsk Olje Historie, vol. 1., Oslo: Norsk

Petroleumsforening.

International Energy Agency (1997), *Energy Policies of IEA Countries*, Paris: OECD.

Johnsen, A. (1990), *Gjennombrudd og Vekst*, vol. 1, Oslo: Gyldendal Norsk Forlag.

Lind, T. and A. Mackay (1980), *Norwegian Oil Policies*, vol. 1, London: Hurst and Co.

Maisonnier, G. (1997), *The European Gas Market Players*, Paris: CEDIGAZ.

Mallakh, R. El-, O. Noreng, and B.B. Poulson (1984), *Petroleum and Economic Development: The Cases of Mexico and Norway*, vol. 1, Lexington MA: Lexington Books.

Naerings- og Energidepartementet (1995–96), Stortingsproposisjon No. 50: Olje- og Gassvirksomhet, Utbygging og Drift av Åsgardfeltet samt Disponering av Innretningene pa Odinfeltet., Olso.

Noreng, O. (1980), *The Oil Industry and Government Strategy in the North Sea*, vol. 1, London: Croom Helm.

Norsk Olje Revy (Several Years) Oil Industry Monthly.

Olje- og Energidepartementet (1986–87), Stortingsmelding No. 46: Om Petroleumsvirksomheten pa Mellomlang Sikt., Oslo.

Petroleum Economist (several years), monthly trade press, London: Petroleum Economist.

Royal Norwegian Ministry of Finance (1973–74), Parliamentary Report No. 25: Petroleum Industry in Norwegian Society, Oslo.

Royal Norwegian Ministry of Petroleum and Energy (1998), Norwegian Petroleum Activity Fact Sheet 1997, Oslo.

— (1997), Memorandum on the Establishment and Functioning of the GFU., Oslo.

— (1969–70), Report No. 95 To the Norwegian Storting: On the Exploration for and Exploitation of Submarine Natural Resources on the Norwegian Continental Shelf, etc., Oslo.

Saeter, M. and I. Smart, eds (1975), *The Political Implications of North Sea Oil and Gas*, vol. 1, Oslo: Universitetsforlaget.

CHAPTER 6

WHAT DOES THE FUTURE HOLD FOR THE EUROPEAN
GAS BUSINESS?

Ian Wybrew-Bond

How far can one meaningfully look ahead? In many ways it is easier
to look ten rather than five years into the future for although change
will certainly take place and its general direction is becoming clearer,
its pace in different markets is difficult to forecast.

In the preceding chapters the authors have given their assessment
of the stances that the four producing states have taken to date and
are likely to take in the future. They and all exporters to the European
gas market are facing a much more uncertain world than they have
known so far. Changes in the business environment are affecting both
their main customers, that is the large gas companies, and their own
direct selling activities; and they will all feel less in control than they
have become accustomed to. The conjunction of the development and
enlargement of the European Union, the market liberalization process
now under way in all utility sectors and the prospect of significantly
lower than expected energy prices have created a very uncertain
business environment.

In this chapter the key changes in the business environment are
assessed and the positions of the four states as producers are
summarized and reviewed.

1. Business Environment in the Coming Decade

Whatever happens to gas, Europe as a region will face an increasingly
competitive business environment, particularly as the Far East and
South Asian countries recover from the economic upheavals of 1998
and become even more economically formidable than in the past.
Europe will therefore need to pursue liberalization policies in all its
markets to achieve lower industrial costs. Some governments are
already recognizing the economic benefits of putting state-owned

monopolies in all utility areas into private commercial hands. This will change many of the accepted business structures and practices that have prevailed since the Second World War. New players will enter the scene.

Let us now discuss the main areas of change faced by the gas industry.

(i) *The place of gas in the European energy mix*. Gas will continue to hold, if not enhance, its place in all non-transport market sectors. There will be a continued push for stricter emission control standards driven by growing public environmental concerns. Gas has a major role to play in helping to achieve the ambitious CO_2 targets being considered and this, coupled with the economic benefits of the improved gas turbine technology now available, will mean that gas will be the prime fuel choice for incremental power generation.

Southern and Eastern Europe are already offering major growth opportunities for gas as these areas catch up with the economic development of the North, a process in which the EU is playing an active part through regional support policies.

(ii) *Market liberalization*. Although many observers will see the 1998 EU gas directive as a weak compromise with a long lead time for its implementation, the very fact of its existence legitimizes the development of competition. Before the directive was approved a strong case to maintain the existing structures and understandings between the established main gas players could be made. This is no longer the case. The 1997 EU electricity directive has already led to the development of electricity trading pools with published prices in a number of European countries, further to those already established in England/Wales and the Nordic states. The potential benefits of this growing price transparency will not be lost on customers, particularly those with significant energy purchases of both gas and electricity. This awareness will be further heightened by the introduction of the Euro, allowing customers in the eleven Euro countries to make international price comparisons with great ease.

Transparency in gas transportation as required by the directive is the key to the creation of real competition. One of the perceived weaknesses of the Gas Directive is that each country is permitted to decide the form of third-party access (TPA), either negotiated or regulated, that will be introduced into its market. Negotiated TPA does not go far enough for those wanting open transportation markets because the transmission/distribution system owners would still retain a competitive advantage over other gas suppliers wishing to use their system. Though the systems' owners are required to unbundle the transmission and distribution accounts from other gas activities, they are not asked to make them public. Without this transparency there is no guarantee of a level playing field for all system users. Regulated TPA provides this transparency but the establishment of an independent regulator causes concern amongst some governments that, as in the UK, it can develop a life of its own. The UK government supported its regulators' freedom of action to promote an open competitive arena following the privatization of its state-owned utilities. However, a similar process of privatization is only in its infancy on the Continent where there has been much less dissatisfaction with the way utility monopolies have managed their affairs. The concept of an independent regulator who may create additional uncertainty in already changing markets is therefore not welcomed everywhere.

The European Commission is already bringing together the various countries' energy and, where appointed, regulatory authorities to provide a forum for discussion of their progress in implementing the Directive. This appears to be a 'softly softly' approach using encouragement and peer pressure to achieve change. Although not all countries have decided to establish regulatory authorities, no one wants to provide the EU Commission with a pretext for establishing a Brussels-based regulator. Failure to provide the competitive environment in their markets as required by the Directive could constitute such a pretext.

(iii) *Customer behaviour.* Now that the directives are in place, there is no longer any unrequited political drive as such for liberalization. It is now up to customers to use the opportunities that liberalization will provide to seek suppliers who will offer them gas at reduced costs. Large companies are likely to aggregate their energy requirements in order to improve their bargaining positions. In many cases this will involve subsidiaries in a number of countries. Smaller companies may seek to enhance their market power through the creation of alliances and buyer consortia.

Further changes are likely to affect municipalities where utilities covering the residential sector have a monopoly over supplies. Some are considering selling their utility business to raise finance.

(iv) *Existing and new players.* There will be new players in the gas business: suppliers or large customers who decide to build their own transmission/distribution systems as has happened recently in the Netherlands; traders who will take advantage of the shorter-term contracting opportunities that are likely to emerge; and companies that decide to develop a multi-utility approach. The obvious examples of the latter are power generators/distributors who are investing in existing gas companies.

A number of existing players are in the process of repositioning themselves to take advantage of new opportunities. From past experience in the USA and the UK we know that old structures may break and new coalitions form as companies develop strategies different from those of their existing partners. These changes will often be the most unsettling for the companies that are in some ways left behind. In most European markets transmission and distribution were established as state monopolies and some are now being privatized. Germany was the exception as the gas transmission and distribution industry was divided into monopoly areas through demarcation agreements between private gas companies. Furthermore interlocking shareholdings between many suppliers, transporters and their customers (the distribution companies and local municipalities), provide an unusual binding together of everyone traditionally involved in the gas industry.[1]

The pattern of these relationships may be reshuffled drastically should any player abandon these arrangements seeing greater commercial gain from becoming, for example, a multi-utility supplier. Openness and transparency in Germany will lead to a completely different market structure in time. This could have a radical effect outside Germany and lead customers and suppliers to seek similar freedoms.

Some players may decide to integrate vertically such as transmission companies deciding to go upstream.[2] Others may decide to take a similar position in the value chain in one or more of the electricity, water and telecom industries. In the UK a number of the regional electricity companies (RECs) also decided to be in all parts of the electricity supply chain and so integrated upstream in the electricity business by becoming generators. Having done so they then bought into the gas production sector too. They also became active traders in the new electricity pool and with that experience welcomed and facilitated the development of short-term gas trading. Some used both their new CCGT outputs and contracted gas supplies as trading commodities deciding whether to market gas or electricity on virtually a daily basis depending on the price they could achieve in either market. At the same time US utilities were actively acquiring RECs to establish a base in the UK from which to take advantage of potential continental opportunities. Later, many of them thought better of this when it became clear that the European market was going to liberalize more slowly than they had expected. Their departure then presented opportunities for consolidation of some of the RECs amongst themselves. Several RECs and PowerGen then withdrew totally or in part from the gas production business.

A further and somewhat unexpected development in the second half of 1998 has been the recent spate of mergers of major oil companies. Before their mergers, the partners in Exxon-Mobil, and BP-Amoco-ARCO had significant but diverging interests and approaches to the European gas business and it is not yet clear what form their merged gas strategies will take compared to the past. Immediate questions come to mind. Will Exxon allow the continuation of the more entrepreneurial approach that Mobil has taken to new market situations or insist that the Mobil position follows the Exxon policy of avoiding taking market risk wherever possible? What will be the effect on the Shell-Esso (as Exxon is known in Europe) relationship in situations where Mobil is also involved such as in Germany, the UK and, to a lesser extent, the Netherlands? These are important questions bearing in mind the strong positions that Shell and Esso hold through their joint and equal shareholdings in a number of existing major gas companies such as Gasunie, Ruhrgas, BEB, and Thyssengas. Mobil also has a direct interest in Ruhrgas and collaborates with BEB in production joint ventures in Germany, and is active in the UK downstream gas business as well as offshore. Furthermore there are signs that Shell and Esso are taking different attitudes to the liberalizing market place. Shell has bought Esso's share of Quadrant, their joint venture UK downstream gas company, to form Shell Gas Direct and subsequently added Texaco and part of Total's gas business to that. Shell has also bought 50 per cent of the power project developer, Intergen, which it now shares with Bechtel. This company is increasingly active in the power market on a worldwide basis. The implications for the joint Shell-Esso participations in the European gas business are not clear but differences there certainly are and these must cause strains for all concerned.

Some producers have long-standing shareholdings in a number of gas companies and for them there is the dilemma of how to avoid being the 'prisoner' of such positions. These may prevent them taking control of their own downstream destiny now that the balance of risk in the gas business is moving from the technical arena to the market place. Companies such as Enron have neither upstream positions nor any established value chain to protect. They are therefore free to take advantage of and promote the opportunities that a liberalized market can bring. This is also true of electricity companies who are increasingly active in the gas world, be it as potential traders of their existing gas supplies or developing a gas business utilizing their access to electricity customers.

(v) *Gas prices, contracting terms and availability.* It makes sense to discuss these issues together as they are all subject to the uncertainties of the changing market and so obviously interdependent.

The bedrock of the European gas business has been long-term supply contracts, and many of the existing agreements have expiry dates well into the next century. These will continue although the major buyers, the gas companies, face a loss of market share with the liberalization of their hitherto captive markets. Their ability to place all the gas which they have contracted will be weakened. The UK-Continent Interconnector will export to North West Europe what some regard as the 'British Disease' of short-term and spot market trading. Whilst many may be locked into long-term contracts, there will nevertheless be a growing knowledge of what is happening to gas prices elsewhere through the ever increasing amount of data published on a daily basis. This cannot but have an effect on existing customer-supplier relationships.

There is currently no shortage of gas and the key transmission infrastructure is in place to transport all the gas that the market would require for the foreseeable future. Security of supply is therefore no longer the immediate concern that it has been in the past. Some worries remain of course about possible political developments notably in Russia and Algeria. Had not the major infrastructure investments been made in recent years against a backdrop of higher energy prices then we would not be quite as sanguine about short-term supply security as we can now be. However if energy prices remain at their current depressed levels for some time then concerns will re-emerge, particularly if there is a significant increase in demand for gas from the power sector.

Gas prices in most European countries have hitherto been linked to oil prices through indexation formulae which reflect the role of oil as the principal competitor to gas. The recent trend of falling oil prices is therefore having a downward effect on gas prices. In existing continental gas contracts there are normally re-openers which allow price adjustments every three years. The liberalization of the gas market is likely to lead eventually to the decoupling of gas and oil prices following the development of gas-to-gas competition. Whether gas prices then develop a life of their own, or become partly coupled to another energy such as electricity remains to be seen. Either way a less predictable and, in the short term, volatile gas pricing environment will have to be faced when planning new investments.

As it takes a long time to bring gas projects on stream, the question arises of what does a gas producer assume for the long-term price of gas. When market liberalization and short-term gas trading began in the UK, price movements were obviously not related to the then accepted longer-term supply/demand norms. The effect was to cause confusion as to what was the 'real' price of gas. Distinctions between longer- and shorter-term pricing were not clear or predictable particularly to those planning gas projects. Although initially gas volumes traded on a short-term basis were relatively small, their pricing prior to the establishment of a more structured and transparent market became one more based on rumour than solid fact. At the beginning of gas-to-gas competition in the UK, the volumes involved were small and there was therefore little impact on the overall supply/demand balance. This has now changed to a degree and gas pricing has become more transparent and a distinction can be made between seasonal price variations and the pricing of long-term supplies. In the UK, the transition was long, however, as it took time for the seasonal gas market and its related pricing basis to grow and become understood. For the continental market and North Western Europe in particular, the situation is different. The basis on which new long-term, long distance supplies will be priced is not yet clear. The speed at which gas-to-gas competition will develop until it becomes a substantial market with well established fundamentals is also uncertain. Without it producers will have difficulties in making pricing assumptions to support project development.

The UK experience in terms of ensuring new gas supplies during a time of market liberalization is not relevant to the continent. The UK was fortunate that during this period there were a number of southern North Sea fields that were small, relatively cheap and quick to bring onstream, and therefore easy to place on the market. Had only large and expensive new UKCS fields been available in the early 1990s then it is questionable whether enough producers would have taken the risk to develop sufficient new supplies to provide for the 'dash for gas' that the newly privatized RECs sparked off in their desire to become CCGT generators as well as distributors.

As Table 1 shows there will be a significant supply gap opening up throughout Europe by the end of the next decade. Although the regional supply gaps are fairly equal, the incremental increase in the north west is much smaller than the other two regions and represents much smaller growth rates. The new battlefields are therefore in the

Table 1: Currently Contracted Gas Supplies to Europe in 2010. Billion Cubic Metres

Suppliers	Supply Gap	Others	Norway	Algeria	Russia	Netherlands	Domestic	Total
NW Europe								
Austria			1		5			6
Belgium	6		6	*5*		4		21
Denmark	4						2	6
Finland	2				4			6
France	3	1	15	*10*	12	5	2	47
Germany		4	31		45	22	14	116
Ireland	5	1						5
Netherlands			6		4		36	46
Sweden	2	1						3
Switzerland	1	1			0	1		4
UK			2			2	115	119
Total NW Europe	23	7	61	15	70	34	169	378
Southern Europe								
Italy		4	6	25	27	8	15	85
Spain	10	3	2	10				25
Greece	1			1	2			4
Portugal	1			3				3
Turkey	10	11		4	30			55
Total South	21	18	8	42	59	8	15	171

Note: Italics indicates contracts run out just before 2010.

Source: Ulrich Bartsch

Table 1: Continued

Suppliers	Supply Gap	Others	Norway	Algeria	Russia	Netherlands	Domestic	Total
Central Europe								
Poland	4		3		11	2	4	20
Bulgaria	3				6			10
Estonia	1				1			4
Latvia	7				1			2
Lithuania	8				3			9
Romania	2		3		5		12	25
Czech Rep.	1	1			8		0	14
Hungary	4				10		2	13
Slovakia					6		0	11
Total Centre	29	1	6		51	2	19	108
Others				3				3
Total	73	26	75	60	181	44	203	661

Note: Italics indicates contracts run out just before 2010.

Source: Ulrich Bartsch

southern and central European gas markets. While much of the required infrastructure is in place, it is not clear in these uncertain pricing times which producers will be prepared to invest in project development to take advantage of demand in these markets.

2.   How will the Producers be Affected and Behave?

The interplay between market changes and long-established gas contracting arrangements is a major strategic concern for the four national companies discussed in earlier chapters as well as their national governments. The natural gas trade involves large amounts of money which lead to complex and delicate relationships between the producing countries and their key consuming countries. Each consuming country has so far achieved security of supply through a balance of contractual commitments between the producing countries.

Each national producer has a portfolio of long-term contracts already in place which are being extended whenever possible and especially where the required transitional export pipelines are already in place. There is a strong incentive to keep such lines fully utilized, particularly in those instances where they run close to gas fields that can therefore be readily developed. Furthermore much time and energy has been expended over a long period in establishing commercial relationships and developing trust between the producers and their principal customers.

Supply that is already contracted will build up significantly over the next five years as a result of the new Trans-Med/GME, Maghreb– Europe pipelines and increased LNG capacity from Algeria, the build up of Troll volumes, and new sales to Italy and Czechia from Norway, and the extension of the old Soviet contracts and the first Yamal gas volumes from Russia through the new Belarus–Poland line. Although Dutch production volumes will probably remain constant, existing contracts are being extended wherever possible, and the loss of internal market share to competitors will be compensated by increases in exports. There will be competition from new suppliers mainly from the UKCS, from Nigeria and Trinidad (LNG) and possibly from the Middle East in the longer term. However new LNG supplies even from the expansion of existing projects will have difficulties to compete with pipeline gas given high regasification costs.

There is always the possibility that a big new field either in or close to Europe will be discovered but low gas prices and liberalization will make it difficult or impossible to justify its development.

The interplay between the emerging market changes and the long-established gas arrangements outlined above will be a major determinant of the growth of the short-term gas market. Other factors such as climate change, inter-fuel price relationships, and individual government energy policies will also have their influence on future growth.

In covering each producing country in more detail we have looked at the way each is adapting its upstream expansion to the changing business environment; what are their marketing strategies; what if anything they are doing in the 'downstream' which means anywhere in the value chain beyond production; and what are the institutional changes that could be foreseen, particularly changes in the role of government? In summary we have drawn the following conclusions.

3.   Algeria

Algeria already has a long-established history as both a pipeline and the principal LNG supplier to Europe. Its objective to expand annual gas exports to 60 bcm will be achieved within the framework of its existing long-term contracts, and it has more gas resources than those already contracted and both the LNG and pipeline infrastructure in place for further gas exports. It is geographically the best placed of any supplier to take advantage of the growth markets of southern Europe and it wishes to maintain its pre-eminent supplier position to this region. While the Spanish authorities have said that they wish to limit their dependency on Algerian supplies to a maximum of 60 per cent as currently contracted, there should be opportunities for additional Algerian gas sales as the Spanish market rapidly expands.

Although Algeria's gas reserves appear relatively large, its gas dominated economy and long-term domestic requirements have tempered its gas export ambitions. At the same time, Sonatrach is under considerable government pressure to expand its hydrocarbon exports to provide additional foreign exchange earnings. Their difficulty lies in deciding whether to expand gas exports or go for the higher rent generated from oil. Partnerships with foreign oil companies are increasingly being recognized as the way forward although defining what is a fair return for them, while Algeria retains what it regards as an appropriate share of the rent, is not easy. It would be to Sonatrach's benefit if the management of such 'resource rental' issues could be given to a separate government agency which would allow Sonatrach to develop like any other oil and gas company taking geological, investment and market risks. This would force it to face up to its cost base without the protection of high resource rents.

Sonatrach has come to recognize that it cannot avoid taking some market risk in a liberalizing world if it wishes to protect its market positions and the income flow that gas exports provide. New contracts may have to become more flexible with shorter durations, lower 'take-or-pay' requirements, market related indexation, and lower prices without the protection for the supplier of a floor price. Its marketing joint venture with BP-Amoco-ARCO, In Salah Gas, certainly faces these issues as part of its marketing challenge.

Although Sonatrach has a new corporate structure which in theory should give it more freedom and provide for some separation of politics and business, it is not clear that Sonatrach itself sought this change and therefore whether in reality it will influence the way the corporation thinks and acts. This will be critical to Sonatrach's success and destiny.

4.   Netherlands

The Dutch as the lowest cost producer can weather a period of low gas prices better than anyone else. All the infrastructure required to service their internal and export markets is in place together with recently expanded storage capabilities to allow them to upgrade gas to meet short-term seasonal market needs that may emerge. However, they are no longer prepared to act as the swing producer for Europe without an appropriate reward. Any significant increase in Dutch gas activities is therefore more likely to be in the area of capacity providers than gas production with the government maintaining an 80 bcm overall annual production target. Gasunie, for example, is promoting a pipeline link between the Netherlands and the UK to provide seasonal load balancing for the UK market.

Gasunie has accepted that they will no longer be able to retain their past degree of dominance of the Dutch market and have published tariffs for third party use of their infrastructure. Irrespective of whether or not the levels set are fair and equitable, the publication of these rates says much about the changing attitudes within Gasunie towards accepting liberalization as a fact of life.

As a result of the erosion of their inland market position, Gasunie will have more gas available for export within the 80 bcm annual production limit and they are seeking to expand and extend their contracts accordingly.

It will be interesting to see whether Gasunie retains its existing financial structure which limits its net income to D.Fl.80 million per year with the balance passing to the government and upstream producers, predominantly NAM, the Shell-Esso company which owns Groningen. The government takes its rent through an involved taxation and corporate structure. The current Gasunie income limitation seems hardly likely to encourage the entrepreneurial flair which a liberalizing market would demand. So how does Gasunie measure its success? As yet it has shown no interest in developing direct marketing outside the Netherlands as it is thought that this would prejudice its relationships with its existing clients. So is Gasunie trapped, a prisoner of its shareholders' wishes and not able to generate any incremental income for itself? The shareholders, Shell and Esso, may have diverging views of how they wish to position themselves and the companies in which they have substantial interests in terms of market risk.

An interesting development would be if the Dutch government were to privatize Gasunie but not allow Shell or Esso to increase their combined 50 per cent shareholding. This would require the introduction of a new mechanism to provide the Dutch government with rent, income via taxation and to retain control over depletion through production limits.

There is a problem however. The current 'small fields policy' followed by the Netherlands allows independent producers to bring fields forward with Groningen acting as the swing producer. If the independent producers seek to market their gas to their own chosen markets, and there are signs that this may be about to happen on a measurable scale, the Dutch government would then face a depletion policy management issue.

5.   Russia

The most important of the nation producers but the one about which there is the greatest uncertainty. It is not yet clear what economic structure will finally emerge following the major political changes that already have taken place and those that are yet to come. Not only does Russia face the same low energy price challenges as other producers, but it has to decide how and in what form its gas industry will operate. That will in part depend on the economic environment in which Russia decides to operate.

If it finally decides to pursue market-based economic reform, which would have general international support and would therefore lead to the provision of further international financial aid, then one of the conditions attached to such assistance is likely to be the requirement for vertically integrated organizations such as Gazprom to be broken up. If the government were to agree, competition would emerge in the domestic market from other Russian gas producers (providing economic reform also leads to Russian consumers agreeing to pay for their gas supplies). Once this is achieved, the collection of payments for domestic supplies would also have the effect of making the Russian domestic market more attractive than gas exports. The break-up of Gazprom would create great uncertainty for the rest of Europe, the question being: who, post Gazprom as we know it, would be the residual holder(s) of the current Russian long-term contracts which provide over a quarter of European gas demand?

If in the shorter term Russia decides to continue with centralized management of its economy then Gazprom's income flow will continue to be very important for the country and it is unlikely that any break-up of its structure would be contemplated which could jeopardize this revenue flow. However, even under centralized management market mechanisms must come into effect in the longer term and Gazprom will be subject to demerging pressures – albeit somewhat later than under a market-based economy.

A further issue, considering that virtually all Russian gas exports transit the Ukraine, is whether the relationship between the two countries will become less confrontational. Russia is also clearly dominant in supplying Turkey, the fastest growing European gas market, and its proposed new supply routes to this country are intended to pre-empt imports from other sources.

Gazprom's management of these issues is critical to Russia remaining the dominant force in gas supplies to Europe and possibly to Gazprom retaining its position as the sole, or at the very least, the pre-eminent exporter of Russian gas. Although the other principal suppliers to Europe cannot replace Russia entirely, they will attempt to increase their supplies when Gazprom's customers start to feel any uncertainty. The recent buy-in of some 4 per cent of Gazprom stock by Ruhrgas, however, may steady customer confidence. Ruhrgas in return could be seen as trying to neutralize Wingas's position and its special relationship with Gazprom.[3]

The strengthening of Gazprom's relationship with Ruhrgas, coupled with its hold through Wingas, will give the Russian giant a powerful influence in maintaining a market structure which provides security of offtake. Since 1990 its Wingas shareholding has provided Gazprom with market intelligence on true costs and margins as well as a learning platform for its executives.[4] Establishing Wingas in the backyard of Ruhrgas had a major impact on other traditional Gazprom customers. The Volta joint venture with Edison was set up to increase Gazprom sales to Italy and the very threat of its establishment led SNAM to sign for additional supplies. Gazprom has since established trading houses in all markets except the UK and the Czech republic, with partners involved in marketing, pipelines, and trading. This gives Gazprom knowledge and a degree of control over the placement of its gas.

With available gas, increasing transmission capacity, and established marketing ventures in virtually every country where it currently sells gas, Gazprom would seem to be ideally prepared to meet the brave new world of competitive European gas markets. The reality is somewhat different. The company has yet to provide an indication as to whether it intends to be a leader or a follower in the move towards gas-to-gas competition and access to networks. With a few exceptions (principally in Germany and Hungary) it is not clear what role its joint venture marketing companies are playing, or indeed whether many of them are active at all. Ideally, the company should be preparing these companies for the increase in short-term trading opportunities. Gazprom is handicapped in that political and economic instability in Russia (and other CIS countries) are a serious distraction for senior management, and divert attention away from the changing nature of the company's export business. Where management time is being spent on exports, it is on new projects such as Blue Stream where the challenges are technical and financial, rather than commercial. If Gazprom intends to wait to see 'how things turn out' it risks losing market share to faster and more aggressive players. The company needs to understand that in the gas market development anticipated in Europe, it is the quickest, rather than the biggest, which will prosper.

6. Norway

Through the Troll Sales Agreements Norway is the principal potential source of incremental gas supply from within Europe and exports should increase from 45 bcm to 75 bcm by the middle of the next decade. Beyond that Norway has the reserves to increase its gas exports by a similar quantity again, but will no doubt balance the need to maintain its market position against the impact on prices of adopting too aggressive a marketing stance.

From time to time Norwegian domestic politics dictate that there are limits put on the level of hydrocarbon exports. They have a small population and, compared to other resource holders, have a relatively lower level of total national income needs. However, continued low oil and gas prices are likely to weaken this resolve over time and agreement to increased sales is probable, providing prices will not be further depressed as a result. With an extensive export infrastructure already in place it is unlikely that Norway will eventually hold back on gas exports.

The perennial question surrounding the future of Norwegian gas exports concerns that of the GFU, the gas negotiating committee. This is coming under increasing scrutiny from the EU because of its potentially anti-competitive nature. It is often said that if the GFU were disbanded, then this would allow Norwegian sector producers to place their gas individually in the liberalizing European gas market. This would increase gas-to-gas competition and would mean that the government would have little if any control over its gas exports. This is theoretically true. However, whether the GFU as such is retained as a formal structure or not, it is clear that the Norwegian government intends to retain a controlling position over the disposition of its gas resources. The marketing arrangements for gas are established in the government's original approval for each project. The only way around this is for an individual producer to be able to demonstrate that it would achieve a greater return by selling to its own downstream affiliate than through the collective arrangement negotiated by the GFU. It should also be borne in mind that Norway is a very socially cohesive country. All Norwegians involved in the hydrocarbon sector have strong informal links and would be unlikely to take any steps or suggest any way forward which would not be widely acceptable. To repeat the point made above, independent steps in marketing gas that could prejudice the overall return on Norwegian gas will not be allowed.

Statoil entered the downstream gas business in the UK, initially in a joint venture with BP which was later split up. It has no doubt learnt much about the gas trading world from its ownership of the US Eastern energy group. It is a player in the Nordic power pool. Statoil and Norsk Hydro are partners in the NETRA pipeline and storage system linking Emden and the VNG network in what was East Germany – involving also Ruhrgas and BEB from Germany. Statoil and therefore Norway are aware from their US and UK experience what a liberalizing world will mean but there are no signs at present that Statoil will become a more active downstream player in the continental gas market.

However Norway is not isolated from the rest of the world. It can be assumed that when the continent moves towards a more liberalized market, the Norwegians will not allow themselves to be left behind.

7. Future Certainties and Uncertainties

It is now widely recognized that the question is no longer whether the utilities markets will liberalize, but when. The time is past when gas could be thought of as a 'noble fuel'. It is now regarded as a tradable commodity like many others. The 'Gas Club' – a small number of companies who could determine the structure and shape of this industry – is still powerful but no longer the dominant force that it once was. It is reported that the competition authorities (DG IV) in the European Commission are in the process of investigating allegedly uncompetitive behaviour on the part of Ruhrgas, BEB, Thyssengas, Gaz de France and Gasunie. To many this investigation is welcome and they seek to erode further the 'Club's' power, but it should not be forgotten that the industry that has developed over the past forty years owes much to the foresight, vision and commercial courage of the original gas players.

That said, there have been great rewards for these founders of the gas industry and it is hardly surprising, first, that others now want to have a share of the pie and, secondly, that the original key players want to hold on to what they have created for as long as possible. To many of them their whole world began to be threatened when the UK embarked on its privatization programme and opened up its hitherto monopolistic utility industries to competition. For the purposes of this book the UK has only been mentioned in passing as it is not expected to become a major gas exporter to (or importer from) the Continent in the coming years. However, despite its limited involvement in trans-European gas trade, this most liberalized of all European gas markets, may have a great influence on the evolution of other European markets. Many lessons have been learnt but, perhaps more importantly, many people have learnt how to participate profitably in the gas industry. Many of these are new to the business and therefore unhampered by past traditions and understandings and as a result think of doing things in new ways. They are willing and determined to bring their new approaches to the Continent.

The European gas industry is special in that it is predominantly the supply province of four national producers who control the resources of their countries even though private companies are involved to some extent in their development. There is therefore a political overlay to what in any event is a complex business environment. The liberalization of all utility markets, the formation processes and the enlargement of the EU, the uncertainties surrounding Russia, and lower than expected energy prices putting pressure on the national incomes of producing countries, are important political factors that cloud the horizon.

Although market liberalization is not in question, its pace in different countries is uncertain and will be determined largely by the form of access to the existing pipeline systems. Regulated TPA will provide a transparency that will facilitate the opening of the markets but it is not certain that all countries will adopt this approach.

Low oil and therefore gas prices may also in the short term reduce some customers' appetites for change and their need to access suppliers outside the existing accepted structures. Should gas prices rise again this could quickly change.

The current gas company aggregators have lost some degree of control. The value of the gas chain will shrink and this will put pressure on all players to the benefit of the end-user. This is not unknown in other industries where companies have managed to adapt and survive, albeit on thinner margins.

Each player, new and old, will have to embrace uncertainty in the protection of their commercial position. This will place existing coalitions of interests under strain and some may break and new ones form as each seeks to establish its own best commercial position. The only prediction that can be made with any certainty is that commercial imperatives will ensure that a dynamic world will emerge which will be different from the predictable one with which we have become familiar. Gas will continue to be needed and new contracting arrangements will emerge. They will provide security for producers but in new ways and providing they are prepared to take a degree of market risk themselves.

This whole process will bring to the fore those people who can embrace change and seek to maximize the opportunities it will bring. To hide behind continued 'denial' will only hand these opportunities to others.

The only two serious uncertainties are related firstly and most importantly to the future of Gazprom and secondly to the possible break-up of the existing interlocking German market structure. Were Gazprom to be demerged in a way that left its international customers unsure as to who in Russia was responsible for the provision of secure supplies, this would create a supply vacuum from which the Norwegians in particular could benefit in the long term.

The structure of the German market is considered important, as earlier discussed, because it involves a number of private monopolies. Although the demarcation agreements, which up to now have prevented what has been described as 'inefficient competition' between the gas companies are being dismantled, their intent will continue to be supported by the ongoing interlocking shareholdings between suppliers, transporters and customers. No one 'rocks the boat' as a result. That may not continue. If a significant company were to decide to follow an independent and probably multi-utility strategy, major cracks would appear in the market structure. This would have a ripple effect on other markets and speed the process of European liberalization. If, on the other hand, the current German structure were to hold, the pace of liberalization may well slow down but it will not, even then, stop.

Notes

1. Wingas as the new usurper has no such relationships although there are signs, now that it is established and accepted as a fact of life, that it would like to be part of 'the system'.
2. For example, some time ago Ruhrgas took a small position in the UK offshore and more recently bought into Gazprom.
3. Ruhrgas will have a legitimate right to information which will not be available to non shareholders. What its position will be vis-à-vis Shell – one of Ruhrgas's shareholders who itself owns 1 per cent in Gazprom – will be an interesting question. As Esso's holding will increase because of the merger between Exxon and Mobil, the pressure within Germany for the maintenance of the status quo in its market structure will be strengthened.
4. Competition between Wingas and Ruhrgas also had the effect of reducing prices in the German market and therefore since 1998 Gazprom has taken a more even-handed view of the two companies.

INDEX

ABB (Sweden) 180
Afghanistan 149, 180
AGIP 18, 161, 177
Air Liquide 74
Air Products and Chemicals 74
Aït-Laoussine, N. 61, 69
Algeria 7, 17–18, 34–92, 242, 264, 265–6
Algerian LNG 6, 13–14, 18, 36, 41, 174
Allcock, J. 210
Alliance Gas (UK) 221, 235–6, 241
Alrar field 57
Ammonia production 74
Amoco 63, 66, 79, 203
AOOT Moldova Gas 160
Arab-Maghreb Union 58
Arco 178
Armenia 155
Åsgard pipeline 249
'Asset management' 249, 251
Astrakhan gas 177
Atlantic LNG (Trinidad) 71
Austria 118, 218
Azerbaidzhan 155

Baltic States 157
Barents Sea 235, 248
Barter trade 137
BASF 17, 164, 243
BEB 162, 208, 218, 241, 259, 270, 271
Bechtel 41, 259
Belarus 60, 155, 157–60, 173, 184
    (see also Yamal pipeline)
Belgium 18
Beltransgaz 159
Berkine field 66, 80
Blue Stream pipeline 166, 172, 175–6, 185, 187–8, 248, 270
Botas (Turkey) 174–5
Boumediene, President H. 42, 49
BP 16, 37, 63, 70, 79–80, 210–12, 239, 249
BP-Amoco merger 66, 70, 83, 130, 259
BP-Sonatrach joint venture 18
Bratstvo (Brotherhood) pipeline 149
British Gas Corporation (BGC) 11, 14, 19, 20, 37, 125, 161, 210, 239
Bulgaria 169–71, 175, 185
Bulgargaz 169

Calorific value 94, 151
CAMEL (Compagnie Algérienne du Méthane Liquide) 37
Capital investment 57, 59
Caspian production region 179
Central Electricity Generation Board (CEGB) 11, 19–20
Centrica 115, 126
Chadli, President B. 49
Chemical and fertilizer industry 74
Chernomyrdin, V. 136, 140, 163, 189
China 235
Coal generated electricity 22

Columbia Gas 55
Combined-cycle Gas Turbine power 11–12, 19–20, 22, 30, 56, 112, 258, 261
Comecon (CAME) 147, 149
Competition 2, 5, 15, 20–3, 124–5, 186–7, 189–90, 193, 201, 212, 246, 255–6, 268
Competition between producer countries 242, 248
Conflict between producing and consuming countries 39
Conoco 179, 217
Conservation policy 105, 251
Continental buyers'consortium 239
Cooper, D.F. 210
Cooperation between producer countries 127
Corporate alliances 135
Cove Point Terminal (USA) 14, 55, 62
Czechoslovakia 240
Czech Republic 118, 168–70, 242, 244, 248, 264, 270

de Korte's Energy Bill 122
de Pous, J.W. 99; Memorandum 100, 121; Natural Gas Bill 105
Delta 115
Denationalization 61
Department of Energy (UK) 211
Depletion policy 34, 36, 43, 82, 208, 226, 228, 230, 251, 267
Deregulation 55, 68, 155
DETG (Germany) 98
Distrigas (Boston) 14, 42, 55–6
Distrigaz (Belgium) 15, 18, 46, 68, 72, 98, 116, 120, 208, 218, 224, 240
Downstream integration 69–70, 73, 128, 135, 162, 236, 241, 250–1, 270
Draupner-S riser platform 224
DSM (Nederlandse Staatsmijnen) 97, 102
'Dutch disease' 101

East Asian market 186–8, 235
Eastern Gas 237
EBN (Energie Beheer Nederland B.V.) 97–8
Ecofuel 74
Edon 110, 129
Eemshaven power plant 115
EFTA Surveillance Authority (ESA) 245, 247
Eggar, T. 235
Egypt 71
Egyptian Petroleum Corporation 72
Ekofisk field 9, 10, 203–5, 208, 209–10, 219, 223, 225
Ekofisk oil pipeline 209
El Paso Natural Gas Company 38, 42
Electricité de France 17
Electricity demand 113
Electricity, nuclear generated 7, 17
Elf Aquitaine 203, 219, 239–40, 244
Elsta 115
EMPL Ltd. 71
Enagas (Spain) 42, 46, 57, 218
ENEL 17–18, 64, 66, 70
Enercom 110

Energy Charter Treaty 159
Energy consumption 115
Energy demand 115
EnergyNed 108, 109
ENI (Italy) 18, 42, 145, 176, 178, 188
ENIP (Algeria) 74, 76
EnTrade 115, 126
Environmental impact 22, 228, 231
Equity policies 227
Esso/Exxon 16, 18, 38, 79, 97–9, 127, 128–9, 203, 259
Ethylene production 74
Etzel storage facility 216
Euro 120, 256
European Economic Area 245
European Energy Market 60
European gas market 15
European Surveillance Agency 217
European Union (formerly Community) 11, 58–9, 174,
    257; competition policy 15, 222, 240–1, 245–8, 271;
    Electricity Directive 12, 22–4, 31, 256; enlargement
    271; energy policy 60, 83
    environment policy 12; Gas Directive 12, 22–4, 32,
    69, 123, 126, 245, 247, 256; gas policy 21;
    Hydrocarbon Directive 106
Europipe 224–5
Europol Gaz 166
EVE (Basque Country) 71
Exploration 80
Export policy 34, 67, 135, 147, 192–4, 270
Export taxes 138
Exports to Europe 53, 56, 67, 70, 102, 127, 148–9, 151,
    162–76, 172–81, 192–4, 211
Exports to Japan 153–4
Exports to North America 38, 42, 53, 55, 65, 67–8, 153–4,
    237

Federal Energy Commission (FEC) (Russia) 139
Fertilizer industry 73
Field depletion contracts 208, 213
Financing of gas industry 57, 141
Fiscal regime (also see Tax payments) 207
FLN 49
Foreign debt 48, 156, 184
Foreign investment 48, 62, 63
Former Soviet Union (USSR) 6, 7, 13–14, 235
Foster Wheeler 43
Fragaz 166
France 17, 57
Frigg field 204, 209, 219
Frigg pipeline 224
Frigg treaty 209, 212–5
Froy field 235
FU (Forsyningsutvalget) 222

Gas and electricity markets 12, 20
'Gas banker' 116
'Gas battle' 35, 36, 42–7
'Gas bubble' 46
'Gas club' 271
Gas consumption 24
Gas exports 41, 48, 83, 116–7, 148, 219, 270
Gas-fired power generation (see also CCGT) 146, 222, 236
'Gas for pipes' 15
Gas futures 21, 130
Gas imports 148
Gas injection 207, 215, 225
Gas policy 121–2
Gas prices 21, 55, 112–3, 119–21, 137, 140, 187, 215, 260,
    270, 272
Gas production 146
Gas production, history 6, 94–5, 142
Gas reserves 51, 54, 66, 83, 107, 143, 204–5, 265

Gas supplies 261–3
Gas storage 129, 216, 266
Gas transmission systems 9, 103–4
Gas transport systems 247, 256
Gas turbine technology 256
Gasum 166
Gasunie 15, 17–8, 31, 42–3, 98–101, 106, 108–19, 126–
    32, 179, 185, 208, 218, 259, 266–7
Gaz de France (GdF) 15, 17, 37, 42, 46, 72, 98, 116, 119,
    151, 168, 208, 218, 240
Gazexport 178, 183
Gazprom 15, 31, 69, 79, 115, 128, 135–6, 141, 143, 145,
    147, 154, 159–94, 242–3, 268–9, 272; foreign
    investment 167; joint ventures and alliances 166–8,
    176–80, 188–9; relations with Russian governments
    137
Gaz Trading 166
Gelsenberg 210, 239
Georgia 155
Germany 13, 16, 163–8, 185–6, 188, 245, 258, 272
GFU (Gassforhandlingsvutvalget) 169, 202, 212, 220–1,
    243, 245–6, 270
Global warming 12, 125
Greece 57
Greenhouse growers 110–1
Groningen field 6, 7, 13, 93–4, 96–8, 100, 101, 104–5,
    107–8, 116, 121, 129, 131, 215, 267
Gullfaks field 205, 209–10, 233
GWH 166

Haltenbanken basin 249
Hamra field 62
Hamrouche government (Algeria) 81
Hansen, B.L. 207
Hard currency earnings (Russia) 171, 182
Hassi Messaoud field 37
Hassi R'Mel field 37, 51, 57
Hassi R'Mel hub 64
Heimdal field 210, 224–5
Helios 74
Household (residential) market 110, 125, 140, 146
Hubs 179, 225
Hungary 168–70, 240, 244

Iberdrola 71
IEA (International Energy Agency) 10, 152
IMF 189–90
In Amenas field 41, 63–4
In Salah field 41, 63–4, 66, 70, 83–4
In Salah Gas Services 64, 83–4, 266
Indexation 22, 39, 42, 112, 260, 266; absolute and relative
    46
Industrialization 36, 42, 44
Industrial sector 111
Integrated resource management 249
Internal Energy Market 60
International Petroleum Exchange 20
Iran 174, 180–1
Iranian gas trunkline (IGAT) 147–8
Iran-Soviet gas trade 147–8
Irkutsk 188
Italy 57, 242, 248, 264
Itera 161, 193

Jagal pipeline 164–5
Johnsen, A. 210, 217, 226, 233
Joint ventures 16, 269

Kaliningrad 157
Karachaganak field 161–2, 179
Kazakhstan 155, 160–2, 183
Khadduri, W. 47

Kristiansen, Kåre 211
Kyrgyzstan 155

Lacq field 17
Liberalization 2, 5, 15, 17–8, 21, 22–24, 30, 60, 68–9, 108, 112, 116, 122–7, 132, 139–41, 189–90, 201, 212, 220, 227, 236–7, 243, 248–51, 255–6, 260–1, 270, 271–3
Licensing rounds 229
Liesen, K. 217, 239
Lignite-based generation 22
Liquefaction plants 43
Liquid helium 74
Lituvos Dujos (Lithuania) 157
LNG vs. pipeline 43
Lubbers, R. 60
Lubbers Energy Bill 105, 121
Lukoil 178–9, 189

'Maatschap' 97–8, 100–1, 130–2
Maghreb-Europe pipeline (GME) 14, 57, 60, 66, 70–1, 79, 84
Marathon 212, 217, 247
Marketing policy 46, 218, 239
Massad, A. 227
Mediterranean market 56, 60
Mega 126
Methane 7
Mezhregiongaz 139, 191
MIDAL pipeline 164–5, 243–4
Midgard field 212
Ministry of Energy (Algeria) 77–8
Ministry of Petroleum and Energy (Norway) 209, 212, 216, 218, 222, 233, 246, 250
Mobil 16, 115, 118, 129, 226–7, 259
Mobil Erdgas Erdol 118
Mobil Exxon merger 127, 130, 258
MOL (Hungary) 170
Moldova 157–60, 184
Monopolies and Mergers Commission (UK) 19–20
Monopolies Commission (Netherlands) 126
Monopoly and monopolization 16–17, 23, 68, 96, 118, 126, 189–90, 222, 241, 243–8, 256, 271–2
Morocco 14, 38, 58, 70
Morrison, P. 213
Moynihan, C. 213
MTBE (Methyl tertiary-butyl ether) production 74
Munnekezijl concession 118

Nadymgazprom 139
NAFTAL 76
NAFTEC 76
NAM (Nederlandse Aardolie Maatschappij) 38, 94, 97–8, 100–1, 106, 118, 267
National Committee for Energy (NCE) 50
National Consultative Committee on Energy (NCCE) 49–50
National Energy Council (NEC) 49–50, 76–9
National Grid 19
National Power (UK) 19, 212, 235
Nationalization 52, 61–2
NATO embargo 150
NCS (Norwegian Continental Shelf) 203–4, 209
Netherlands 6, 13, 17–8, 93–133, 266–7
Netherlands Mining Act 1810 95
Netra pipeline 186, 221, 240–2, 270
Nigeria 24, 264
Nigerian LNG 18, 174
Nitrogen content 94, 104
Nofra 225
Non-payment of debts 138, 191, 269
Nordic Gas Grid 174, 185
Norpipe 112, 223, 225

Norsk Hydro 115, 179, 202, 207, 212, 220–2, 232, 235–6, 241–2, 245–6, 249, 270
North Trangas pipeline 166, 173, 185, 187
North West Shelf project (Australia) 18
Northern Lights pipeline system 172
Norvik, H. 236, 245
Norway 6–9, 13–4, 17, 201–53, 264, 269–70
Nuclear industry 22

Office of Gas Supply (UK) 19
Ofgas 21
Øien, A. 207, 229
Oil and Gas Act (UK) 19
Oil prices 7, 11–14, 21, 34, 38, 43, 46, 48–9, 58, 69, 101, 111–2, 118–120, 130, 222, 229, 249, 260, 270, 272
Oil-fired stations 22
OMV (Austria) 218, 244
OPEC 44, 49
Optimal recovery scheme 52
Orenburg field 143, 168
Orenburg gas processing plant 179
Orenburg ('Soyuz') pipeline 150, 181
Orkney Islands 211
Ormen Lange field 249
Oseberg field 205, 207, 209, 215

Pacific Basin 130
Panhandle Eastern Pipeline Company 55
Panrusgas 166–7
Partnership with foreign companies 80, 265–6
Pauwels, J.-P. 45
Petroleum Directorate (Norway) 209
Phillips 203–4, 209, 219, 224
Pipelines 8–9, 24, 27–9, 33, 127, 223
PMG (Netherlands) 129
Pnem 126
Poland 168, 170–1, 240, 242, 244, 248
Polish Oil and Gas Company (PGNiG) 170
Polyethylene production 74
Polymed 74
Portugal 12, 14, 57–8, 70
Power generation 21–2
Powergen 19, 259
Pricing policies 14, 45–7, 56–7, 68, 117, 119–20, 209, 249, 261
Principal-agent problems 217, 237
Privatization 18–9, 99, 125, 227, 238, 271
Progresgaz Trading 166
Promgaz 166–7

Quadrant 259

Reagan, President R. 10, 43–4, 152
Redirected Mediterranean Policy (EU) 60
Regional electricity companies (RECs) 19–20
Regulation 44, 125, 139–41, 214, 257
Rehden storage facility 164, 244
Repsol 63, 71, 79
Repsol-Quimica 74
Rhourde Nouss field 57, 61
Romgaz 169
Rosneft 179
Ruhrgas 15–6, 42, 53, 98, 116, 151, 162, 166, 168–70, 178, 188, 208, 217–8, 236, 239–41, 243, 259, 270, 271
Russia 18, 135–99, 248, 267–9
Russia-Ukraine trade 157

Saga 202–3, 220, 232–3, 241, 244–6
Sakha 188
Sakhalin Island 153, 188
Scandinavian pipeline 242
Schoonebeek concession 116

Scottish Power 212, 235
Self-determination 226
SEP (Netherlands) 108, 112
Shatlyk field (Turkmenistan) 143
Shell 14, 16–8, 38, 55–6, 79, 97–9, 128, 129, 145, 176,
    178–9, 188, 203, 211–2
Shell Esso relation 259
Shell Gas Direct 259
Shtomanovskoye field 174, 187
Siberia 6, 144, 151, 191
Sleipner fields 14, 18, 211, 215–6, 221, 240
Slovakia 118, 171, 185, 244
Slovrusgaz 166, 171
small gas fields 17, 105–6, 192, 208, 215, 267
SN Repal 37–8
SNAM (Italy) 15, 17–18, 46, 57, 98, 116, 151, 167, 218,
    242, 270
Snøvit field 237
Social policies 39, 82, 226–8
Sonatrach 14, 34–84, 265; relations with BP Amoco 71,
    83–4, 266
Sonatrach-Amoco partnership 35, 63–4
Sonatrach-BP partnership 35, 63–64, 70, 236
Sonatrading 56
Sour El Guelta 63
Sovereignty over natural resources 47
Soyuzgazexport 43, 147
Soyuznefteexport 147
Spain 12, 14, 57, 58, 70, 242, 248, 265
Spitzbergen 228
Spot market 20, 68, 119, 130, 250, 260
SROG (Netherlands) 109, 111
State Direct Financial Interest (SDFI) 234
State Gas Board (SGB) 96, 102
Statfjord field 13, 209–10, 217, 224–5, 239
Statoil 179, 202, 203, 210, 212, 215–7, 220–1, 226, 229–
    38, 241–2, 245–6, 270; relation with BP 235
Statkraft 236
Statpipe system 217, 224–5
STEGAL pipeline 164–5, 244
Stern, J. 72
Strike on Norwegian platforms 1986 216
Supply diversification 186
Supply gap 261–3
Swing supplier/producer 108, 127, 129, 208, 215, 220–1,
    250, 266–7
Switzerland 242

Tadzhikistan 155
'take or pay' 23
Tax payments 138
Technip 43
Teesside terminal 208
Texaco 16, 259
Third-party access (TPA) 23, 214, 241, 245, 256, 272
Thyssengas 98, 116, 129, 208, 218, 259, 271
Timan-Pechora production region 179
Tin Fouye Tabenkort field 63
Topenergy 170
Total 37, 62, 74, 79, 203, 259
Total Oil Marine UK 224
Total/Repsol 63
Town gas 6, 142
Tractobel 18
Trade between former Soviet Republics 154–7
Transgas 169, 242
Transit crises 184
Trans-European Network (TEN) 60
Trans-Med pipeline 13, 42–3, 57, 60, 64, 66, 70–1, 79, 84,
    264
Transit Convention (Algeria and Morocco) 71

Transmission companies 191
Transparency 257
Trinidad 24, 264
Troll field 18, 202, 205, 207, 215–7, 220–1, 240, 249–50,
    264, 269
Troll/Sleipner Gas Agreements 207
Trunkline Gas Corporation 14, 42, 55, 56
Turkey 47, 174–6, 185, 248, 268
Turkmengazprom 160
Turkmenistan 155, 158, 160–2, 183, 193
Turkmenrosgaz 160

UK 6, 258, 266, 269; gas market 19–21; government
    policy 18, 24, 30
UK-Belgium (Bacton-Zeebrugge) Interconnector 18–9, 21,
    30, 60, 68, 102, 109, 115, 126, 164, 166, 215, 236, 260
UK Continental Shelf (UKCS) 215, 236, 264
UK North Sea 3
Ukraine 151, 155, 157–60, 173, 184, 193, 268
Ukrgazprom 158
Ula field 210, 239
Unified Gas Supply System (UGSS) 146
Urengoy field 10, 14, 139, 143, 152–3
Urengoy pipeline 152–3, 182
Urengoygazprom 139
US-Canada trade 157
US Eastern energy group 270
US-Soviet relations 10, 43, 152
US trade sanctions 152
USA (see also Exports to North America) 14, 258
Uzbekistan 155

VALHYD (Valorisation des Hydrocarbures) 35–6, 41–2
van Aardene's Review 121
VEEN (Netherlands) 109
VEGIN (Netherlands) 109
VEP Gazexport 147, 154
Vertical integration (also see Downstream integration) 20,
    236, 258
VESTIN (Netherlands) 109
Vietnam 235
Visund field 212
VNG (Verbundnetzgas) 163, 240–1, 244
VNG pipeline 240
Vyakhirev, R. 137, 186–7

Walker, P. 211
Wedal pipeline 164–5
Western Sahara 58
Wijers, H. 122
Wingas 16–7, 128, 164, 166, 185–6, 241, 243–5, 268–9
Wintershall 17, 128, 163–4, 243–4
Wintershall Erdgas Handelshaus (WIEH) 164, 166
Wintershall/Gazprom joint venture 16, 164
Wirom 166
World Bank 189

Yakutia project 153
Yamal Europe project 167–8, 248
Yamal-Nenets production region 179, 191
Yamal Peninsula fields 143, 172
Yamal (Belarus-Poland) pipeline 156–7, 159–60, 180, 185,
    187–8, 264
Yamburg field 139, 143, 152, 168
Yamburg ('Progress') pipeline 150, 181
Yamburggazodobycha 139
Yugorosgaz 166

Zapolyarnoye field 143, 176
Zeepipe 18, 224–5, 240, 242, 247